DATE DUE	
	AUG 2 5 2005
MAR 0 7 2000	DEC 1 2 2005
1/29/02	AUG 25 2005
5/4/02	FEB 1 1 2006
APR 2 4 2003	APR 1 8 2006
NOV 0 6 2003	JUL 2 3 2007
AUG 1 6 2004	
MAR 1 6 2005	FEB 2 6 2008
HIGHSMITH #45114	NOV 1 7 2008

Health and
Sexuality Education
in Schools

Health and Sexuality Education in Schools

The Process of Social Change

Steven P. Ridini

Foreword by Charles V. Willie

BERGIN & GARVEY
Westport, Connecticut • London

Library of Congress Cataloging-in-Publication Data

Ridini, Steven P., 1962–
    Health and sexuality education in schools : the process of social
change / Steven P. Ridini ; foreword by Charles V. Willie.
        p.   cm.
    Includes bibliographical references and index.
    ISBN 0–89789–570–3 (alk. paper)
    1. Sex instruction—United States.   2. AIDS (Disease)—Prevention—
Study and teaching—United States.   3. Health education—United
States.   4. Community and school—United States.   I. Title.
HQ57.5.A3R54   1998
613.9'071—dc21   98–9536

British Library Cataloguing in Publication Data is available.

Library of Congress Catalog Card Number: 98–9536
ISBN: 0–89789–570–3

First published in 1998

Bergin & Garvey, 88 Post Road West, Westport, CT 06881
An imprint of Greenwood Publishing Group, Inc.

Printed in the United States of America

The paper used in this book complies with the
Permanent Paper Standard issued by the National
Information Standards Organization (Z39.48–1984).

10 9 8 7 6 5 4 3 2 1

For my parents,
Kathleen Althea and Leonard Michael

Contents

Foreword *by Charles V. Willie*   ix

Acknowledgments   xiii

I. Introduction   1

1. Introduction   3

II. Case Studies of Alpha and Beta   19

2. Alpha Case Study: Students and Adults Working Together   21

3. Beta Case Study: If at First You Don't Succeed, Try,
   Try Again   37

III. Findings and Comparative Analysis   53

4. A Call for Health and Sexuality Education Programs   59

5. Obtaining Community Support for Health and Sexuality
   Education Programs   91

6. Opposition to Health and Sexuality Education Programs   111

7. Neutralizing Opposition   137

8. Implementing School-Based Health and Sexuality
   Education Programs   159

IV. Conclusion and Implications   **171**

  9. Conclusion and Implications   173

Appendices   **181**

  A. Methodology   183

  B. Coding Categories   192

  C. List of Primary Interviewees in Alpha   194

  D. List of Primary Interviewees in Beta   196

  E. Interview Guide   198

Selected Bibliography   201

Index   205

Foreword

Several years ago, I served on the President's Commission on Mental Health by appointment from President Jimmy Carter. Also serving on the Commission was Dr. Julius B. Richmond, a magnificent clinician, scientist, administrator, and policymaker. Dr. Richmond has been a professor, university department chair, medical school dean, guidance center director, and chief of a medical specialty in a hospital for children. In federal government, Dr. Richmond was the first director of Head Start and eventually served as assistant secretary of health and surgeon general in the U.S. Department of Health and Human Services. He is a teacher, researcher, author, and wise counselor. Despite these expert credentials (or, maybe, because of them), Dr. Richmond said during the first meeting of the Commission at the White House that we want the people to appear and give testimony at the hearing and to know that what they say will be taken seriously. His remarks reflected the sentiments of most Commission members.

These remarks reminded me of a saying expressed by many public health practitioners that health is a community affair and is too important to be left entirely to the will of experts and professionals. The case studies of community action examined in this book demonstrate the validity of this idea.

Steven Ridini provides a fascinating analysis of how two communities developed a comprehensive health curriculum designed to promote well-being among adolescent students and prevent HIV/AIDS. His detailed analysis examines a series of events that facilitated and impaired implementation of a public policy that was recommended by state educational authorities.

Ridini's study indicates that public education, like public health, cannot be limited to the will of experts and professionals. Ridini effectively guides us through the data that support and sustain this allegation because of his professional training in public health and public education. Two important conclusions are revealed in this book: (1) teaching and learning experiences about health and human sexuality are difficult to implement in public school systems; (2) teaching and learning experiences about health and human sexuality are possible in public education, if appropriate attention is given to the process of community decision-making.

Most of the discussion in this book focuses on the process of community decision-making, to which limited attention has been given in the past. Ridini adopts a process model developed by Christopher Sower which divides community decision-making into three separate but interrelated stages—initiation, legitmation, and implementation. Based on this study, Ridini adds a fourth state—evaluation that encourages a locality to reflect upon what it has done. Using this model to analyze community decision-making pertaining to the development of a curriculim on health and human sexuality, one understands not only what decisions are made and who makes them but also how and why decisions are made, and how and why they are accepted or rejected by the community at large. This, therefore, is a study of the process and structure of community decision-making. As such, it is a comprehensive, timely, and needed study that may equip school districts and their communities with useful conflict-resolution methods and techniques.

The issues discussed are deeply anchored in individual and institutional values that may seem to be incompatible and in conflict. However, this study shows that valid differences may be accommodated through continuous negotiation in each stage of the community action process. Effective negotiation, of course, requires open communication, the absence of which may lead to distrust that jeopardizes cooperation and the building of alliances and coalitions. Ridini discovered that collaboration is essential in effective community action.

The two communities studied eventually implemented acceptable programs on HIV/AIDS prevention because information on this and other topics was included in a comprehensive health education curriculum. The comprehensive approach moderated some resistance to specific topics. A very important finding is that neither a top-down bureaucratic decision-making method nor a bottom-up consensus decision-making method alone is sufficient. Probably, both communities investigated would have been reluctant to take up controversial issues like health and human sexuality education if state educational authorities had not recommended it. In this respect, a top-down, bureaucratic approach has merit in generating effective community action. It should be noted, however, that the community that made the most rapid progress in developing an acceptable and comprehensive health education curriculum was one in which the issue was initiated from the bottom up by a "grass roots" group of students who pursued a solution jointly with their families and the public school bureaucracy. In this community, consensus-oriented decision-making and bureaucratic authority formed a complementary relationship that may be described as a collaborative approach.

Careful analysis by Ridini of the collaborative way that both school districts eventually handled this controversial public education/public health issue indicates that, in a pluralistic community, the goal should be achievement of a "double victory" for dominant as well as subdominant people of power, as opposed to a "winner-take-all" philosophy. The double victory (a phrase popularized by Martin Luther King, Jr.) is obtained by way of open communication, continuous negotiation, and democratic decision-making.

Finally, this study reveals that success in public health or public education programs is attributed to interaction between individuals and groups or institutions. In one community, the attitudes of individual students regarding the need for some type of school-based sexuality education program were insufficient to bring about the desired change. However, when the attitudes of individuals were incorporated into recommendations of a ten-month study by a task force appointed by the School Board, the School Board—a permanent institution in the community—voted to support the recommendations concerning the human sexuality–HIV/AIDS curriculum.

In the other community, the school system—the local educational agency—took initiating responsibility for revising and implementing the curriculum guidelines on HIV/AIDS suggested by state authorities. It did this by establishing an AIDS Advisory Committee dominated by education professionals. This group held meetings to review state guidelines and to suggest changes in these but did not obtain and assess the views of individuals in the community on this matter. When the School Board held public hearings on the recommendations of its AIDS Advisory Committee, disagreement by individuals was loud and extensive and caused the School Board to reject the recommendations. School authorities then devised a process that took into consideration the attitudes of individuals in the community and developed a curriculum from this process, on which consensus was achieved.

These case studies show that individuals on the one hand, and groups and institutions on the other, are interdependent in community organization and are mutually influenced by each other. According to the theory of complementarity, we ignore either component of this couplet at our peril.

Charles V. Willie
Harvard Graduate School of Education

Acknowledgments

I would like to acknowledge with great appreciation those individuals who have assisted me in making this research study a reality: my parents, Kathleen and Leonard, who have provided me with endless support and love over the past 36 years; my grandparents, Mary Helen and Leonard John, who always stressed the importance of education and attaining one's dreams; my uncle Michael and aunt Josephine; my sisters and brothers, Maryann, Lenny, Carol, Kathy, Fred, Chris, Kris, David, and Jill; and my nieces, Jennifer, Kimberly, Carley, and my nephew Dylan.

I would also like to thank Susan Johnson and Caesar McDowell for their endless support and guidance.

I would like to thank Dr. Charles V. Willie, who many times went beyond the role of advisor and mentor to provide me with the support, advice, and motivation to pursue my dreams. Additionally, I would like to thank Kathy George, who assisted me with the transcription of data, and more importantly was always there to listen, provide comfort food, and help me navigate through uncharted waters.

I would also like to acknowledge the assistance of Norma Diala, on whom I could always count for support and a good laugh.

I would like to acknowledge the support of Susan Downey, who as colleague and friend allowed me the opportunity to continue with my studies while providing me the chance to stay in the field doing the work I love most.

I would like to thank my friends, Janice Jackson, Gladys Morales, Teresa Madden, Hannah Feldman, Dennis Holtschneider, Karen Mapp, Inge Ameer, Karen Gould, Ira Thomas, John Veere, and Sean Haley.

Finally, I would like to thank the community members from Alpha and Beta who welcomed me into their respective communities and homes. Special thanks go to Natalie Dixon and Jane Alexander.

ACKNOWLEDGMENTS

PART I

Introduction

CHAPTER 1

Introduction

HEALTH AND SEXUALITY EDUCATION AS A COMMUNITY ISSUE

In April 1990, the Massachusetts Board of Education urged all public schools to provide HIV/AIDS prevention education to every student in every grade.[1] At the secondary level, the Board of Education stated that "HIV/AIDS education should be part of a more complete sexuality education curriculum, that includes information about sexually transmitted diseases, and the value of both sexual abstinence and the use of condoms as disease prevention methods." The Board also suggested that the scope and sequence of the curriculum remain under local control.[2] One year later, the Alpha School Committee approved a condom availability program and charged the school administration with developing recommendations for a comprehensive health and sexuality education curriculum. In March 1992, Beta school administrators responded by creating an AIDS Advisory Committee to develop recommendations for an AIDS curriculum. In both communities, individuals opposed to the curriculum began to voice concerns. After months of debate the Alpha School Committee voted in May 1993 to implement the first stage of a comprehensive plan, a ninth-grade pilot program. However, in June 1993, the Beta School Committee voted 4–3 against the adoption of a comprehensive K–12 HIV/AIDS education curriculum.

For the past few years, there has been much debate over the adoption, implementation, and maintenance of comprehensive health and sexuality education programs in Massachusetts public schools. Advocates of school-based comprehensive health education programs often use a public health approach to substantiate their position. They cite national and statewide statistics about adolescent sexual activity and unsafe sexual practice as a basis for providing students with the facts and the skills to make decisions to prevent pregnancy and the spread of sexually transmitted diseases.[3] Opponents often speak about the parents' role in educating their sons/daughters and object to public school instruction that regards homosexuality and safe sex as acceptable lifestyles.

This issue will be used as a framework to learn more about how communities and the groups within them organize for social change.[4] In review of the literature, many models of community organization focus on the decision-making structure within the community rather than on the process of social change. Therefore, we often know who makes community decisions, yet know very little about how decisions are made and why. The process of social change will be explored by conducting comparative case studies of two Massachusetts communities. In Alpha, School Committee members, school administrators, and community members are currently implementing a comprehensive health and sexuality education program. In comparison, Beta School Committee members defeated a similar initiative in June 1993. However, presently Beta School Committee members are working with school administrators and community members toward the implementation of a school-based comprehensive health education program.

In this study, I analyze the process by which individuals, community-based groups, and institutions influenced the development and implementation of Alpha's health and sexuality education program. I also analyze the process of events that initially prevented the adoption of an HIV/AIDS education curriculum in Beta's schools and ultimately led to the adoption of a comprehensive health education program. Additionally, I compare how, why, and to what effect community members in both Alpha and Beta formed community-based groups and worked with established institutions to support or oppose the development of these initiatives. I use community organization theory—Sower's Community Action model—to guide my investigation and to compare the experiences of these two communities. According to this model, community organization is a process consisting of three stages: Initiation, Legitimation, and Implementation.[5]

CONCEPTUALIZATION OF COMMUNITY ORGANIZATION

As I conducted research in Alpha and Beta it was helpful to think of the community as a social system composed of different individuals, groups, and institutions.[6] C. M. Moore (1991) discusses the significance of interactions within social systems. He writes, "community exists when people who are interdependent struggle with the traditions that bind them and the interests that separate them so they can realize a future that is an improvement on the present."[7]

Models of Community Organization

Definitions of community organization and conceptions of its nature vary markedly in the literature. In their anthology, Harper and Dunham (1959) list thirteen definitions of community organization and indicate that at least one hundred definitions have been projected in sociological literature in the past 35 years.[8] Miller, Rein, and Levitt (1990) identify seven forms of community organizing.[9] It is more helpful to capture the variety of theories and conceptions than attempt to establish an all-embracing theory. The implication, according to Rothman and Tropman (1987), is to examine community organization *methods* rather than *the* community organization method.[10] Morris and Binstock (1966) and Rothman (1968) present three important orientations to deliberate community change: community development, social planning, and social action.

Community development is concerned with the creation of improved social and economic conditions through emphasis on voluntary cooperation and self-help efforts of local residents.[11-14] The term "community development" came into use after World War II in the efforts to improve village life in newly independent developing countries. The model has been used to address the problems of American cities. Clinard (1970) discusses these components in urban community development.[15] Community development is based on an optimistic view of people and community change. But in most communities there are constraints which can prevent cooperation and consensus from achieving constructive change. These constraints can include inadequate time, money, and organized opposition.[16-18]

Social planning is a technical process of problem solving largely concerned with the delivery of goods and services to people who need them. Rational deliberation and controlled change have a central place in this model. Community participation may vary, depending on how problems present themselves and what organizational variables are present.[19] This approach assumes that planned change requires the technical skills of "experts." There are a series of models that employ social planning practice[20, 21] including Watzlawick, Weakland, and Fisch's Model of Planned Change (1974), Green's System-Centered Education Model (1985), and Pentz's Expanded Model of Community Organization (1986). These models are similar in that they discuss: the importance of the identification and training of community/opinion leaders, the completion of a formal decision-making process for program adoption, establishment of an organizational structure for decision-making, the provision of training and technical assistance to community leaders through outside experts, and allowance for ongoing program monitoring and evaluation.[22-24]

Social action occurs when a disadvantaged segment of the population becomes organized, perhaps in alliance with others, to make demands on the dominant community institutions for increased resources or treatment in accordance with social justice. It sometimes aims at making basic changes in major institutions or community practices. The goal of social action is to ensure a more equitable distribution of power, resources, or decision-making in the community.[25] Alinsky (1972) states this goal in simple terms by pointing out that the battle is between the "haves and the have-nots."[26]

Many community organization models, which can be classified under one of these three orientations to purposive community change, tend to focus on the decision-making structure in the community.[27, 28] Therefore, we often know who is involved in decision-making. For example, in community development, community change is pursued through the broad participation of community members. The social planning approach emphasizes the technical skills of experts and the training of community leaders. Social action involves the mobilization and organization of a disadvantaged segment of the population.

Although this focus on the structure of community organization reveals who is involved in decision-making, it tells little about how the decisions are made and why. By favoring structure over process, we develop an incomplete picture of the nature of community organization.[29] Fox, Forbing, and Anderson (1988) write, "In most cases, lack of significant [programmatic] success can be attributed to inadequate understanding of both the process and content of comprehensive planning and implementation."[30] For example, in Alpha much of the debate over a school-based condom availability program and comprehensive K–12 health and sexuality education curriculum occurred among adults at open forums of the Alpha School Committee. While School Committee members would ultimately decide the fate of these initiatives, it was Alpha High School students who initiated social change when they petitioned the School Committee for a condom availability program and an expanded health and sexuality education curriculum. Further study revealed the students' motivation for becoming involved in this issue and how their relationships with peers and other adults influenced their decision to drop plans to distribute condoms in school in favor of adopting a broader public health vision.[31, 32] The impact of the students' action is reflected in the comments made by the Alpha School Committee Chairwoman Sonya Schultz, who stated, " If it were not for the students' requests, I don't think you would have seen this kind of vote."[33] In studying social change in Beta, it is important to understand how and why the Beta School Committee and other community members initially prevented the adoption of a comprehensive K–12 HIV/AIDS education curriculum. Additionally, it is important to analyze how individuals and community-based groups in Beta who advocated for a school-based

HIV/AIDS curriculum realized their goal when the Beta School Committee voted to implement the first part of a comprehensive health education program in Beta's schools.

Christopher Sower and associates conducted an investigation of community organization as a process and concluded that the process contains three stages: Initiation, Legitimation, and Implementation.[34] In the initiation stage, a "convergence of interest" occurs among people holding similar feelings and beliefs about a problem. A group is formed to deal with an idea possessed by one or more individuals. Subsequent events include development of common goals/objectives, identification of proposed action, and creation of external relationships within the larger community. *Legitimation* involves getting approval for the proposed action. Persons who propose community action must show that such proposals will benefit the community at large. This is accomplished by obtaining approval and support from respected groups and organizations. This stage may also include, if necessary, dealing with opposition. A plan is executed during the *implementation stage*. To be effective, access to personnel, techniques, and other resources, usually from more than one organization, is necessary.

Sower's stage theory provides a way of understanding how Alpha implemented a sexuality and HIV/AIDS education program while other communities such as Beta initially failed. Specifically, analysis revealed interrelationships between individuals and groups in each of the three stages and demonstrated how the action in one stage became the foundation for action in subsequent stages. For example, Alpha students initiated action by organizing and petitioning the Alpha School Committee to make condoms readily available at the city's two high schools. This action was legitimized by the School Committee's affirmative vote, in January 1992, to make condoms available and begin the development of a health and sexuality education curriculum. In Beta, school administrators initiated action by forming a nineteen-member Advisory Committee to develop recommendations for an AIDS curriculum. In contrast to Alpha, however, there were few opportunities for Beta community members to take ownership of the Advisory Committee's work. As a result, there was no organized student or parent movement that publicly supported the Advisory Committee's recommendations. These recommendations, however, were opposed by members of Concerned Parents and Citizens of Beta (CPCB)—a grassroots parent organization. Through their organizing efforts at both public forums and School Committee meetings, CPCB members were successful in mobilizing public opposition. The CPCB's efforts were realized when the Beta School Committee voted against the adoption of a K–12 HIV/AIDS education curriculum in June 1993. Within months, however, another grassroots parent group emerged in Beta—Community Advocates for Responsible Education (CARE). According to CARE spokesperson Ellen Nagel, the mission of this group was, "[the belief] in the importance of a sequential, comprehensive, and developmentally appropriate health education curriculum for students in grades K through 12 enrolled in the Beta schools."[35] For two more years, Beta community members debated each other over the benefits and drawbacks of a school-based comprehensive K–12 health education program. The debate came to an end in June 1995 when the Beta School Committee adopted *The Great Body Shop*, a health curriculum for students in grades K–5.

WHY STUDY HEALTH AND SEXUALITY EDUCATION?

During the past few years my professional experiences have provided me with the opportunity to work in various communities throughout Massachusetts. Through my travels, my conversations, and what I have read in statewide reports and newspaper accounts, the issue of school-based sexuality and HIV/AIDS education programs has captured much attention at public meetings and in the media around the state. Combining my passion for community organization with such an abundance of information, I use the issue of school-based sexuality and HIV/AIDS education programs to learn more about how individuals and community-based groups organize for social change.

SEXUALITY EDUCATION: A HISTORICAL CONTEXT

For almost a century, schools have developed programs aimed at reducing sexual behaviors which place youth at risk of pregnancy and sexually transmitted diseases (STDs). In the early 1900s, concern surfaced that young people were having sex prior to marriage and that venereal disease was increasing. Believing that accurate information about venereal disease would prevent youth from engaging in sex, schools introduced sex education.[36]

Both during and since the decades that followed, a variety of school-based health programs have been implemented. The length of these programs has varied from one-hour, didactic presentations on sexuality education to semester-long, comprehensive health education programs.[37] The content of these programs has ranged from discussions about abstinence until marriage to the acquisition of knowledge/skills to comprehensive programs that include the dispensing of contraceptives.[38]

Two reports brought teenage pregnancy and sex education into the arena of national debate. The National Research Council of the National Academy of Sciences released a series of recommendations that dealt with "problems posed by growing numbers of unmarried, teenage mothers."[39, 40] In another report, Surgeon General C. Everett Koop called for sex education in schools that "must include information on heterosexual and homosexual relationships."[41, 42] In September 1991, the U. S. Department of Health and

Human Services set forth national health objectives. These objectives which were outlined in *Healthy People 2000: National Health Promotion and Disease Prevention Objectives* included: family planning, and the prevention of HIV infection and STDs. The report mentioned that schools could directly contribute to the attainment of these objectives.[43]

Then, in 1991, the Massachusetts Departments of Education and Public Health issued a joint communication urging all local school districts to "create programs which make instruction about HIV/AIDS available to every student at every grade level."[44] It was recommended that every school committee, in consultation with school administrators, faculty, parents, and students consider making condoms available in their secondary schools. That November, the Massachusetts Board of Education announced new guidelines for sex education urging schools to teach children as early as kindergarten about sex organs and AIDS.[45]

DATA ON ADOLESCENT SEXUAL ACTIVITY, EDUCATION, AND PRACTICE: A PUBLIC HEALTH ISSUE

To understand the need for sexuality education in public schools, it is helpful to examine national and statewide data. A national study conducted by the Alan Guttmacher Institute concluded that one-fourth of all adolescent females and one-third of all adolescent males have intercourse by age 15.[46] In Massachusetts, one-half of the 3,000 high school students surveyed in 1993 reported having had sexual intercourse. Among students who had sexual intercourse in the preceding three months, 52% reported using a condom and 33% reported not using any contraceptive method.[47]

Data quantifying the consequences of practicing unsafe sex are also available. Nationally, in 1992, one million adolescent women between the ages of 15 and 19 became pregnant. An additional 30,000 became pregnant before age 15.[48, 49] In Massachusetts, approximately 17,000 adolescent women become pregnant annually.[50] Furthermore, 513,486 people have been diagnosed with AIDS in the United States, and more than 300,000 Americans have died of AIDS-related complications.[51] In Massachusetts, 10,154 people have been diagnosed with AIDS. One-fifth of these cases are among people in their twenties, and the majority of these individuals were infected during their adolescence.[52, 53] These figures underscore the importance of developing and extending comprehensive health and sexuality education programs to all students.

Forty-seven states either require or encourage the teaching of sexuality and AIDS education in the public schools. Massachusetts officials just recently recommended the development and implementation of comprehensive sexuality education in all public schools at all grade levels.[54, 55] However, in a survey of 179 urban school districts, Sonnenstein and Pittman (1984) found that, while sex education was offered, most instruction was limited to ten hours or less, with content focused on anatomy.[56] Donovan (1989) concluded that less than 10% of all public school students are exposed to what might be considered comprehensive programs. In a national survey of 4,200 sexuality education teachers, nearly all felt that their programs provided "too little, too late."[57, 58]

In the spring of 1995, the Planned Parenthood League of Massachusetts sent a Sexuality Education Assessment questionnaire to health education coordinators in all 351 school districts in Massachusetts. Usable questionnaires were obtained from respondents in 109 school districts, representing 55% of all cities and towns in Massachusetts and more than 400,000 students. Almost all school districts (94%) that responded to the assessment questionnaire have developed and/or implemented a sexuality education program in their public schools. Most health educators described both their middle/junior high school and high school sexuality education programs as abstinence-based (78%), and/or knowledge-based (73%). Approximately half also described their programs as skills-based and/or comprehensive.[59]

THE RELATIONSHIP BETWEEN SEXUALITY EDUCATION AND ADOLESCENT SEXUAL ACTIVITY

Sexuality education curricula have been developed and implemented in junior and senior high schools during the past 15 to 20 years. These curricula can be loosely divided into four groups.[60] These include knowledge-based,[61-65] values clarification and decision-making,[66-72] abstinence-only,[73-75] and social learning theory.[76-80]

The belief that sexuality and AIDS education may encourage sexual activity in young people is a powerful barrier to the introduction of HIV/STD prevention programs.[81] Yet, the data suggest that sex education does not promote an earlier onset or increase in sexual activity[82] and may postpone intercourse.[83, 84] In fact, research indicates that sex education and access to contraceptives can help reduce the rates of unintended and unwanted adolescent pregnancy.[85-87]

COMMUNITY VIEWS ON SEXUALITY EDUCATION

A variety of social, economic, and political factors foster risk behaviors that result in one million adolescent pregnancies and three million teens being infected with STDs annually.[88] Many communities look to education as a way to address these issues. However, the two most common arguments used by opponents of sexuality education are that it both undermines the family unit and causes sexual activity and pregnancy in young people.[89]

Resistance to sex education is both less vocal and less active within schools and parents' groups.[90] In fact, support for sexuality education in the schools has increased steadily in recent years.[91-93] Clearly, parents prefer to have some say about whether or not their youngsters will be exposed to sex education and what form that instruction will take. Interestingly, public support for sex education drops significantly if it's offered without parental consent.[94, 95] While parents may support sexuality education, national polls reveal that only 30% of children, aged 13–15 receive information about sex from their parents. The majority learn from friends (26%), at school (26%), or from books and entertainment (15%).[96]

In Massachusetts almost all health educators (89%) who responded to the 1995 Planned Parenthood League of Massachusetts Sexuality Education Assessment believe that their community, as well as their local school committee, support the sexuality education plan currently in place in their school district, even though 20% report that they observed some controversy regarding sexuality education in their community during the past year.[97]

These statistics help to illustrate the importance of providing students with the information and skills they need to prevent unwanted pregnancies, HIV/AIDS, and other STDs. While all the individuals I interviewed in Alpha and Beta supported some type of school-based health education program, individuals differed on curriculum content and its age-appropriateness. This comparative case study analysis is used as a means to understand how individuals and community-based groups from both Alpha and Beta created community support for school-based comprehensive health and sexuality education programs. More specifically, this study explores how and why community members formed particular groups and worked with established institutions to support or oppose the development of such programs.

NOTES

1. Massachusetts Department of Education, *Policy on AIDS/HIV Prevention Education* (Quincy, MA: Massachusetts Department of Education, April 24, 1990).

2. Massachusetts Department of Public Health, *Comprehensive Curriculum Guidelines on HIV/AIDS: Grades K–12* (Boston: Massachusetts Department of Public Health, September 1991).

3. In the *Massachusetts 1993 Youth Risk Behavior Survey* of nearly 3,000 high school students from 39 cities/towns within the Commonwealth, it was reported that, "One-half of the Massachusetts high school students surveyed reported having had sexual intercourse. One-third of the students who had sexual intercourse in the past three months did not use any contraceptive method the last time they had intercourse." *Massachusetts 1993 Youth Risk Behavior Survey* (Malden, MA: Massachusetts Department of Education, Bureau of Student Development and Health, June 1994).

4. Social change takes place through a set of activities that sometimes focuses on a single organization, sometimes on a community, and sometimes on a society as a whole. C. D. Garvin and F. M. Cox, "A History of Community Organizing

Since the Civil War with Special Reference to Oppressed Communities," in F. M. Cox, J. R. Erlich, J. Rothman, and J. E. Tropman, eds., *Strategies of Community Organization: A Book of Readings* (Itasca, IL: F. E. Peacock Publishers, 1970), p. 4.

5. C. Sower, J. Holland, K. Tiedke, and W. Freeman, *Community Involvement* (New York: The Free Press, 1957), pp. 61–234.

6. C. L. Perry, "Community-wide Health Promotion and Drug Abuse Prevention," *Journal of School Health*, 56(9) (November 1986), pp. 359–363.

7. C. M. Moore, *Working Paper on Community*, The National Conference on Peacemaking and Conflict Resolution (Fairfax, VA: George Mason University, 1991), p. 2.

8. E. B. Harper and A. Dunham, *Community Organization in Action: Basic Literature and Critical Comments* (New York: Associated Press, 1959).

9. S. M. Miller, M. Rein, and P. Levitt, "Community Action in the United States," *Community Development Journal*, 25(4) (1990), pp. 356–368.

10. J. Rothman and J. E. Tropman, "Models of Community Organization and Macro Practice Perspectives: Their Mixing and Phasing," in F. M. Cox, J. R. Erlich, J. Rothman, and J. E. Tropman, eds., *Strategies of Community Organization: Macro Practice* (Itasca, IL: F. E. Peacock Publishers, 1987), pp. 3–26.

11. K. Heller, R. Price, S. Reinharz, S. Riger, and A. Wandersman, *Psychology and Community Change* (Homewood, IL: Pursey, 1984).

12. A. Dunham, "Some Principles of Community Development," *International Review of Community Development*, No. 11 (1963), pp. 141–151.

13. D. A. Kotze, "Contradictions and Assumptions in Community Development," *Community Development Journal*, 22(1) (1987), pp. 31–35.

14. C. Mitchell-Weaver, "Community Development in North America: Survey and Prospect for the 1990s," *Community Development Journal*, 25(4) (1990), pp. 345–354.

15. M. B. Clinard, *Slums and Community Development: Experiments in Self-Help* (New York: Free Press, 1970).

16. Heller, Price, Reinharz, Riger, and Wandersman, *Psychology and Community Change*.

17. W. W. Biddle and L. J. Biddle, *The Community Development Process: The Rediscovery of Local Initiative* (New York: Holt, Rinehart & Winston, 1965).

18. P. Henderson and D. N. Thomas, *Skills in Neighborhood Work* (Winchester, MA: Allen & Unwin, 1980).

19. Rothman and Tropman, "Models of Community Organization and Macro Practice Perspectives," pp. 3–26.

20. H. S. Perloff, *Planning and the Urban Community* (Pittsburgh: Carnegie Institute of Technology, 1961).

21. R. Morris and R. H. Binstock, *Feasible Planning for Social Change* (New York: Columbia University Press, 1966).

22. F. Watzlawick, J. H. Weakland, and R. Fisch, *Change Principles of Problem Formation and Problem Resolution* (New York: W. W. Norton, 1974).

23. L. W. Green, *Toward A Healthy Community: Organizing Events for Community Health Promotion* (Washington, DC: U.S. Department of Health and Human Service, U.S. Public Health Service, 1985, 80–50113).

24. M. Pentz, "Community Organization and School Liaisons: How to Get Programs Started," *Journal of School Health*, 56(9) (1986), pp. 382–388.

25. F. M. Cox, J. R. Erlich, J. Rothman, and J. E. Thompson eds., *Strategies of Community Organization: A Book of Readings* (Itasca, IL: F. E. Peacock Publishers, 1970), p. 4.

26. S. D. Alinsky, *Rules for Radicals* (New York: Random House, 1972), p. 19.

27. Rothman and Tropman, "Models of Community Organization and Macro Practice Perspectives," pp. 3–26; and J. Rothman, "Three Models of Community Organization Practice," in K. Heller, R. Price, S. Reinharz, S. Riger, and A. Wandersman, eds., *Psychology and Community Change* (Homewood, IL: Pursey, 1984).

28. J. W. Selsky, "Lessons in Community Development: An Activist Approach to Stimulating Inter Organizational Collaboration," *Journal of Applied Behavioral Research*, 27(1) (1991), pp. 91–115.

29. C. V. Willie, *Theories of Human Social Action* (Dix Hills, NY: General Hall, Inc., 1994), p. 54.

30. C. L. Fox, S. E. Forbing, and P. S. Anderson (1988), "A Comprehensive Approach to Drug-Free Schools and Communities," *Journal of School Health*, 58(9) (1990), pp. 365–369.

31. D.W. Merenda, *A Practical Guide to Creating and Managing Community Coalitions for Drug Abuse Prevention* (Alexandria, VA: ACTION: The Federal Domestic Volunteer Agency, n.d.).

32. R. Lear, "Sex Ed Debate Heats Up," *Tab*, 1/21/92, pp. 1, 6, and 12.

33. Schultz Interview, 8/29/95.

34. Sower, Holland, Tiedke, and Freeman, *Community Involvement*, pp. 61–234.

35. Nagel Interview, 10/27/95.

36. D. Kirby, "School-Based Programs to Reduce Sexual Risk-Taking Behaviors," *Journal of School Health*, 62(7) (1992), pp. 280–287.

37. Sexuality education refers to any program which provides information about sexuality, sexual development, and/or sexual health. Comprehensive health education refers to a planned, sequential, kindergarten through grade 12 curriculum that addresses and integrates education about a range of categorical health problems and issues (i.e., HIV infection, drug abuse, tobacco use, drinking and driving, emotional health) at developmentally appropriate ages.

38. Kirby, "School-Based Programs to Reduce Sexual Risk-Taking Behaviors," p. 280.

39. R. P. Hey, "Major U.S. Effort Urged to Handle Problems of Teen Parenthood," *Christian Science Monitor*, 12/10/86, p. 9.

40. Recommendations emphasized the need for more educational programs dealing with sexual activity and safe usage of contraceptive devices, greater access to contraceptive services for teens, and the establishment of supportive services for teenage parents. National Research Council, *Risking the Future: Adolescent Sexuality, Pregnancy and Childbearing* (Washington, DC: National Academy Press, 1987) Tables 2–10.

41. C. E. Koop, *Surgeon General's Report on Acquired Immune Deficiency Syndrome* (Washington DC: Office of the Surgeon General, 1986).

42. J. Leo, "Sex And Schools," *Time*, 11/24/86, p. 54.

43. "Healthy People 2000: National Health Promotion and Disease Prevention

Objectives and Healthy Schools," *Journal of School Health* 61(7) (1991), pp. 298–328.

44. The Commonwealth of Massachusetts Board of Education, *Policy on AIDS/HIV Prevention Education*, 1991.

45. Today in the United States, 47 states mandate or explicitly encourage sexuality education in schools. In D. deMauro, "Sexuality Education 1990: A Review of State Sexuality and AIDS Education Curricula," *SIECUS Reports*, 18(2), pp. 1–9.

46. The Alan Guttmacher Institute, *Facts in Brief: Teenage Sexual and Reproductive Behavior in the United States* (New York, 1992).

47. In 1994 the Massachusetts Department Of Education released findings from *Massachusetts 1993 Youth Risk Behavior Survey*. The survey was conducted with nearly 3,000 Massachusetts high school students from 39 cities/towns in the Commonwealth. The findings include:

• One half of Massachussetts high school students surveyed reported having had sexual intercourse.

• 31% of ninth-grade adolescent men and 25% of ninth-grade adolescent women have had sexual intercourse.

• By twelfth grade 70% of adolescent men and 67% of adolescent women have had sexual intercourse.

• 60% of students who have ever had sexual intercourse have had more than one sexual partner, and over one-third have had three or more sexual partners.

• Among students who had sexual intercourse in the past three months, 52% reported using a condom.

• 33% of students who had sexual intercourse in the past three months did not use any contraceptive method the last time they had intercourse.

• 75% of ninth graders reported condom use at last sexual intercourse compared to 49% of twelfth graders. (*Source*: Massachusetts Department of Education, Bureau of Student Development and Health, January 1993 and June 1994).

48. M. E. Mecklenburg and P. G. Thompson, "The Adolescent Family Life Program as a Prevention Measure," *Public Health Reports*, 98 (1983), pp. 21–29.

49. The Alan Guttachmer Institute, *Facts in Brief.*

50. Planned Parenthood League of Massachusetts, *Heart-to-Heart Program Overview*, 1992.

51. AIDS and HIV Fact Sheet, AIDS Action Committee, 1/1/95, and CDC National AIDS Hotline, December, 1995.

52. Ibid.

53. Massachusetts Department of Public Health, AIDS Bureau, 1994.

54. A. M. Kenney et al., "Sex Education and AIDS Education in the Schools: What States and Large School Districts Are Doing," *Family Planning Perspectives*, 21(2) (1989).

55. DeMauro, "Sexuality Education 1990," pp. 1–9.

56. F. L. Sonnenstein and K. J. Pittman, "The Availability of Sex Education in Large City School Districts," *Family Planning Perspectives*, 16(2) (1984), p. 19.

57. P. Donovan, "Risk and Responsibility: Teaching Sex Education in America's Schools Today" (New York: The Alan Guttmacher Institute, 1989). In D. Kirby,

"Sexuality Education: It Can Reduce Unprotected Intercourse," *SIECUS Report*, December 1992/January 1993.

58. J. D. Forrest and J. Silverman, "What Public School Teachers Teach About Preventing Pregnancy, AIDS and Sexually Transmitted Diseases," *Family Planning Perspectives*, 21(2) (1989), pp. 65–72.

59. Sexuality education may incorporate any one of the following strategies:

- *Abstinence-only*: Abstinence-only education refers to sexuality education programs which promote the message that refraining from all sexual activity until marriage is the correct option. These programs do not include information about contraception.

- *Abstinence-based*: Abstinence-based education refers to sexuality education programs which emphasize the benefits of postponing sexual involvement and refraining from intercourse. These programs also include information about contraception.

- *Knowledge-based*: Knowledge-based education refers to programs which focus on the acquisition of factual information about health, sexuality, pregnancy, and disease prevention.

- *Skills-based*: Skills-based education refers to programs which utilize classroom activities that provide students with the behavioral skills that will enable them to act upon responsible decisions about their sexual health. In Planned Parenthood League of Massachusetts Sexuality Assessment Report, *The Status of Sexuality Education In Massachusetts Public Schools*, 1995.

60. D. Kirby, "Sexuality Education: It Can Reduce Unprotected Intercourse," *SIECUS Report* (1993), pp. 19–25.

61. D. Kirby, J. Alter, and P. Scales, *Analysis of U.S. Sex Education and Evaluation Methods* (Washington, DC: U.S. Department of Health Education and Welfare, 1979).

62. D. Kirby, "Evaluating Sexuality Education," *Independent School*, (41) (1981), p. 21.

63. D. Kirby, *Sexuality Education: An Evaluation of Programs and Their Effects* (Santa Cruz, CA: Network Publications. 1984).

64. M. Zelnick and J. Kanter, "Sexual and Contraceptive Experience of Young Unmarried Women in the U.S., 1976 and 1971," *Family Planning Perspectives* (1977), p. 55.

65. G. S. Parcel and D. Luttmann, "Evaluation of a Sex Education Course for Young Adolescents." *Family Relations* (1981), p. 55.

66. G. S. Parcel and D. Luttman, "Effects of Sex Education on Sexual Attitudes," *Journal of Current Adolescent Medicine* (2) (1980), pp. 38–46.

67. Parcel and Luttman, "Evaluation of a Sex Education Course for Young Adolescents," pp. 55–60.

68. L. Hoch, "Attitude Change as A Result of Sex Education," *Journal of Research in Science Teaching* (8) (1971), pp. 363–367.

69. Kirby, *Sexuality Education: An Evaluation of Programs and Their Effects.*

70. A. M. Kenney and M. T. Orr, "Sex Education: An Overview of Current Programs, Policies and Research," *Phi Delta Kappan* (March 1984), pp. 491–496.

71. L. Cooper, *Final Report on the Secondary Component of the Family-Life Education Program Development Project* (Santa Cruz, CA: ETR Associates, 1982).

72. D. Kirby, "The Effects of School Sex Education Programs: A Review of the Literature," *Journal of School Health* (December 1980), p. 559.

73. S. E. Weed, J. A. Olsen, and J. Hooper, *Sex Respect First Year Evaluation Report* (Salt Lake City: Institute for Research and Evaluation, 1987).

74. B. Trudell and M. Whatley, "Sex Respect: A Problematic Public School Sexuality Curriculum," *Journal of Sex Education and Therapy*, 17(2) (1986), pp. 125–140.

75. F. S. Christopher and M. W. Roosa, "An Evaluation of an Adolescent Pregnancy Prevention Program: Is 'Just Say No' Enough?" *Family Relations*, 39(1) (1990), pp. 68–72.

76. P. Brick, *Adolescence in Perspective: A Lifespan Approach to Sexuality Education* (Planned Parenthood/ Bergen County, NJ: Thieme-Stratton, 1985).

77. M. Eisen, G. L. Zellman, and A. L. McAlister, "Evaluating the Impact of a Theory-Based Sexuality and Contraceptive Education Program," *Family Planning Perspectives*, (22) (1990), p. 262.

78. M. Howard and J. B. McCabe, "Helping Teenagers Postpone Sexual Involvement," *Family Planning Perspectives*, 22(1) (1990), pp. 21–26.

79. D. Kirby, R. Barth, N. Leland, and J. Fetro, "Reducing the Risk: Impact of a New Curriculum on Sexual Risk-Taking," *Family Planning Perspectives*, 23(6) (1991), pp. 253–263.

80. Kirby, "Sexuality Education: It Can Reduce Unprotected Intercourse," pp. 19–25.

81. M. Baldo, P. Aggleton, and G. Slutkin, "Does Sex Education Lead To Earlier or Increased Sexual Activity On Youth?" Poster presentation at IXth International Conference on AIDS, Berlin, 1993.

82. M. Zelnick and Y. J. Kim, "Sex Education and Its Association with Teenage Sexual Activity, Sexual Activity, Pregnancy, and Contraceptive Use," *Family Planning Perspectives*, 16(3) (1982), p. 116.

83. L. S. Zabin, M. B. Hirsch, E. A. Smith, R. Street, and J. B. Hardy, "Evaluation of a Pregnancy Prevention Program for Urban Teenagers," *Family Planning Perspectives*, 18(3) (1986), pp. 119–126.

84. J. Dryfoos, "School-Based Health Clinics: A New Approach to Preventing Adolescent Pregnancy?" *Family Planning Perspectives*, 17(2) (1985), pp. 70–75.

85. National Research Council, *Risking the Future: Adolescent Sexuality, Pregnancy and Childbearing* (vol. 1) (Washington, DC: National Academy Press, 1987).

86. Kirby, "Sexuality Education: It Can Reduce Unprotected Intercourse," pp. 19–25.

87. Researchers from the World Health Organization reviewed nineteen studies that evaluated the sexual behavior of students who had experienced sexuality education. They found no evidence of sex education leading to earlier or increased sexual activity. In fact, sex education led either to a delay in the onset of sexual activity or to a decrease in overall sexual activity. In addition, access to counseling and contraceptive services did not encourage earlier or increased sexual activity. Sex education increased adoption of safer sex practices by sexually active youth. These researchers concluded that school programs which promoted both postponement and protected sex to sexually active students were more effective than those promoting abstinence alone. In addition, school-based sex education programs for the prevention of pregnancy and STDs were found to be more effective when offered before young people become sexually active. In M. Baldo, P. Aggleton, and G. Slutkin, "Does Sex Education Lead to Earlier or Increased Sexual Activity on Youth?" in Planned Parenthood League of Massachusetts, *PURPOSE Massachusetts Advocacy Kit* (Cambridge, MA, 1994).

88. Centers for Disease Control and Prevention, Division of STD/HIV Prevention, *Annual Report*, 1990.

89. P. C. Scales, "Where Is Sexuality Education Today?" *Independent School*, (41) (1981), pp. 10–12.

90. J. Hottois and N. Milner, *The Sex Education Controversy* (Lexington, MA: Lexington Books, 1975); in M. Fine, "The Missing Discourse of Desire," *Harvard Educational Review*, 58(1) (1988), pp. 29–53.

91. Leo, "Sex and Schools," pp. 54–63.

92. More than 85% of the American public in 1989 approved of such instruction, compared with 76% in 1975 and 69% in 1965. In Louis Harris and Associates, "Public Attitudes Toward Teenage Pregnancy, Sex Education and Birth Control," poll conducted for the Planned Parenthood Federation of America, New York.

93. Approximately nine out of ten parents want their children to have sexuality education in school. In P. Donovan, *Risk and Responsibility: Teaching Sex Education in America's Schools Today* (New York: The Alan Guttmacher Institute, 1989).

94. A 1980 Gallup poll found that 79% of adults supported sex education with parental consent while only 34% approved of such instruction without parental consent. In Gallup Organization, *American Families—1980*, report submitted to the White House Conference on Families, Princeton, NJ, 1980.

95. 94% of parents approve of AIDS education in schools. In A. Gallup, "The 19th Annual Gallup Polls of the Public's Attitudes toward the Public School," Gallup Poll (69) (1987), p. 1.

96. T. Andre, R. L. Frevert, and D. Schuchmann, "From Whom Have College Students Learned What About Sex?" *Youth and Society*, 20 (1993), pp. 241–268.

97. Planned Parenthood League of Massachusetts Sexuality Assessment Report, *The Status of Sexuality Education in Massachusetts Public Schools*, 1995.

PART II

Case Studies of Alpha and Beta

Alpha Case Study: Students and Adults Working Together

COMMUNITY PROFILE OF ALPHA

Alpha, a city of approximately 83,000 residents, is located six miles from Boston, Massachusetts. This suburban community is a collection of fourteen distinct villages incorporated into the City of Alpha over three hundred years ago. Each of the villages has its own distinct flavor. In Alpha Lakes, home to many Italian-American families, red, green, and white lines—colors of the Italian flag—run down the median of the main thoroughfare. Alpha also has a large Jewish population. There are five synagogues in various parts of the city. A 1990 census found that 75,410 Alpha residents identified themselves as white, which included Irish, Russian, Italian, English, and German ethnic groups. The former mayor boasted of 54 nationalities living in the city. However, people of color (African Americans, Asian Americans, Latinos, and Native Americans) comprised less than 9% of the city's population.[1] Nevertheless, the presence of racial groups has a history in Alpha. According to the pastor of a local historically black church, "This church is celebrating its 120th anniversary. There have been Black people in Alpha since the late 1600s."[2]

Although often regarded as an affluent community, Alpha has some socioeconomic diversity. Approximately one-third of the households have incomes over $75,000 and 20% of Alpha households have incomes under $25,000.[3] The city's northern and western villages are more ethnically and economically mixed and traditionally have had significant working-class populations. The southern villages are considered the wealthiest parts of the city.[4] Nearly 70% of Alpha adults are college educated.

During the 1993–1994 school year, 10,571 students were enrolled in

Alpha Public Schools. There were fifteen elementary schools, two junior high, and two senior high schools.[5] The system employs more than 800 classroom teachers with a $63 million budget. Per pupil expenditure in Alpha is $6,714 compared with $5,034 statewide.[6]

The Alpha Public Schools are governed by an eight-member School Committee elected at-large from the city's eight wards for two-year terms. The mayor presides as an ex-officio member and the superintendent and two high school students also serve on the committee. During 1993–1994, the committee was comprised of five women and three men, all of whom were white. Four committee members were Jewish, three Catholic, and one Protestant. This reflects the religious diversity of Alpha. At least six members have children who attend or have graduated from Alpha schools. Key community organizations and leaders are listed in Figure 2.1.

A LOOK AT SEXUALITY EDUCATION IN ALPHA PUBLIC SCHOOLS

In 1986, Alpha schools offered sex education in seventh and tenth grades.[7] Within a year, AIDS education was integrated into each school's science curriculum.[8, 9] But some Alpha residents wondered if enough was being done. Verna Schock, an Alpha North guidance counselor, stated, "They're [the students] not informed. They're very naive. They're all vulnerable and think this can't happen to them."[10] Lisa Bradbury, a PTO president, commented, "Sex education should be made mandatory in every elementary school. It is a 'cop out' for teachers not to teach sex education."[11] Like many school systems, Alpha had a range of health education/human service programs; however, the city-wide coordination of curricula and service components did not exist.

In 1987, Alpha School Committee member Sandra Riley researched the extent of sex education in Alpha schools and concluded that there were no "system-wide policies or guidelines." She commented, "I think we need more [sex education] and perhaps something more structured."[12] While members of the community continued to discuss teaching sex education in public schools, it was in the fall of 1991 when this issue gained community-wide attention.[13]

STUDENT VOICES

In September 1991, seniors Mark Fleming and Regina Sidell were discussing the results of a student survey of sexual activity and condom use published in an Alpha South school newspaper, the *Advocate*. Sidell recalled, "Mark and I read this *Advocate* article where they took a poll of sexual activity among students. We were shocked." In their conversation, Fleming noted that while nearly half of juniors and seniors said they were

Figure 2.1
Key Community Organizations and Leaders in Alpha

Student Committee on Sexual Awareness
• Mark Fleming, former Alpha South High School student;
• Regina Sidell, former Alpha South High School student;

Committee on the Prevention of AIDS
• John Kurtis, former Alpha North High School student;
• Jamie Sinclair, former Alpha North High School student;

Health Education Task Force
• Caren Burke, Health Education consultant;
• Natalie Dixon, Health Education specialist;

Health Advisory Council
• Natalie Dixon, Health Education specialist;
• Bill Parker, Alpha South High School History and Sexuality Education teacher;
• Susan Simon, Alpha parent;
• Rob Pike, Alpha parent;

Committee '93
• Daniel Colin, Massachusetts State Representative;
• Martha Kaplan, parent, past co-president, City-wide PTA Council;

Alpha School Committee
• Diane Eisen, Alpha School Committee member;
• Howard Rosen, Alpha School Committee member;
• Sandra Riley, Alpha School Committee member;
• Sonya Schultz, chairwoman, Alpha School Committee;

Alpha School Administration
• Ivan Brown, superintendent, Alpha Public Schools;
• Paul Redman, assistant superintendent, Alpha Public Schools;

Alpha Citizens for Public Education (ACPE)
• Bob Carr, co-director;
• Mary Citron, spokeswoman;
• Linda Hale, co-director;

Supporters of Student Health Education in Alpha (SSHEA)
• Hanah Golden, local activist;
• Sarah Kanner, chairwoman;

Alpha Clergy Association
• Reverend Jack Andrews, president, Alpha Clergy Association;
• Reverend Matthew Barker, pastor, Second United Church of Christ.

sexually active, "a lot of freshmen said they were active too."[14] He added, "Then it popped into my head. I read [in a related story] that Cambridge Rindge and Latin [High School] had condoms. . . . We decided to do something."[15]

These individuals formed the Student Committee on Sexual Awareness, a group of 22 Alpha South students, who brought the idea of an expanded AIDS education program to the community's attention. The initial goal of this group, according to co-founder Mark Fleming, was to "have condoms available at school." A few days later the student group approached Edward Vanderbilt, Principal of Alpha South High School, with their plan. His response, according to Sidell, was, "I can see where you are coming from and I agree with your position, but I think the way you're going about this is wrong, and, by the way, you'll be suspended." Sidell remembered,

I ran home that day [after the meeting with Vanderbilt] and said, "Mom, guess what, I'm going to get suspended. I'm so happy." And my mother said, "No, Regina, you haven't spent your whole life working so hard doing so well. You'll get your first mark on your record, and you're not going to get into college." So I was a little angry with her. I said, "Come on, this is ridiculous, you gotta be radical." But on the other hand I started thinking about it. She was saying to me, "Regina, the officials and the educators and the adults, they want you to fly off the handle. They want you to run around and hand things out. It will solidify their beliefs that you're not responsible. Why don't you go through the proper channels. Use your resources. Use your town to your advantage and you'll gain the respect of the community and you'll find people behind you, supporting you, the numbers are going to grow." So that's what we did.[16]

Members of the Student Committee on Sexual Awareness used the resources within their community. They developed relationships with members from both inside and outside the community, collaborating with faculty, parents, school administrators, peers, and outside experts to accomplish their goal.

The students solicited the support of faculty members. They repeatedly met with Bill Parker, an Alpha South High School teacher. One afternoon, Parker told Fleming, "The best way for change to occur is to come from the people who are most affected. You can have enormous power if you choose to exercise it, particularly in one collective voice." While the students were initially interested in condom distribution, through their conversations with Parker they created a broader vision that called for the expansion of health and sexuality education in Alpha's schools.[17] In a period of two weeks, they collected 630 student, 31 faculty, and 15 parent signatures to support their position.[18]

The students also obtained support from parents inside and outside the community.[19] One such parent was Sylvia Healey, president of the Alpha South High School Parent Teachers Association. She stated, "Mark and

Regina came to me. At first they were interested in guerrilla tactics. They wanted to provide a gross of condoms and start distributing them. I talked with them about the parents and the administration and said, 'Let's work with the system. Come to the PTA and let's get support from parents.' "[20]

While the students received support from both parents and school personnel, they also met resistance. When they requested to be put on the School Committee's docket to discuss the issue of condom availability and sexuality education, Sidell recalled, "We called up a woman we were told was in charge of [making the appointments]. She was so mean to us. We had to call back three times, 'cause we got hung up on and were put on hold. We weren't treated with respect. She said, 'We have this docket and we can put you wherever we want. So we can do this tomorrow or we can do it next year.' "[21] Through persistence, the students were successful in getting their issues docketed for the January 1992 meeting.

The students also developed relationships with their peers from Alpha North. Sidell recalled, "Patrick Lawson called us up and said, 'Let me help you, I tried to do this. It didn't work.' He basically saved our butts because he was the bridge between North and South. He was older and because he went to both schools. He had a lot more insight. He knew the community."[22] Within three days, Jamie Sinclair and John Kurtis, co-presidents of Committee on the Prevention of AIDS, organized students to collect over 1,000 signatures at Alpha North. Sinclair stated, "We wanted at least 700 signatures and we ended up with over 1,000." Kurtis added, "Although there are different social groups in school, the issue was felt strongly in the whole school."[23]

The student groups also worked together to conduct various awareness activities within school and the community. Hours before the School Committee's second Open Forum, the students co-sponsored a rally outside City Hall to demonstrate support for a condom availability program. They passed out over 400 condoms.[24]

PUBLIC HEARINGS ON CONDOM AVAILABILITY

Due to the students' request for a school-based condom availability program and the new guidelines on sexuality education developed by the Massachusetts Board of Education in 1990, the Alpha School Committee solicited community input. Initially, a notice went "out to all interested members in the community."[25] Eighty-nine individuals and organizations wrote letters or made telephone calls to the School Committee to voice their position.[26] The majority of supporters favored such a program within the context of a "sound comprehensive educational program." Opponents cited "ethical and religious" reasons and their belief that this action was not "an appropriate function of an educational institution."[27, 28]

Additionally, the School Committee also publicized and hosted two city-wide meetings. These Open Forums attracted nearly 300 adults and students. Interestingly, adults were more divided on this issue than the students.[29, 30]

Students from both high schools were vocal in calling on adults to make condoms available in the city's two high schools.[31] Jamie Sinclair, co-president of Alpha North's Committee on the Prevention of AIDS stated, "AIDS is not discriminating and children are not immune nor invincible. It is important to instill the message of abstinence, but there will always be teenagers who will not listen to that message and they need to be protected."[32] Through their persistence in attending meetings and forums, the larger community eventually heard the student voices.[33]

While adult members of the community wrestled with this issue, School Committee members also debated it. In their discussion that followed the Open Forum, one member of the School Committee, Howard Rosen, and Ivan Brown, the School Superintendent, verbalized their opposition to a condom availability program in the schools.[34–36] The complexity of this issue is reflected in Chairwoman Schultz's comments. She said, "This is the first issue where a decision has not been obvious to me. My own position is clear in terms of supporting availability, but it's not finalized in terms of availability within schools. I am concerned about mixed messages, the increasing demands placed on schools and the lack of financial support."[37]

At the School Committee's second Open Forum on the issue, students presented a petition to the Alpha School Committee with over 1,600 student and faculty signatures supporting condom availability in the city's high schools. Jason Wiseman, Alpha South Student Faculty Association member, commented, "There is nothing immoral or improper about saving lives."[38] Sidell summed up the evening: "I think what really clinched it was when we said, boom, students, teachers and parents from both schools were concerned [about this issue]."

After soliciting community input, the School Committee approved, in a 7–1 vote, a measure to make condoms available to students at Alpha's two high schools. Sonya Schultz, School Committee chairwoman, recalled that evening: "This was student initiated. If it were not for the students' request, I don't think you would have seen this kind of vote. They were asking for help and doing it in the most appropriate way possible."[39] Throughout the coming months, school administrators and city Health Department officials developed and implemented a condom availability program.[40] The Alpha School Committee also charged school administrators with forming a task force to explore the components of a comprehensive sexuality and HIV/AIDS curriculum.

CREATION OF THE HEALTH EDUCATION TASK FORCE

In February 1992, Assistant Superintendent Paul Redman sent an invitation letter to interested students, school personnel, and community members to join the Task Force. This group, which began meeting in March 1992, was comprised of 50 parents, teachers, students, administrators, physicians, social service professionals, clergy, and other residents. Redman stated, "We wanted to include people from broad perspectives, so that we could have some dialogue."[41] The goal of this group was to recommend a comprehensive K–12 health education curriculum to the School Committee.

In an initial interview of Alpha faculty, many staff noted that they wanted support in dealing with health education issues. Others expressed concern about the importance of these topics and the lack of time to teach them.[42] In October 1992, Task Force members met with parents at six of Alpha's nineteen schools to assess their attitudes and concerns on sexuality education topics. Overwhelmingly, those surveyed supported a comprehensive sex education program. Additionally, they requested parent workshops.[43] In October 1992, the Task Force also conducted a survey of a representative sample of eighth and ninth graders about their knowledge, attitudes, behaviors, and needs.[44] However, the school administration never completed the analysis of these data. These results have never officially been reported or utilized. Teachers were again surveyed in March 1993. When the results from the initial teacher/administrator survey were analyzed, Dixon commented, "Gaps in Alpha's program were obvious and glaring."[45] Results from the parent and second teacher surveys provided additional evidence to verify the need for an expanded sexuality education program in Alpha's schools.

OBTAINING COMMUNITY SUPPORT

Through the early work of the Task Force it became apparent that the majority of those surveyed supported some type of school-based sexuality education program. Even though students' views were not analyzed, approximately two-thirds of the Alpha High School students endorsed the petition presented to the School Committee. After ten months of data collection, the Task Force recommended to the School Committee in January 1993 that it pilot test a health and sexuality education program at the ninth-grade level and eventually implement age-appropriate materials for all grades.[46] At this same meeting, individuals representing community groups verbalized their support of the Task Force.[47]

The School Committee voted unanimously to support the Task Force's recommendations concerning the human sexuality–HIV/AIDS curriculum. Over the next few months, other individuals and community groups emerged to support the Task Force's work.[48]

EMERGENCE OF ALPHA CITIZENS FOR
PUBLIC EDUCATION

Amidst this support, opposition arose. Individuals demonstrated their opposition in various ways. Some individuals requested to join the Task

Force with the hopes of influencing the curriculum development process. Others demonstrated their opposition by removing their children from the pilot program, from the Alpha Public Schools, or by remaining publicly silent on the subject. Still others expressed their dissatisfaction by voicing their opposition at public meetings and through the media.

One of the first public opportunities for Alpha residents to voice their concerns over the proposed curriculum was at the School Committee's Open Forum in January 1993. Of the 22 individuals who addressed the School Committee, eight opposed to the development of the curriculum had the opportunity to present their opinions.[49] Linda Hale, an Alpha parent who was instrumental in organizing the opposition, stated, "We did get twenty to thirty bodies to that meeting." Many of those who opposed the plan later became the "core group" of Alpha Citizens for Public Education (ACPE)—a grassroots parent organization founded by Linda Hale and Bob Carr opposed to the ninth-grade curriculum. Over time, ACPE would take on the administration's "opt in/opt out" policy and its requirements for participation on the Task Force, and ultimately the School Committee by running a slate of candidates in the 1993 elections.

Over the next few months, as the Task Force held a series of parent meetings to solicit community input, ACPE members remained outside and distributed their own materials. The flyers called school plans "propaganda" and "double speak."

After the School Committee adopted the Task Force's recommendations, Superintendent Brown stated, "Parents have the option to have their child opt out." Carr took issue with school officials because the program was designed to be integrated into other curricula. Carr discussed the option of developing an "opt in" policy. He commented, "If schools insist on having faculty members introduce oral sex, homosexual lifestyles, sexual response, and similarly intimate subjects to children, plus hand out condoms, I would not deny [others] any of it. But make it an elective, something that parents can sign their kids into, not something they have to expend time and energy to get their kids out."[50] Despite ACPE's criticisms the "opt out" policy remained.

ACPE also expressed frustration because it felt it had been "shut out" of the Task Force. Specifically, Bob Carr, ACPE co-director, was angry that members of his group were not asked to join. He stated, "They haven't contacted anyone from our group despite the fact that I publicly asked to be included." He continued, "Parents feel shut out of a 'mad rush' by educators to stop teen pregnancy and gay bashing."[51] Hale also expressed her frustration. She recounted, "I requested to serve on the Task Force and was turned down. I called Assistant Superintendent Redman and he said that they had already chosen all the people and that there were no more places left."[52]

In an *Alpha Graphic* article, "Group Set to Fight Sex Ed," Dixon responded to some of ACPE's accusations. She commented, "It doesn't make sense that they think the process is closed. We're taking the time to get a lot of input."[53]

COUNTERING ACPE ACTIVITIES

Many Alpha residents and community groups demonstrated support of the curriculum by counteracting ACPE activities. Less than a month after ACPE's forum, entitled "What's Wrong with Sex Education Anyway?", a more formalized organization, Supporters of Student Health Education in Alpha (SSHEA), was created to support the Task Force's efforts.[54] The members of this organization sponsored an evening telethon to explain the facts about the pilot program to Alpha residents. The group also gathered over 800 pledges of support. With these funds, SSHEA took out a full-page ad in the two local newspapers supporting the Task Force's efforts. Members of SSHEA also successfully recruited curriculum supporters to the School Committee's May meeting. At this meeting the School Committee was to vote on the Task Force's recommendations. Kanner, an Alpha parent and founding member of SSHEA, commented, "We worked hard to get people to the meeting."[55]

In response to ACPE's media campaign, Sheila Fenn, an educator and local video producer, developed "Response to the Gay Agenda," a panel discussion on homophobia with Alpha clergy, parents, and school activists. Fenn stated, "Whatever she [Pam Ferguson, a local producer and ACPE member] puts on, I will counter-program. Because I think that you should see both sides." ACPE's media tactics compelled private citizens to speak out. Nadine Nadler, an Alpha resident, stated, "After weeks of following the media blitz of a small but vocal minority of Alpha parents bombarding the press with alarmingly malevolent misinformation, I feel compelled to speak out."[56] Even the local newspapers responded. An editorial in the *Alpha Graphic* a week later was entitled "No Place for Hate."[57]

In response to ACPE's slate of School Committee candidates, members of Alpha's political establishment became active and formed Committee '93. This political action committee, comprised of activists and parents, interviewed all sixteen candidates and endorsed a slate of candidates for the November elections.[58] State Representative Daniel Colin (D-Alpha) felt the slate card increased the vote total of all the candidates. He concluded, "It was clear that individuals were voting the slate card. All of our candidates won."

Another method used to counteract ACPE's activities was to link its members' associations with the right wing. The earliest accusations made *Tab* front-page headlines: "Officials fear religious right targeting schools."[59] In his address to the School Committee in May, Melvin Caan, Chairman, State Board of Education and Alpha resident, made a series of comments linking ACPE to the "religious right." He stated, "The material that has been distributed by ACPE is very similar to material appearing in many communities nationwide in opposition to any comprehensive health and sex education in the public schools."[60] Mary Citron, ACPE spokeswoman, charged that Caan's comments were intended to incite hatred. She said, "He came in an official capacity to increase fears based on totally untrue allegations and inferences."[61]

THE MAY 10 SCHOOL COMMITTEE MEETING

The mobilization efforts of supporters and opponents of the curriculum culminated in May. Over 600 people filled Bell Junior High auditorium to voice their positions and hear the Task Force's final recommendations. More than half of the speakers voiced their support.[62] State Senator Lisa Pell (D-Alpha), who recognized the School Committee's leadership role, commented: "We cannot stand idly by while our children make serious decisions without understanding the nature of their choices. This program will ensure that they have accurate information and a respect for themselves and others."[63]

After four hours of public testimony, the Health Education Task Force submitted its final recommendations. In a 9–0 vote, School Committee members approved "the report from the Health Education Task Force, including the proposed outline for the ninth grade human sexuality course."

IMPLEMENTATION OF THE *HEALTH AND SEXUALITY* CURRICULUM

Solicitation of funds occurred at the federal, state, and local levels. In spring 1992, Task Force members worked with the Alpha School Department to submit grant applications for curriculum and staff development.

Task Force members worked collaboratively with school administrators to obtain possible funding. Members of this grant-writing team were successful in securing $45,000 from the Massachusetts Department of Education. In a memo to Superintendent Ivan Brown, Phil Redman announced that these funds would support the development of a comprehensive health education curriculum.[64, 65] In another attempt to locate funding, Jean Fisk, co-chair of the Task Force's curriculum subcommittee, informed the School Committee of funds available through the Massachusetts Department of Education's Health Protection Grant program. She noted that Alpha was eligible for $300,000. Eligibility required that the Health Education Task Force be renamed and its composition slightly revised to represent a broader segment of the community. Three additional individuals—Bill Parker, Susan Simon, and Rob Pike—were asked to become members. Later that summer, the Alpha Public Schools received $310,000 from this grant program.

Over the next year, the Task Force worked to develop the curriculum for the ninth-grade pilot program. Dixon wrote, "We examined many commercially developed curricula, reviewed programs from other school systems and searched through the professional literature to identify effective researched-based programs. Our study led us to the decision to design our own curriculum and to integrate the commercially published skills-based curriculum, *Reducing the Risk* into the course."[66-68] The ninth-grade curriculum was entitled *Sexuality and Health*. The key concepts included human development, relationships, personal skills, sexual behavior, health, and society and culture. Approximately 800 ninth-grade students at Alpha North and Alpha South were enrolled in the program. Approximately 162 (17%) ninth-grade students opted out of the program, many due to scheduling conflicts. In anticipation of full implementation in fall 1994, thirteen faculty members and other interested colleagues participated in a five-day summer training.

In December 1993, the School Committee approved the new curriculum. In a memo to the School Committee, Brown wrote, "I am extremely pleased and proud of the work that these people have done . . . in developing this pilot program. It is a program that will meet the needs of Alpha students and represents efforts that we should all be proud to support."[69] This sentiment was echoed in an editorial in the *Tab* entitled "Sex ed long overdue." The author wrote, "This is a thorough pilot program dealing with a complex, controversial subject. It is a subject that can no longer be ignored by schools or taught as a small section of health class. It is well thought out and represents careful, methodical work by the Task Force."[70]

NOTES

1. E. R. Hornor, *Massachusetts Municipal Profiles 1993–1994* (Palo Alto, CA: Information Publications, 1993).

2. Howard Interview, 9/15/94.

3. Hornor, *Massachusetts Municipal Profiles 1993–1994*.

4. C. Cleary, "Alpha More Than Wealthy Neighborhoods," *The Boston Globe*, 11/11/90, p. 25.

5. Telephone Interview, Alpha School Department, October 1994.

6. Telephone Interview, Massachusetts Department of Education, November 1992.

7. J. Duman, "Sex in School," *Tab*, 12/16/86, p. 16.

8. H. Altman, "AIDS: Communities Consider Education," *Alpha Graphic*, 7/29/87, p. 8.

9. J. Berkofsky, "AIDS Education in All Grades," *Alpha Graphic*, 11/11/87, p. 7.

10. L. McFalls, "Opinions Definite, Varied on Sex Ed," *Alpha Graphic*, 9/24/86, p. 1.

11. Ibid.

12. M. Azzato, "Sex Education Programs Criticized," *Alpha Graphic*, 3/18/87, p. 8.

13. Editorial, "Sex Education Needed," *Alpha Graphic*, 3/4/93, p. 16.

14. A random survey of students conducted by the Alpha South High School newspaper the *Advocate* (9/30/91) found that 18% of freshmen, 27% of sophomores, 45% of juniors, and 48% of seniors described themselves as sexually active and one fourth of all sexually active students used no birth control.

15. In a related article in the *Advocate* entitled "Cambridge leads the way in condom distribution," the authors mention the outreach work of a group of peer leaders at Cambridge Rindge and Latin High School who had handed out envelopes containing condoms with instructions and information about AIDS prevention. In R. Wand, B. Stern, and D. Mirsky, "Cambridge leads the way in condom availability," *Advocate*, 9/30/91.

16. Sidell Interview, 12/22/94.

17. Student Petition, 1991.

18. P. Mahoney and R. Telegen, "School Committee Votes to Make Condoms Available," *The Capsule*, 1/31/92, p. 3.

19. Through Fleming's father the students came in contact with Beverly Wiggins, director of the Center for Prevention, who provided the group with information and strategy on how to deal with the School Committee. Beverly Wiggins and Kevin Crane co-authored "Condom Availability in a Small Town: Lessons Learned from Falmouth, Massachusetts," *SIECUS Report*, October/November 1992. This article outlines suggestions for holding public hearings on condom availability.

20. Healey Interview, 8/19/94.

21. Sidell Interview, 12/22/94.

22. Ibid.

23. R. Lear, "Sex Ed Debate Heats Up," *Tab*, 1/21/92, pp. 1, 6, and 12.

24. Mahoney and Telegen, "School Committee Votes to Make Condoms Available," p. 1.

25. Initially, a letter went "out to all interested members in the community," including community agencies, parents, youth groups, religious leaders, and elected officials, inviting written opinions on this issue. In Alpha School Committee Minutes, 1/27/92, p. 3.

26. Of those responses, 40 favored condom availability within the schools as compared to 49 who opposed it. Alpha School Committee Minutes, 11/25/91, p. 4.

27. Letters from the community, 1991–1992.

28. Another opponent of a school-based condom availability program was John McCarthy, principal of the Alpha North High School. He wrote in a letter, "For those who are sexually active the use of condoms is strongly recommended as safe practice. I support that recommendation. However, in my view, condoms are already available to anyone who wants them through a pharmacy." In letter, 1/6/92.

29. Of the 39 people who addressed the Alpha School Committee at the Open Forums on January 13 and 27, 1992, 24 individuals (17 adults and 7 youths) supported a condom availability program within the high school setting compared

to 15 individuals (15 adults) who did not support such a program. In Alpha School Committee Records, 1991–1992.

30. Nearly one-half of the 40 people who spoke voiced their opposition to condom availability based on religious beliefs, moral grounds, the lack of school resources, and a conviction that this was not a responsibility of the schools. For example, Nina Hanover supported AIDS education but did not believe dispensing condoms was the school's role. She stated, "There are fourteen pharmacies in Alpha where condoms are available." Alpha School Committee Minutes, 1/13/93, p. 13.

31. Ibid., p. 14.

32. Ibid., p. 9.

33. Eisen Interview, 8/24/93.

34. H. Rosen, Alpha School Committee Meeting videotape, 1/27/94.

35. J. Brown, Alpha School Committee Meeting videotape, 1/27/94.

36. At this same meeting, Sandra Riley commented that she had a great deal of respect for people on both sides of the issue. She went on to state, "The driving issue for me was not moral or religious, but rather the public health aspect." Riley Interview, 9/7/94.

37. R. Lear, "Sex Ed Gets Go-Ahead amid Debate," *Tab*, 1/19/93, p. 3.

38. *Alpha School Committee Minutes*, 1/27/92, p. 9.

39. R. Lear, "Sex Ed Debate Heats Up," *Tab*, 1/21/92, pp. 1, 6, and 12.

40. Alpha School Committee Minutes, 1992, p. 12.

41. Fifty people out of approximately 80 candidates who had spoken or written to the School Committee during the deliberations about this program were selected to sit on the Task Force. Of the 32 members who sat on subcommittees, 8 were identified as parents, 10 as teachers, 2 as students, 1 as an administrator, 3 physicians and 2 nurses, 5 social/health service professionals and 1 clergy. Interestingly, all members supported a comprehensive health and sexuality education program in the schools. In *Alpha School Committee Minutes* Attachment C, 5/26/92.

The goal of the School Climate/Environment subcommittee was to examine gender and racial issues, including homophobia, abuse, racial conflicts, and teacher sensitivity. In a memo to the School Committee, the members of this subcommittee wrote, "[We] believe that it is our responsibility to provide a healthful, supportive environment for all our students." The Community Resources subcommittee looked at ways to address the adult community. They stated, "There will be a need to not only convey what is being taught in the schools, but to provide information geared towards giving better insight relevant to the issues." The School Health Services subcommittee examined the definition of school health services by looking at what services were provided by the Health Department in the schools and how to enhance current services. In Alpha School Committee Memo, May 1992.

42. Alpha Health Education Task Force, *Report and Recommendations*, December 1992.

43. Other results from the parent questionnaire included:

• While almost all parents were comfortable with students in grades 4–6 learning about reproductive anatomy and puberty, a small number did not want their children taught specifics about sexual physiology and behavior;

• A majority of parents did not want information about sexual orientation given to children in grades K–3. A smaller number did not want this topic discussed in grades 4–6. Parents of older children supported teaching about this topic;

• Many parents urged that the physical, emotional, and spiritual aspects of sex be integrated into the curriculum;

• Many parents wanted the topic of personal responsibility addressed in relationships and abstinence as the healthier choice to be emphasized in the curriculum;

• Parents were also concerned about the expertise of the teacher. (*Source*: Alpha Health Education Task Force, *Report and Recommendations*).

44. *Alpha School Committee Minutes*, 5/26/92, p. 10.

45. N. Dixon, *Educating for Life: Implementing Sexuality and HIV/AIDS Education in the Alpha Schools* (Master's Thesis, Cambridge, MA: Cambridge College, 1993), p. 38.

46. Alpha Health Education Task Force, *Report and Recommendations*.

47. In particular, Fern Mendon, co-president of the Alpha PTA Council, stated, "We unanimously support: (1) the process for developing the curriculum; and (2) the work of the Task Force in the implementation of a city-wide health education curriculum to meet the needs of Alpha's children." *Alpha School Committee Minutes*, 3/94; *Alpha School Committee Minutes*, 1/11/93, p. 4.

48. In an editorial in the *Alpha Graphic* (3/4/93, p. 1) entitled, "Sex Education Is Needed," the author writes, "Listen to the students. It's not enough just to teach them about the basics anymore. Students should be trusted with as much information as available, taught in a frank and honest atmosphere."

49. *Alpha School Committee Minutes*, 1/11/93, pp. 2–23.

50. Carr Interview, 8/18/94.

51. M. Houston and R. Lear, "Officials Fear Religious Right Targeting Schools," *Tab*, 3/23/93, p. 8.

52. Hale Interview, 8/24/94.

53. S. Lyons, "Group Set to Fight Sex Ed," *Alpha Graphic*, 3/25/93, p. 20.

54. Sara Kanner, an Alpha parent and one of the group's founders, outlined why citizens of Alpha should support the effort. In summary, Kanner stated, (1) the Task Force is made up of a cross-section of professionals from the community who have long been involved in health and sexuality education, (2) children need to learn about sexuality in a healthy context, and (3) the statistics on adolescent sexual activity are alarming. In S. Kanner, Viewpoint: "Safe Crossing for Students," *Tab*, 5/4/93, p. 29.

55. Kanner Interview, 8/19/94.

56. N. Nadler (letter), "A Matter of Life and Death," *Tab*, 5/25/93, p. 29.

57. Members of SSHEA responded by co-sponsoring a public forum with the Alpha Human Rights Commission and the Alpha Substance Abuse and AIDS Coalition, entitled "A Partnership: Sexuality Education in the Home, Schools, and Community," in October 1993. The purpose of this event was to increase awareness around HIV/AIDS and foster better communication between parents, schools, and children. Editorial, "No Place for Hate," *Alpha Graphic*, 4/8/93, p. 18.

58. Colin Interview, 1/23/95.

59. Houston and Lear, "Officials Fear Religious Right Targeting Schools," p. 1.

60. *Alpha School Committee Minutes*, 5/10/93.

61. L. Pappano, "Alpha to Try Sex Education in 9th Grade," *The Boston Globe*, 5/11/93, p. 21.

62. These individuals represented groups such as Alpha Teacher's Association, Alpha Substance Abuse/AIDS Coalition, Alpha Human Rights Commission, Alpha School Nurses Association, the Unitarian Society of Alpha, Second Church of Alpha, Temple Emanuel, Gay and Lesbian Advocate Defenders (GLAD). Alpha School Committee Minutes, 5/10/93.

63. Ibid., p. 7.

64. Redman Memo, 9/12/92.

65. A press release from the Office of Grants Management/Alpha Public Schools read, "The grant will support the first year of a three-year project to plan and implement a course on human sexuality for 650 ninth graders in Alpha's two high schools. Central to this project is the development of an effective curriculum, staff development and in-service trainings for teachers who will teach the curriculum. . . . A part-time health education consultant will assist teachers and coordinators in conducting this project." Alpha School Department Press Release, 9/14/92.

66. Dixon, *Educating for Life: Implementing Sexuality and HIV/AIDS Education in the Alpha Schools*, p. 59.

67. *Reducing the Risk* curriculum is based on active learning and skill-building. This curriculum uses fifteen structured lessons to help teenagers gain skills and confidence to either abstain from sex or if sexually active to use birth control.

68. Dixon, *Educating for Life: Implementing Sexuality and HIV/AIDS Education in the Alpha Schools*, p. 55.

69. Brown memo to the Alpha School Committee, 12/93.

70. "Sex Ed Long Overdue," *Tab*, 12/28/93, p. 30.

CHAPTER 3

Beta Case Study: If at First You Don't Succeed, Try, Try Again

COMMUNITY PROFILE OF BETA

The town of Beta is a suburban community located twelve miles from Boston, Massachusetts. Incorporated in 1640, Beta was the birthplace of two presidents, John Adams and John Quincy Adams, as well as John Hancock and General Sylvanus Thayer, the founder of West Point. Today, the town of Beta is situated at the crossroads of I-93 (Route 128) and Route 3. Office and industrial parks have sprung up along the major thoroughfares that run through the northern and eastern regions of town. In 1980, the Massachusetts Bay Transportation Authority extended its train service from Boston to Beta.

One resident described Beta as "three different parts."[1] East Beta is regarded as a lower-income and more industrial section of town. In this area one notices the striking similarity among the Cape Cod–style homes. Only exterior colors or plantings distinguish one home from its neighbor. Occasionally, these homes give way to larger, more stately Victorian homes built before World War II. Beta Highlands, located in the northern and western parts of town, is considered one of the wealthier areas. In these neighborhoods large oak and maple trees shade elegant brick and cedar shake colonial-style homes. According to Beta resident Michael Murphy, "South Beta is also like the Highlands. This part of town has some of the much larger houses."

In the past 50 years Beta's population has more than doubled to 34,000.[2] Alice Dowling, a Beta parent, explained: "A lot of people moved here from an urban community and felt it was a safe community. They could throw up a fence around their house and protect their children from everything."

A 1990 census found that 32,750 Beta residents identified themselves as white, which included: Irish and Italian ethnic groups. People of color (African Americans, Asian Americans, Latinos, and Native Americans) comprised less than 3% of the city's population.[3] When asked to describe the town's demographic composition, a Beta School Committee member stated, "We're a Catholic town. We have a very small minority population."[4]

Residents feel that people are attracted to Beta because it has an excellent school system. During the 1991–1992 school year, approximately 4,500 students were enrolled in Beta Public Schools. The system employs over 500 professional staff with a $21 million budget.[5] Beta's per pupil expenditure is $5,244 compared with $5,034 statewide.[6] The Beta Public Schools are governed by a seven-member School Committee elected at-large for one-, two-, or three-year terms. The superintendent and two high school students also serve on the committee. During 1991–1992, the committee was comprised of four women and three men, all of whom were white and Catholic. Approximately half of the members had served on the School Committee for more than five years. A listing of key community leaders and organizations appears in Figure 3.1.

AIDS EDUCATION IN BETA PUBLIC SCHOOLS

In 1990, Beta had eight documented cases of AIDS.[7, 8] In less than eighteen months, Beta health officials reported six additional AIDS cases. In the same year, a sampling of schools south of Boston showed that AIDS education was presented in health education, physical education, and science classes in nine out of ten high schools surveyed.[9]

Jim Gray, Beta's former health education director, provided a historical context of health education in Beta. He commented:

The first time we had any health education was about twenty-five years ago. It was called Sociobiology. A few years passed before they asked me to continue the program under the name Health and Human Development. The first thing I did was to form a committee to send out a survey to all the parents. When the surveys came back there was no question in anybody's mind that parents wanted it. We drew up the original curriculum. It included: physical, mental, social, environmental and emotional health.[10]

Some years later, Assistant Superintendent Michael Moore discussed Beta's AIDS Education Program at the AIDS Advisory Committee's initial meeting. He commented, "AIDS education presently starts in grade seven and eight in the Health and Human Development Program and is infused into the subject disciplines of biology, physical education, psychology, and sociology."[11] Beta School Committee member Maureen Casey remembered, "Our kids were taught about AIDS in the high school, in many different

Figure 3.1
Key Community Organizations and Leaders in Beta

Students
- Ann Murphy, former Beta High School student;
- Sharon Whitmire, former Beta High School student;

AIDS Advisory Committee (AAC)
- Jane Alexander, chairwoman and health educator, Beta Public Schools;
- Shirley Bowman, parent;
- Alice Dowling, parent;
- Elaine Kane, parent;
- Mary McPherson, parent;
- Ellen Nagel, parent;
- Dorothy Nedrick, parent, future Beta School Committee member;
- Chris Valley, home economics educator, Beta High School;

Health Advisory Council
- Jane Alexander, chairwoman and health educator, Beta Public Schools;

Beta School Committee
- Jean Anderson, member for 16 years;
- Maureen Casey, member;
- Joseph Ponds, chairman;

Beta School Administration
- Peter Kurtz, superintendent;
- Michael Moore, assistant superintendent;

Concerned Parents and Citizens of Beta (CPCB)
- Carolyn Banner, co-founder;
- Mary Custer, co-founder;
- Thomas Hampton, founding member and founder, Restore American Values in Education (RAVE);
- Elaine Kane, leader of CPCB;
- Linda Whitmire, spokeswoman;

Community Advocates for Responsible Education (CARE)
- Kathy Bartow, member;
- Shirley Bowman, founding member;
- Valerie Devine, founder;
- Ellen Nagel, member, spokeswoman;
- Bill O'Neff, member;

Religious Institutions
- Bill O'Neff, Unitarian Universalist Church, Social Action Committee;
- Reverend Richard Riding, pastor, Second Church of Christ;
- James Russo, pastor, St. Timothy's Roman Catholic Church.

classes. I know my daughter had a biology class where they discussed AIDS. So it was going on in our school system, in a very quiet, biological kind of way." Beta's Health and Human Development specialist Jane Alexander added:

But we were putting an AIDS prevention education program into a very, very informal health education program. And it spelled disaster from the beginning. We were doing another issue-of-the-month kind of thing. All of our health programs were integrated, multidisciplinary, and unorganized.[12]

PUTTING STATE POLICY INTO ACTION

In the early 1990s, as AIDS became a public health issue at both the national and state levels, a series of statewide initiatives motivated Beta administrators to initiate action on the development of an AIDS curriculum. In 1990, the Massachusetts Board of Education urged all public schools to provide HIV/AIDS prevention education to every student at every grade level. At the secondary level it was recommended that HIV/AIDS education should be part of a more complete sexuality education program that included information about sexually transmitted diseases and the value of both sexual abstinence and the use of condoms as disease prevention methods.[13] This suggestion met with local opposition from School Committee candidates at a rally in March 1992. "It's a health issue," responded one candidate, Patricia Dorman. "Have the health department pass them [condoms] out or the drug stores." She went on to say the distribution of condoms "does not belong in the public schools."[14]

These communications were followed by a copy of *Comprehensive Curriculum Guidelines on HIV/AIDS for Grades K–12*, which was forwarded to all school superintendents. The guidelines were intended to be a resource for school personnel and advisory groups as they developed their own respective curricula. Jane Alexander recalled, "Michael [Moore] and I went to a few statewide meetings and we were both convinced that we needed to address this issue." She continued, "We felt that if we didn't have our own policies and programs that this AIDS epidemic was serious enough that somebody else would be telling us what to do. So our intent was to form an AIDS Advisory Committee." As a result they worked with Dr. Peter Kurtz, superintendent of Beta schools, to form an AIDS Advisory Committee (AAC).

FORMATION OF THE AIDS ADVISORY COMMITTEE

The AAC was created through advertisements in the local town newspaper, notices were sent out in school newsletters, and public announcements were made at School Committee and Parent Advisory Council (PAC) meetings. Beta School Committee member Maureen Casey recalled, "The school administration wanted it [the AAC] to be truly representative [of the community]. They wanted a representative from each one of the elementary schools, the middle schools, and the high school." AAC member Shirley Bowman continued, "There was supposed to be a representative from every school who would then go back to their own PTO to report on the AAC's work." Alexander added, "We let everybody on the Committee. No one was excluded. Amazingly, we got about twenty-six volunteers."

Some community residents, however, felt the AAC was overrepresented with community members who formed part of an established parent network in Beta. Mary McPherson, a Beta parent and AAC member, said, "I assumed that others on the Committee were parents like myself. Then it came out that so many of the parents were also on the Parent Advisory Committee (PAC). My eyes opened up and I realized that this was already a stacked committee." [15] Another Beta parent and AAC member, Elaine Kane, added, "I didn't notice it right away that everyone seemed to know everyone else. I just attributed it to the fact that I was new to the town. I did notice though that there was only me and one other person [Mary McPherson] who ever said, 'What does this mean?' "[16]

Beginning in February 1992, AAC members held monthly meetings to review and discuss the development of an HIV/AIDS education curriculum. The group's purpose was articulated by Assistant Superintendent Moore at the AAC's initial meeting. Moore stated, "The goal of the Committee is to recommend to the School Committee curriculum components for a K–12 AIDS education program."[17] Unlike in other communities, the AAC did not assess the views of a broader constituency on the need and content of a K–12 AIDS curriculum. The AAC's leadership felt that Beta residents wanted a school-based HIV/AIDS curriculum. According to AAC Chairwoman Alexander, "I knew from living in the town, that the majority wanted this. I knew our current AIDS curriculum wasn't explicit enough. Parents knew I'd been telling their kids for years not to have sex, so I knew the majority of the parents trusted me."[18] The AAC went on to develop a K–12 HIV/AIDS education curriculum it felt met the needs of Beta residents based on the state guidelines.

EMERGENCE OF CONFLICT

During the summer months, three members of the AAC, Jane Alexander, Mary Sanders, and Dorothy Nedrick, developed the AAC's HIV/AIDS curriculum based upon the recommendations made by the group's three subcommittees.[19]

This action was met with complaints by AAC members who expressed an interest in working on this curriculum. According to Elaine Kane,

We broke in June for the summer, and we were told that those people who were interested in working on the curriculum would be contacted over the summer. So we [McPherson and I] signed up but we were never called. I didn't think anything of it. I assumed that not much was being done and we'd just pick up in the fall. But when I was handed this completed curriculum [in the fall], I was rather shocked.[20]

Beta educator and AAC member Chris Valley recalled, "I didn't feel it was done in any way to keep them out. They [AAC members] had their input."

The exclusionary nature of this action created conflict among AAC members. The infighting among group members pushed one AAC member to resign. Other group members coalesced. AAC member Ellen Nagel recalled, "The more outspoken Elaine [Kane] became, the more we realized how together we were. She caused our side to really solidify."

EMERGENCE OF THE CONCERNED PARENTS AND CITIZENS OF BETA

Unsuccessful in swaying the AAC membership to support their positions, Kane and McPherson tried to enlist support within the larger Beta community. "They [Kane and McPherson] got the ball rolling and brought people together," recalled Beta parent Tom Hampton. In May 1993, they formed the Concerned Parents and Citizens of Beta (CPCB). Kane stated, "I started telling people what was going on in the AAC and my concerns. People were shocked. We decided to get together and talk about what we were going to do. We were just a bunch of parents who felt a certain way. We knew we had to inform parents of what was exactly in that curriculum."[21]Linda Whitmire, who became the CPCB's spokesperson, added, "We wanted to show the School Committee that we didn't want *this* [AIDS] curriculum."

The goal of CPCB was to influence the content of AIDS education in Beta's schools. Kane stated: "Somebody or some group has to speak out for upholding morals and values and we want to be heard."[22]

To achieve their goal of influencing the content of AIDS education in Beta, CPCB members raised concerns regarding the development of the HIV/AIDS curriculum at AAC meetings. The group also conducted a series of outreach activities to raise community awareness about the AAC's HIV/AIDS education plan.

Mary Custer, a Beta parent who befriended Kane, mentioned, "It was at the April [AAC] meeting that 50 people showed up. At this meeting, one Beta parent asked, 'How come I didn't know about this Committee?' Another Beta parent was more accusatory. She shouted: 'You're doing this behind our backs!' After the meeting, Elaine Kane was quoted in the paper as saying: 'Parents are beginning to wake up. And there's a lot of concern that this is just the beginning. Gay and lesbian awareness could be next.' "

As Kane and others reached out to parents in the Beta community, more adults wanted to become involved in the AAC. "We met for two years and we didn't have any problems," said Alexander. "Then when all of the noise began, all these people from out of the sky wanted to join." Some of the parental concerns appeared justified since there were no public forums to build community support for the AAC's HIV/AIDS education curriculum. Beta School Committee member Maureen Casey stated, "There were no mini-presentations made along the way leading up to the curriculum presentation, except for one presentation [the parent education night] and that . was just an update." Alice Dowling added, "I think that some PR should have been done previously. This curriculum was coming."[23]

In June, a week before the School Committee vote, the CPCB hosted two Information Nights. Whitmire summed up the sessions: "People were aghast when they came and found out what was in the curriculum."[24]

CPCB members also conducted a series of outreach activities which included: collecting signatures from residents opposed to the HIV/AIDS curriculum, having messages printed in church bulletins and read on the local airwaves, passing out information at ballfields and parking lots, and conducting a telethon. Each of these activities was meant to raise community awareness and opposition to the AAC's HIV/AIDS education plan.

PUBLIC HEARINGS

On June 14 and 21, 1993, the Beta School Committee held two public hearings to provide an overview of the proposed HIV/AIDS curriculum and to listen to parents' concerns. More than 600 people, mostly parents, attended these public sessions. Health and Human Development specialist and AAC chairwoman Jane Alexander provided the audience with an overview of the proposed curriculum. She concluded her comments by stating, "This is just a proposal, it is not formal school policy yet. There is plenty of room for change." Superintendent Kurtz emphasized that the "material does not advocate dispensing of condoms and promotes sexual abstinence and avoidance of IV drug use as a way to avoid the virus."[25-27]

During the public testimony, the loudest contingent opposed the AAC's proposed HIV/AIDS curriculum. One Beta parent, William Conner, pleaded with the Committee: "My children still have boogey men in their closets and monsters under their beds. We don't need to introduce them to death and disease. We shouldn't throw fear into them."[28] Another Beta parent Brenda Burns commented, "Only parents have the right to teach their children about AIDS. Teachers should teach my children to read."[29] One former Beta High School student, Sharon Whitmire, agreed. She stated, "I know and understand the pressures of today's teens, for I am one. I am here to sort of testify that when taught and expected to wait, teens *can* and *will* wait."[30]

However, several high school students and parents urged the School Committee to approve the plan. "We all have to put away our phobias and fears," pleaded Beta High School student Ann Murphy. "This is about our lives. Abstinence is great, but it's not a realistic goal for a lot of kids. We have to realize many kids are having sex, and unprotected sex. You can't just leave it up to parents, because many don't talk about sex. We students deserve to be told the truth about the disease."[31]

After nearly ten hours of public debate, the Beta School Committee voted 4–3 to reject Superintendent Kurtz's request to revise the proposed plan, saying it could not be salvaged. "We need to start at the beginning," said School Committee member Patricia Dorman.[32-34]

Committee members Maureen Casey, Dan Craig, and Chairman Joseph Ponds also voted to reject the plan. Chairman Joseph Ponds voiced his opposition to the plan, stating, "I'm for AIDS education. I just felt that what we were trying to do was chock full of holes."[35] Committee members Paul Andros, Karen White, and Jean Anderson supported the AIDS curriculum, but asked for revisions.

It was not until after the School Committee vote that individuals and community-based groups within Beta began to organize around the need for a school-based HIV/AIDS education curriculum.[36]

Supporters of the proposed AIDS curriculum vowed to form a grassroots organization that would help them express an organized viewpoint. AAC member Shirley Bowman commented, "I was disappointed with the level of intimidation. It caught us off guard. When this comes up again next school year, maybe our side can be heard and we'll have a stronger voice."[37] Valerie Devine, a Beta parent and Morrison School PTO president, added, "It's absolutely ludicrous to throw away fifteen months of work."[38]

BACK TO THE DRAWING BOARD: SELECTION OF AN AIDS CURRICULUM

On June 28 the Beta School Committee voted unanimously to support Superintendent Kurtz's proposed recommendations around the future development of an AIDS education program in Beta schools. The recommendations included: (1) the parent as the primary teacher of the student, (2) the provision of medically sound information about AIDS, (3) an emphasis on sexual abstinence and non-intravenous drug use as ways to avoid contracting the virus, and (4) discussion of the transmission of HIV/AIDS virus through sexual contact would be limited to middle and high school levels.[39-41]

As Superintendent Kurtz, Assistant Superintendent Moore, and Health and Human Development specialist Jane Alexander used these criteria to assess various curricula, they were provided with resources from community members. Said CPCB member Elaine Kane, "We didn't want to be a group that just came in and said, 'No, No, No.' We wanted an abstinence-based program. We researched different programs, sent away for stuff, and got information." After viewing a series of programs, school administrators decided to select the *Free Teens* program. CPCB spokeswoman Linda Whitmire recalled, "We gave them [the school administration] four different programs. They thought this program [*Free Teens*] was great. They felt this program addressed the problem. They all approved of it." In an interview one week before unveiling this proposed AIDS curriculum, Dr. Kurtz commented, "I feel the [*Free Teens*] program will receive very strong and community-wide support."[42]

At the Beta School Committee's January 24, 1994 meeting, Superintendent Kurtz presented the proposed HIV/AIDS curriculum for seventh and ninth grades. "To truly appreciate and understand the program proposed," Kurtz stated, "it is important to have the material presented in a fashion similar to how students would receive it."[43] As such, a public viewing of the program was scheduled for January 31. Following this presentation, Beta residents had three weeks to review the program and submit written comments on the curriculum to the School Department. Interestingly, "in an effort to avoid a repeat of hearings held in June" school officials decided not to hold public hearings on the proposed curriculum.[44]

While school administrators may have obtained approval from community members including CPCB members on the newly proposed HIV/AIDS education program, they overlooked the sentiments of other Beta parents including members of the newly formed Community Advocates for Responsible Education (CARE). Beta parent and CARE member Bob O'Neff stated, "I also believe abstinence is the best policy. But it's a lot more than putting the fear of AIDS into them. I don't feel this [*Free Teens*] program will address the kids who need to hear it the most."[45]

EMERGENCE OF COMMUNITY ADVOCATES FOR RESPONSIBLE EDUCATION

CARE, a grassroots parent organization, was formed in August 1993 to initiate action around the development of a comprehensive K–12 health education program for the Beta schools.[46, 47] CARE members raised concerns that the *Free Teens* curriculum did not provide information and skills that would enable sexually active students to protect themselves. As such, CARE members provided Dr. Kurtz with an alternative AIDS education course entitled *Preventing AIDS*. This risk reduction[48] curriculum stressed sexual abstinence while telling students who have sex to use condoms.[49, 50] CARE members also provided evidence that the development and publication of the *Free Teens* curriculum was linked to the Unification Church. In a meeting with Superintendent Kurtz, Valerie Devine, president of the Morrison School PTO and a founding member of CARE, alluded to her group's involvement in breaking this story to the media. She recalled, "We said to Kurtz, 'Listen, we're going to tell you right now, this thing *[Free Teens]* is backed by the Moonies. This is not a scare tactic. If you don't deal with this, if you don't at least investigate it, it's going to be in the newspapers tomorrow.' It was in the newspaper the next day."[51] Within ten days from the time the local papers carried the story, Dr. Kurtz withdrew his recommendation for School Committee approval of the *Free Teens* program.

FORMATION OF THE HEALTH ADVISORY COUNCIL

With the emergence of Community Advocates for Responsible Education (CARE) came an organized call from parents within the community for the development of a *comprehensive* K–12 health education program for the Beta schools. At about this same time, Beta school administrators were also interested in receiving state funding for the development of such a program. One of the requirements for state funding was the creation of a community advisory council. Due to the defeat of two proposed HIV/AIDS programs in less than eight months, school administrators and community members learned about the importance of obtaining community approval for a comprehensive health education curriculum.

In February 1994, Superintendent Kurtz formally recommended to the School Committee that it appoint a community Health Advisory Council (HAC) to develop a comprehensive health curriculum based on input from Beta residents.[52] Within a month, the Beta School Committee appointed a 36-member group representing a cross-section of the community.[53, 54] At the HAC's initial meeting, members voted unanimously to study the opinions of students, parents, faculty, and other community members regarding the health education needs of Beta students.[55] Dr. Kurtz commented, "Parents [in Beta] have never been surveyed about this. The survey will help us more clearly define what the role of schools should be in providing health education."[56] Health and Human Development specialist Jane Alexander added: "My hope is that it [the survey] will also bring the community together to show where there is a consensus on health education issues."[57]

Questionnaires were sent to an estimated 2,000 parents, 350 faculty, 2,500 students in grades 8, 10, 12, and select community members in October. Four months later, in a *Report of the Health Education Needs of the Beta Public Schools*, analysis of the survey data revealed that the majority of parents, professional staff, students, and community members surveyed supported some type of comprehensive K–12 health education program.[58, 59]

Commenting on the survey results, Superintendent Kurtz stated, "The results provide a clear direction for the school system in terms of providing health education to the students."[60] Beta School Committee chairperson Jean Anderson added, "When the results of the survey came back, they simply said exactly what we knew all along, but now we had it in black and white to prove it." Based on these results, the HAC voted on March 6 to recommend to the School Committee that a comprehensive K–12 health education curriculum be developed and adopted by the 1995–1996 school year.[61]

COMMUNITY VOICES

Beta community members also publicly expressed support/opposition for a school-based comprehensive health education program. One parent wrote in the *Beta Forum*, "In my opinion, Beta is woefully behind every other community in the area. It's about time given the results of the survey that we develop such a curriculum and get on with it. It's what people want."[62] Along with this call supporting a school-based comprehensive health education program, there were community members who were opposed to such an idea. One parent commented in the *Beta Forum*: "Sexuality should be taught exclusively in the home by parents who love their children. . . . Children's sexual behavior and attitudes should never be taught in a public school setting."[63]

Individuals and groups opposed to the development of a comprehensive health education curriculum employed various strategies and tactics to promote their position. Trying to slow down or halt the HAC's progress, a group of eight Beta citizens filed a complaint with the Norfolk County District Attorney's Office alleging that the Health Advisory Council violated Massachusetts' open meeting law. This complaint sought to invalidate the HAC's March 6 vote.

Due to the complaint, the School Committee avoided direct consideration of the HAC's recommendations. However, it voted 6–1 to accept the results of the health survey.[64]

On the weekend before the 1994 elections, CPCB mailed *The Grassoots Forum* to Beta residents. In this publication, CPCB endorsed the candidacies of Maureen Casey, John Custer, and Lorraine Donovan. They wrote:

We believe School Committee candidates should be consistent in their beliefs and not forsake them for political correctness. Candidates' platforms should not boast of their involvement as CCD leaders if their stand on AIDS education is condom sanctifying—contradictory to fundamental Catholic teachings. Faith must never be checked at the door of a public debate.[65]

Other activities conducted by those opposed to a comprehensive health education curriculum included the use of television and newsprint media including church bulletins to raise community awareness for their position.

Many Beta residents and community groups demonstrated support for the health education program by countering those who opposed the initiative. These strategies included: soliciting expertise to provide legal and programmatic guidance, supporting candidates for political office, the emergence of student voices, dispelling misinformation by providing information through media campaigns and public forums, and linking the CPCB with other conservative groups.

In one instance, proponents of the curriculum initiative supported candidates for political office by forming a political action committee and developing and mailing out a slate card of candidates they supported. According to CARE member Valerie Devine, "We wanted to get people elected to the School Committee who would appreciate our point of view."

As the debate evolved from a discussion around an HIV/AIDS education program to the development of a comprehensive health education curriculum, more students became involved in the issue. Initially, only a handful of Beta students expressed their views on this issue. Over the course of the next year, however, students on both sides of the issue expressed their opinions in writing and at School Committee meetings. On June 5, 1995, Beta High School student Kathy Williams presented the School Committee with a petition signed by over one hundred Beta High School seniors (approximately one-third of the senior class) urging that the health education curriculum be expanded to grades 10, 11, and 12.[66, 67]

Community members also countered the activities of the main opposition group, the CPCB, by linking them with other nationally known conservative groups. CARE member Bill O'Neff made the connection public in his letter to the editor of the *Beta Forum* dated April 6, 1994. He wrote:

My battle is not with Christians, nor is it with those who follow Rev. Moon, it is with those who conduct their devious and destructive political activities under the guise of religion. The activities of the "Religious" Right are no secret in this country. . . . Now let us consider some facts . . . *Free Teens* which was presented by CPCB to Dr. Kurtz, is sponsored by the World Medical Health Foundation, which has also been identified as a Unification Church related organization.[68]

CPCB spokesperson Linda Whitmire felt that being identified as members of the "Religious Right" was "a way to distract from the real issue."

IMPLEMENTATION OF THE COMPREHENSIVE HEALTH EDUCATION CURRICULUM

Interestingly, as School Committee members shunned the idea of developing a piecemeal comprehensive health education program, they voted on implementing various components of the program over a sixteen-month period. While School Committee members voted to implement programs at the elementary and middle school levels, some members expressed concern that the HAC's proposal did not begin to address health education needs for high school students until the 1996–1997 school year. "Instead of beginning in the elementary school," said School Committee member Al Bari, "I think you should begin in the higher grades and then work down. We should focus on HIV/AIDS so more kids don't graduate without having this instruction." School Committee member Karen White also expressed concern. She commented, "We will have another senior class going out ignorant, without having learned this [AIDS education]." [69]

By December 1995, the School Committee was presented with a grade 9–12 curriculum. School Committee members voted to adopt the curriculum. A few months after this vote, Beta school administrators learned that grant money had been reduced and there wasn't enough funding to implement the curriculum in its entirety. Presently, the health education curriculum is in grades 5 and 6 and 7 and 9. CARE member Linda Mazarella commented: "[Jane] Alexander only got half of what she thought the grant was going to be. She could only institute [the curriculum] in two or three grades." School personnel were looking to community resources for support. Kathy Bartow mentioned, "I heard Beta Medical Associates gave some money and somebody else was coming through with funds." Additionally, program supporters are raising money through Beta's Healthy People 2000 initiative.

Shirley Bowman, a Beta parent who has seen the initial request for an HIV/AIDS program evolve into a comprehensive K–12 health education curriculum, commented on the community decision-making process. She stated, "We do have a [grade] 5–6 curriculum. We also have School Committee approval to put in AIDS education for [grades] 9–12. It's been a lot of work, four years worth of work and an epidemic that's been here for twenty years."

NOTES

1. Devine Interview, 10/27/95.

2. E. R. Hornor, *Massachusetts Municipal Profiles 1993–1994* (Palo Alto, CA: Information Publications, 1993).

3. Ibid.

4. Anderson Interview, 12/1/95.

5. Telephone Interview, Beta School Department, September 1995.

6. Massachusetts Department of Education, 1992.

7. Massachusetts Department of Public Health, AIDS Bureau, 1995.

8. S. Coleman, "AIDS Education, Center Stage," *The Boston Globe*, 6/10/90, p. 1.

9. Ibid., p. 1.

10. Gray Interview, 12/8/95.

11. *AIDS Advisory Committee Minutes*, 2/12/92.

12. Alexander Interview, 6/15/95.

13. Massachusetts Department of Education, *Policy on AIDS/HIV Prevention Education* (April 24, 1990).

14. J. Reardon, "School Board Hopefuls Focus on Realignment," *Beta Forum*, 3/11/92, pp. 18, 19.

15. McPherson Interview, 1/8/96.

16. Kane Interview, 12/5/95.

17. Objectives to accomplish this goal were also presented. They included: an assessment of current curricula and programs used in Beta's schools, review of the state guidelines, and the development of a parent guide. *AIDS Advisory Committee Minutes*, 2/12/92.

18. Alexander Interview, 6/15/95.

19. Ibid.

20. Kane Interview, 12/5/95.

21. Ibid.

22. A. Reid, "Foes of Teaching on AIDS Test Clout," *The Boston Globe*, 6/27/93, p. 1.

23. To address some of the parental concerns, Superintendent Kurtz publicly announced that the Beta School Committee would not install an AIDS curriculum without first obtaining parental input. Additionally, in an attempt to dispel the belief that the AIDS Advisory Committee operated secretly in "closed meetings," Kurtz announced that copies of AAC minutes and the proposed curriculum would be made available to the public. "AIDS Course Is Ready for Scrutiny," *Beta Forum*, 4/21/93, p. 1.

24. Whitmire Interview, 12/8/95.

25. *Beta School Committee Minutes*, 6/14/93.

26. J. W. Ferro, "AIDS Curriculum under Fire," *Beta Forum*, 6/16/93, p. 22.

27. A. Reid, "Beta Schools Air AIDS Plan," *The Boston Globe*, 6/20/93, p. 1.

28. S. Patton, "Debate on AIDS Heated," *The Patriot Ledger*, 6/15/93, p. 1.

29. Reid, "Beta Schools Air AIDS Plan," p. 1.

30. Copy Sharon Whitmire testimony, 6/14/93.

31. R. Aicardi, "AIDS Curriculum—Back to Ground Zero," *Beta Forum*, 6/23/93, p. 24.

32. S. Patton, "Beta Rejects Curriculum on AIDS," *The Patriot Ledger*, 6/22/93, p.1

33. S. Patton, "Beta Seeks Compromise on AIDS Curriculum," *The Patriot Ledger*, 6/29/93, p. 19.

34. *Beta School Committee Minutes*, 6/21/93.

35. Aicardi, "AIDS Curriculum—Back to Ground Zero," p. 24.

36. K. Bartow, "Put Away Phobias, Teach Our Children," *Beta Forum*, 7/14/93, p. 10.

37. A. Reid, "Town Takes Breather in AIDS Tussle," *The Boston Globe*, 7/4/93, p. 1.

38. R. Aicardi, "Call for Calm about AIDS Education," *Beta Forum*, 6/30/93, p. 1.

39. *Beta School Committee Minutes*, 6/28/93.

40. Patton, "Beta Seeks Compromise on AIDS Curriculum," p. 19.

41. Aicardi, "Call for Calm about AIDS Education," p. 9.

42. M. Goldberg, "Kurtz to Detail AIDS Curriculum Monday Night," *The Patriot Ledger*, 1/21/94, p. 8.

43. *Beta School Committee Minutes*, 1/24/94.

44. L. Kowalczyk, "Rev. Moon Linked to AIDS Course," *The Patriot Ledger*, 2/17/94, p. 9.

45. M. Goldberg, " Former Foes Accept Class Program," *The Patriot Ledger*, 2/1/94, p. 9.

46. CARE Document, 1993.

47. M. Goldberg, "Parents Take Sides on AIDS Education," *The Patriot Ledger*, 1/26/94, p. 14.

48. Risk reduction according to Jane Alexander, Beta's Health and Human Development specialist, is a term used to discuss various measures students can adopt (i.e., use of a condom) to reduce their chance of contracting STDs such as AIDS.

49. M. Goldberg, "New Lessons Proposed for Beta," *The Patriot Ledger*, 2/17/94, p. 9.

50. M. Goldberg, "Beta to Drop AIDS Course," *The Patriot Ledger*, 2/19–20/94, p. 1

51. Devine Interview, 10/27/95.

52. J. W. Ferro, "AIDS Course Put in Hands of Local Teachers," *Beta Forum*, 3/2/94, p. 20.

53. *Beta School Committee Minutes*, 3/94.

54. *Beta Forum*, 4/1/94, p. 10.

55. *Health Advisory Committee Minutes*, 5/11/94.

56. J. C. Perez, "Schools Seek Parents' Views on Topics for Health Lessons," *The Patriot Ledger*, 10/13/94, p. 8C.

57. M. Goldberg, "Survey Will Seek Health Course Views. Results Are Expected by January," *The Patriot Ledger*, 6/16/94, p. 7C.

58. *Report of the Health Needs of the Beta Public Schools*, February 1995.

59. Health Protection Grant, Beta Public Schools, 1995–96, p. 1.

60. D. Falbo, "Survey Called Mandate for Sex Education," *Beta Forum*, 3/8/95, pp. 1, 24.

61. D. Falbo, "Sex Ed Sparks More Heated Debate," *Beta Forum*, 4/26/95, p. 12.

62. "What People Want," *Beta Forum*, 3/29/95, p. 11.

63. "Teach about Sex in the Home," *Beta Forum*, 5/25/94, p. 11.

64. Opposition was also evident in relation to the development and use of the health education survey instrument. Initially, at an HAC meeting, CPCB member Linda Whitmire proposed that two additional questions be added to the survey based on her argument: "The survey doesn't give anybody an option to say I don't want this, or I think this should be an elective." Whitmire's proposal was rejected by an overwhelming majority of HAC members at their July meeting. *Health Advisory Committee Minutes*, 7/13/94.

65. *The Grassroots Forum*, CPCB, Spring 1994.

66. *Beta School Committee Minutes*, 6/5/95.

67. D. Falbo, "Health Course Books Okayed," *Beta Forum*, 6/7/95, pp. 1, 9.

68. B. O'Neff, "The Free Teens Program Is Where It Belongs—In the Trash Heap," *Beta Forum*, 4/6/94, pp. 10, 11.

69. Falbo, "Health Course Books Okayed," pp. 1, 9.

PART III

Findings and Comparative Analysis

Sower et al.'s stage theory has provided the framework for understanding the process of social change within community. This model helps to explain the impact of national- , state- , and local-level events on the development and implementation of respective comprehensive health education programs in Alpha and Beta. In *The Community in America*, Roland Warren defines these linkages as vertical and horizontal patterns.[1]

At the national level, the U. S. Department of Health and Human Services set forth national health objectives in *Healthy People 2000: National Health Promotion and Disease Prevention Objectives*. Some of these objectives included the prevention of HIV infection and STDs.[2] Today, fifteen years into the AIDS epidemic, there are 513,486 documented cases of HIV/AIDS and over 300,000 deaths attributed to AIDS in the United States.[3] In an article in the *Journal of the American Medical Association* the authors state, "AIDS is the leading cause of death among young adults."[4]

In the past few years, public policy statements made at the state level dealt with high-risk behaviors among adolescents and the need to create a safe school environment for all students. In 1990, the Massachusetts Board of Education urged all public schools to provide HIV/AIDS prevention education to every student in every grade.[5] Less than one year later, in 1991, the Massachusetts Department of Public Health developed guidelines[6] for the development of comprehensive K–12 HIV/AIDS prevention education. These guidelines, which were forwarded to all school superintendents, were intended to be a resource for school personnel and advisory groups as they developed their own respective curricula. In January 1993, the Massachusetts Department of Education released a study detailing the risky behavior of adolescents statewide.[7] One month later, the Governor's Commission on

Gay and Lesbian Youth published its report that recommended secondary schools institute a series of programs to provide a safe environment for homosexual students. These recommendations were backed by the State Board of Education in May 1993.[8]

At the local level, a series of events supported the work of community-based groups in both Alpha and Beta. In 1990, Sex Information and Education Council of the U.S. (SIECUS) launched a nationwide effort to "initiate a special AIDS education project to assist educators and health and mental health professionals in providing sex-positive AIDS education and counseling."[9] Additionally, the Planned Parenthood League of Massachusetts launched the PURPOSE campaign to provide community members with the information and technical assistance they need to develop and maintain high-quality, school-based sexuality education programs.[10]

For those opposed to school-based health education programs or for those who are interested in a program with an abstinence-only message, a number of resources have been available throughout the Commonwealth of Massachusetts. Some of these resources are available through national organizations which have opened field offices in Massachusetts within the past few years. These include the Christian Coalition, Concerned Women for America, American Family Foundation, American Freedom Coalition, and Focus on the Family.[11]

More recently, the Catholic Alliance, a division of the Christian Coalition, hosted a one-day workshop for over 700 people in Boston. Distributed at this training session was a *Citizen Action Manual* which was designed to give the reader "a hands-on working knowledge of the nuts and bolts of grassroots political activism."[12] Within the manual, under the section entitled "Issues," it is written, "Subjects such as sex education, where students are taught that exploring homosexuality and safe sex are acceptable lifestyles, are not appropriate topics of instruction in public schools."[13]

To present a comprehensive view of the community decision-making process in Alpha and Beta, I have focused in each stage on the group that carried the issue successfully through the particular stage and the interactions that occurred between this group and those community groups that supported or opposed the initiative. This framework has allowed for a more thorough analysis of the interactions among a variety of individuals and community groups within both communities.

There were two distinct but interrelated sets of issues within each community. The first set concerned a school-based condom availability program. The second set concerned the development of an HIV/AIDS education curriculum.

For example, in fall 1991, Alpha students initiated action by petitioning the Alpha School Committee to make condoms available at the city's two high schools. After soliciting community input, the School Committee approved the students' request in a 7–1 vote on January 27, 1992. Throughout the coming months, school administrators and city Health Department officials developed and implemented a condom availability program.[14] This was the first phase of a comprehensive program of education and counseling. In Beta, however, the adoption of a condom availability program was not even considered by the School Committee. This supports the findings of the Planned Parenthood League of Massachusetts' 1995 Sexuality Assessment Report which states, "Very little community and school committee support is believed to exist for condom availability programs."[15] At a candidate's rally for the Beta School Committee in March 1992, all three candidates flatly denounced the distribution of condoms by the schools. "It's a health issue," said candidate Lorraine Donovan. "Have the health department pass them out or the drug stores." Another candidate, Patricia Dorman, said that there are sex and AIDS awareness programs in the school system but believed the distribution of condoms "does not belong in the public schools." Candidate Joseph Ponds also commented on a school-based condom availability program: "I would never entertain the thought. It's a rhetorical question as far as I'm concerned. It'll never happen. It's absolutely ludicrous."[16]

With regard to the development of an HIV/AIDS education curriculum, the Alpha School Committee charged school administrators with forming a Health Education Task Force to explore the components of a comprehensive sexuality and HIV/AIDS curriculum. This action supported the students' request for an expanded sex education program. In January 1993, the School Committee legitimized the work of the Task Force by adopting its recommendations. In an emotional meeting in May 1993, the School Committee voted 9–0 to adopt the Task Force's final recommendations concerning the proposed ninth-grade pilot program. The *Health and Sexuality* curriculum was pilot tested in September 1993 and implemented in September 1994.

In January 1992, Beta school superintendent Dr. Peter Kurtz approved the formation of an AIDS Advisory Committee (AAC) to review, discuss, and recommend curriculum components for an HIV/AIDS education program. During the following year, AAC members continued to edit curriculum components for each grade level. The group presented its recommendations to the Beta School Committee in May 1993. After two spirited public hearings in June 1993, the School Committee voted 4–3 against the AAC's proposed K–12 HIV/AIDS education curriculum. Within a year, however, the Beta School Committee charged school administrators with forming a Health Advisory Council to conduct a community-wide assessment about what was needed in a comprehensive K–12 health education curriculum and then charged the group to develop a curriculum based on those needs.

NOTES

1. In *The Community in America*, Roland Warren defines the linkages between communities as vertical and horizontal patterns. These patterns are the structural and functional relation of a community's various social units and subsystems to extra-community systems. The term "vertical" is used to reflect the fact that such relationships often involve different hierarchical levels. The term "horizontal" is used to indicate that the community units tend to be on approximately the same hierarchical level. In R. Warren, *The Community in America* (Chicago: Rand McNally and Company, 1963), pp. 161–166.

2. "Healthy People 2000: National Health Promotion and Disease Prevention Objectives and Healthy Schools," *Journal of School Health*, 61(7) (1991), pp. 298–328.

3. In Massachusetts one-fifth of AIDS cases are among people in their twenties. The majority of these individuals were infected during their adolescence. In the last six years, the number of AIDS cases in Alpha and Beta have doubled. From AIDS Bureau, Massachusetts Department of Public Health, 1995.

4. R. M. Selik, S. Y. Chu, and J. W. Buehler, "HIV Infection as Leading Cause of Death among Adults in U.S. Cities and States," *The Journal of the American Medical Association*, 69(23) (June 16, 1993), pp. 2991–2994.

5. Massachusetts Department of Education, *Policy on AIDS/ HIV Prevention Education* (April 24, 1990).

6. Less than one year later, in 1991, the Massachusetts Department of Public Health created guidelines for the development of comprehensive K–12 HIV/AIDS prevention education programs. In Massachusetts Department of Public Health, *Comprehensive Curriculum Guidelines on HIV/AIDS: Grades K–12* (September, 1991).

7. In the *Massachusetts 1993 Youth Risk Behavior Survey* of nearly 3,000 high students from 39 cities/towns within the Commonwealth, it was reported that "One-half of the Massachusetts high school students surveyed reported having had sexual intercourse. One-third of the students who had sexual intercourse in the past three months did not use any contraceptive method the last time they had intercourse." In Massachusetts Department of Education, *Massachusetts 1993 Youth Risk Behavior Survey*. Bureau of Student Development and Health, June 1994.

8. In February 1993, the Governor's Commission on Gay and Lesbian Youth published its report that recommended secondary schools institute a policy and a series of programs to provide a safe environment for homosexual students. In *Making Schools Safe for Gay and Lesbian Youth, Breaking the Silence in Schools and In Families*, Governor's Commission on Gay and Lesbian Youth (February 1993).

9. *Alpha Tab*, 6/29/93. SIECUS has also widely distributed a publication entitled *Guidelines for Comprehensive Sexuality Education* and the booklet *Winning the Battle: Developing Support for Sexuality and HIV/AIDS Education*.

10. Launched in August 1993, the primary goal of the PURPOSE (Parents United for Responsible Policies On Sexuality Education) program is to bring together community members who want to ensure the development and maintenance of high-quality sexuality education in their public schools and provide them with the information and technical assistance they need to combat opposition. PURPOSE,

coordinator Sarah Kanner stated, was committed to "providing the public with accurate information. It's really important to show that there are good comprehensive sexuality programs out there." R. Lear, "PAC Groups Enter Political Arena," *Tab*, 8/31/93, p. 10. Other resources available to sexuality education proponents were materials developed by The Lighthouse Institute for Public Policy in Sudbury, Massachusetts, and Political Research Associates in Cambridge, Massachusetts. Both groups track the activities of right-wing activists around the nation. "This group [The Lighthouse Institute for Public Policy] formed," said co-founder Hannah Golden, "because we saw an effort to take power in the state through deception. The way to combat deception is to take correct information and get it to [the public]." S. Lyons, "Culture War Comes Home," *Alpha Graphic*, 6/30/94, p. 12.

11. Dan White, director of Massachusetts Family Institute, says his group is dedicated to restoring traditional family values to the public policy process. In a statement to the *Alpha Graphic*, White said, "There are roughly six million people in Massachusetts. It will only take 100,000 committed and involved people to turn things around. . . . To prevail we need organization, hard work, financial resources, courage and above all, prayer." S. Lyons, "Culture War Comes Home," p. 13.

12. Introductory letter, *Citizen Action Seminar Manual* (Chesapeake, VA: Christian Coalition, 1995).

13. Ibid., p. 42

14. Within three months school administrators and city government officials implemented a plan. The city Health Department, through the AIDS Coalition, conducted a series of nine focus groups with students to determine the methods and materials needed to optimize the effectiveness of such a program. The condom availability program started in April 1992. During the first three weeks of the program, over 130 students at both high schools availed themselves of this service.

15. Planned Parenthood League of Massachusetts Sexuality Assessment Report, "The Status of Sexuality Education in Massachusetts Public Schools" (1995).

16. J. Reardon, "School Board Hopefuls Focus on Realignment," *Beta Forum*, 3/11/92, pp. 18, 19.

CHAPTER 4

A Call for Health and Sexuality Education Programs

In Sower et al.'s *initiation stage* a "convergence of interest" occurs among people holding similar feelings and beliefs about a problem. A group is formed to deal with an idea possessed by one or more individuals. Through group discussions, ideas are transformed into specific proposals of action for the community. This group is defined as the initiating set.[1] The central theme in this process is to understand the manner in which an idea held by one or more individuals evolves into a specific proposal of action for the "community" either to accept or reject.

Sower and his associates outline the steps of the initiating process. First, an effective group possesses basic internal and external characteristics. The internal characteristics include an internal organization among people of common interests, the development of common goals and methods for their achievement, and identification of proposed action. The external characteristics include a sufficient number of external relationships within the larger community to accomplish its goals.[2] Second, there are three conditions for initiation of an action. Each plays an important role in determining the probability that the proposed action will move from initiation to legitimation. The first condition is related to the prestige and authority held by the initiators within the community. The second condition is related to gaining access to others whose approval is necessary for the group to fulfill its goals. The third condition is concerned with the extent to which the proposed action is compatible with the existing conceptions of "community welfare."[3]

INTERNAL CHARACTERISTICS OF THE INITIATING SET

In both Alpha and Beta, some School Committee members and school administrators raised concerns about the need for expanded sexuality education programs in their respective schools.

In 1987, Alpha School Committee member Sandra Riley researched the extent of sex education in Alpha schools and concluded that there were no "system-wide policies or guidelines."[4] In the mid-1980s, Jane Alexander, Beta's Health and Human Development specialist, tried to generate community interest in teaching about infectious diseases, specifically AIDS.[5] In both cases, these initiatives did not generate community support to change existing policies and programs. However, in the early 1990s there were a series of national, state, and local events and initiatives that motivated local school committees and school administrators to initiate action on the development of HIV/AIDS curricula.

Internal Organization

In Alpha it was a group of students who brought the idea of an expanded AIDS education program to the community's attention. Their common interest was motivated by their concern for their peers. In Beta, statewide initiatives motivated school administrators to form the AIDS Advisory Committee (AAC). Both groups would be identified by Sower et al. as the initiating set.[6]

In Alpha, students at Alpha South High School shared a common interest in being concerned about the sexual activity and practices of their peers. In September 1991, seniors Mark Fleming and Regina Sidell were discussing the results of a student survey of sexual activity and condom use published in an Alpha South school newspaper, the *Advocate*.[7-11] Sidell summed up the initial meeting by stating, "It was kind of like you put these seventeen-year-olds in a room together and they're going to take on the world. Within thirty minutes this whole idea was born."[12, 13] Over time and with the guidance of adults, the students would form the Student Committee on Sexual Awareness, a 22-member student organization.

As I talked with Alpha School Committee members about their support for a condom availability program and an expanded sexuality education curriculum, many of them mentioned the influence of the students. Prior to the students' request, there were two instances when the School Committee discussed the development of a sexuality education program. In the first instance, the issue was raised by a School Committee member the previous school year. In the second instance, the School Committee received communications from various state agencies announcing new guidelines for sexuality education and a condom availability program. In both cases, the majority of School Committee members agreed that, "Unless it [sexuality education] gets raised [by the public], let's not raise it ourselves."[14] In November 1991, it was the students who would raise this issue at a monthly School Committee meeting.

As AIDS became a public health issue at both the national and state levels, statewide initiatives motivated Beta administrators to initiate action on the development of an HIV/AIDS curriculum.[15] Beta's Health and Human Development specialist Jane Alexander recalled, "[Assistant Superintendent] Michael [Moore] and I went to a few statewide meetings and we were both convinced that we needed to address this issue. We weren't doing enough around HIV/AIDS education. Teachers needed a framework to teach AIDS education." She continued,

After going to these meetings, Michael Moore and myself felt that if we didn't have our own policies, didn't have our own programs, that this AIDS epidemic was just serious enough that there was a chance that somebody else would be telling us what to do. At any given time, we felt that the state or the federal government was going to say, "This is the way it's going to be. Get busy here and do this." So that was our intent and the AIDS Advisory Committee was formed.[16]

Chris Valley, a Beta High School faculty member, recalled, "He [Moore] had just come back from a state conference. He was pretty fired up about the need to do this."[17] As a result of the statewide initiatives, Dr. Peter Kurtz, superintendent of Beta schools, worked with Moore and Alexander to initiate the formation of an AIDS Advisory Committee (AAC). Their common interest was to have an HIV/AIDS curriculum in place before state or federal officials became involved. According to Joseph Ponds, Beta School Committee chairman:

At one point in 1992, the administration came before the School Committee saying that Governor Weld was going to be proposing his own type of health education curriculum and that we would be better served if we took the reins in our own hands. When the administration informed us that they wanted to develop this curriculum, the School Committee then instructed the Superintendent to devise his own committee that he would work with. The findings of that committee would be brought forward by the Superintendent to us.[18]

The common interest among school administrators initiated the formation of the nineteen-member AAC. Beta School Committee member Maureen Casey stated, "The school administration wanted it [the AAC] to be truly representative [of the community]. They wanted a representative from each one of the elementary schools, the middle schools, and the high school."[19] The AAC was created through advertisements in the local town newspaper, notices sent out in school newsletters,[20] and public announcements made at School Committee and Parent Advisory Council (PAC) meetings. Alexander added, "We spread the word. We announced it through the PTO network, because we needed parent input. We let everybody that wanted to come on the Committee, come. No one was excluded."[21]

Of the nineteen members who sat on the AIDS Advisory Committee, more than one-half were Beta parents. According to Chris Valley, one of three educators on the AAC, "It was predominantly a parent group."[22] Some parents, however, felt the AAC was overrepresented with community members who formed part of an established parent network. AAC member Mary McPherson stated, "Elaine [Kane] and I were the two parents on the AIDS Advisory Committee who were unsolicited from the community."[23]

Joe Ponds had another view: "What people tend to forget is that we were always beating the bushes. We tried to get as many people as we could. People might of said this Committee was not fairly representative but when we were looking for people they just weren't there."[24]

In contrast to the administration's motivation for forming the AAC, many parents joined the AAC based on personal reasons and out of concern for community members. One parent member, Alice Dowling, commented, "I think the reason I got involved was because of my kids."[25] Another parent member, Elaine Kane, added: "I went in there very open, thinking we were all coming from a more or less same point of view. Trying to make up this curriculum that was going to be the best thing for our kids and the community."[26] At least four parents on the AAC had lost a family member to AIDS. Each shared a common interest in wanting to educate others about HIV/AIDS prevention. Ellen Nagel, who lost her 25-year-old brother to AIDS, commented, "To see AIDS take a young person breaks your heart. I've seen the suffering firsthand, so I felt I had to do something."[27] Shirley Bowman recounted,

I was just an average citizen. I was going to join the Committee to save a life, so some family wouldn't have to experience what my family experienced. My brother was brilliant. He's dead. So what, that he was class valedictorian and graduated from Yale in three years? Knew five languages. So what? He's not alive. If one kid, from their education can turn around and say, "No. . . . I'm not going to engage in risky behavior," then it's worth it. I felt I had to share what I knew.[28]

Beginning on February 12, 1992, AAC members held monthly meetings to review and discuss the *Comprehensive Curriculum Guidelines on HIV/ AIDS for Grades K–12* and other resource materials.

While the school administration was instrumental in initiating action around the AAC's formation, their organizing capabilities left many AAC members somewhat confused about why this group was convened. Some AAC members said they had been told that the group was convened based on a recommendation from the Massachusetts Department of Education. Kate Pagano, a Beta parent and AAC member, recalled, "When we got our first letter [to serve on the AAC] it said, 'The state *recommends* that you look at this curriculum.' "[29] Other AAC members remembered that the group had been assembled based on a state mandate. AAC member Ellen Nagel recalled, "We had gotten told by the people who put our group together, which was [Jane] Alexander and [Dr. Peter] Kurtz that it was *mandated*. So we thought we had no choice but to come up with a curriculum."[30] Nan Parker, another AAC member, stated, "At one point it was a recommendation, next point it was mandated."[31] While Health and Human Development specialist Alexander confirmed that indeed the group was convened based on a state recommendation, the mixed messages created confusion among group members. Pagano added, "I went in thinking we had no choice but to come up with a curriculum. I didn't understand why some people were rocking the boat when this was mandated by state law."[32] This confusion "killed us," said Ellen Nagel. "It sabotaged our whole effort, because we came together under a mandate and we got watered down."[33]

Development of Common Goals and Objectives

The second internal characteristic of an effective initiating group is its development of common goals and objectives. This becomes the "group charter" of the initiating set, formalizing the relationships that have been established among them. As such, the charter is distinct from the goals of the individual members.[34] While both the Student Committee on Sexual Awareness and the AIDS Advisory Committee had clear goals and objectives, the groups differed in how their goals and objectives were determined. The goals/objectives of the student group were developed by group consensus, whereas, the goal/objectives of the AAC were determined bureaucratically by Beta's school administration.[35]

The goal of the Student Committee on Sexual Awareness was to distribute condoms at their high school. Their motivation came from a series of articles printed in their school newspaper, the *Advocate*, that dealt with the results of a survey on student sexual activity and condom use and what their peers were doing at a nearby high school around HIV/AIDS education. Mark Fleming, who was a co-founder of this student group, recalled his initial reaction after he read that students at a nearby high school were distributing condoms. He suggested, "Wouldn't it be good for us to have condoms available here at school?" He added, "Then we all started really getting into it."[36] The students agreed and then strategized about how they would accomplish this goal. Sidell recalled,

Mark let me know where we could get condoms donated to us. He said, "Maybe we should distribute them in school." And so I was like, "Yeah, that's a great idea. Why don't we pick one week and kind of make it a condom day." And we were going to walk around with envelopes containing a condom and three pieces of literature, on how to use a condom, information on AIDS and sexually transmitted diseases. It was going to be a very radical, intense, one day kind of thing.[37]

The Beta school administration's creation of the AIDS Advisory Committee was primarily policy driven. While Beta's Health and Human Development specialist Jane Alexander had expressed for years her interest in developing a curriculum about infectious disease, Beta school administrators were moved to action before federal and state officials became involved. From its earliest stages of formation, the AAC was guided by the Beta school administration rather than it's members. This was illustrated when Assistant Superintendent Moore chaired the first Committee meeting and indicated that Jane Alexander would be chairperson for subsequent meetings. This was also evident in how the group's goal was determined. At the AAC's initial meeting, Assistant Superintendent Moore stated, "The goal of the Committee is to recommend to the School Committee curriculum components for a K–12 AIDS education program with accompanying resource, reference and media materials."[38] This community group was provided with its goal with no discussion among group members.

The bureaucratic approach adopted by the AAC's leadership was also reflected in the comments made by Elaine Kane, an AAC member. She stated,

At our first meeting we were given the [state] guidelines . . . and we were told we were going to be reviewing the guidelines. We were going to make up a curriculum for school age kids. The point was to come up with something that would be serviceable to the whole town.[39]

Objectives to accomplish this goal were also presented to this group. They included: a review of state guidelines, the development of a curriculum, a presentation to the School Committee, the development of parent guides, and the presentation of a parent program.[40]

While AAC members unanimously supported the need for AIDS education in Beta schools, the school administration's bureaucratic leadership provided little opportunity for AAC members to reach consensus on how this would be accomplished.[41] This leadership style laid the foundation for future conflict among group members. This was alluded to in the comments made by AAC member Alice Dowling in her statement: "There were just different issues that would come up and we would end up in these arguments. There was never concession. That was the problem. We ended up having to finally agree with majority rule."[42]

In effective community group organizing, members typically have the opportunity to reach consensus when defining group goals and objectives.

For members of the AAC, this process was bypassed as the goals and objectives of the group were predetermined by the school administration.

Identification of Proposed Action

The third characteristic of an effective initiating group is its ability to propose action. The proposed action identified by the Alpha students was the distribution of condoms to their peers during a school day. The main action taken by the AAC was curriculum assessment and development.

From interviews it was apparent that Alpha students were ready to transform their idea into specific action. Sidell stated, "We were literally going to walk around the school, handing them out. We really didn't think at all about a lasting effect."[43] Fleming confirmed this plan when he stated, "I did go as far as getting 2,000 condoms from the Department of Public Health and we were going to make up this little packet."[44] However, it was also obvious that the students had not developed external relationships in the community to facilitate the accomplishment of their goal. This was exemplified when the student group learned that they would be suspended by Principal Edward Vanderbilt if they carried out their plan.[45] This was also evident when Fleming recalled, "I made the mistake of calling Jane Graham [Associate Superintendent for Administration and Secondary Education], and I was like, 'Well are we allowed to pass out condoms in school?' She kind of flipped."[46] These accounts were confirmed in interviews with other community members who later offered the students some direction about how to proceed. One of those adults was Sylvia Healey, president of the Alpha South High School Parent Teachers Association.[47]

Based on these accounts it was apparent that the students' inability to develop external relationships within the community potentially jeopardized their plans. Sidell recalled in an interview, "I remember that day. We were so upset. Our plans, we were sitting in Mark's room saying, 'What are we doing? We don't know what to do.'"[48] This period was an important transition for the students. They had a variety of choices. One option was to abide by the words of the school administration and not carry out the plan. A second option was to carry out their plan and risk suspension. This option would identify the group as a discussion or protest group and therefore might deny group members the opportunity to be involved in community change.[49] The third option was identified by Sidell's mother. Heeding the advice of Sidell's mother, members of the Student Committee on Sexual Awareness decided to go through the proper channels and use the resources within their community.[50]

Initially, the AAC conducted an assessment of curricula and programs currently in use in Beta schools and worked toward determining how the state guidelines on HIV/AIDS could be integrated into Beta's existing Health and Human Development program. With regards to this task, Jane

Alexander and Cathy Engel, a Beta High School teacher, provided AAC members with an overview of the Health and Human Development program.[51]

The AAC also began to review the state guidelines. According to Beta parent Shirley Bowman, "We thought we would just go through the guidelines and either approve or disapprove it. We started doing that. . . . It seemed pretty congenial."[52] "However," Elaine Kane mentioned, "It was just such a big amount of information that nobody could go through it in a short amount of time. . . . You'd look through it but to read the whole thing was really cumbersome."[53] As a result of the amount of material for review, Chris Valley went on to add, "We realized what we needed to do to get anywhere was to divide up into subcommittees. So we met as elementary, middle and high school groupings."[54] The task of each group, as defined by Assistant Superintendent Moore, was to find out what actually was being taught in each grade level and to use the state guidelines on HIV/AIDS as a basis to make recommendations to the larger Committee membership.[55] Each subcommittee picked a chairperson and was charged to recommend age-appropriate AIDS educational materials to the larger committee.[56] One month later, these subcommittees reported on their findings and recommendations.[57]

At the School Committee meeting on June 15, 1992, an AIDS Advisory Committee status report and recommendations were presented by Chairperson Jane Alexander.[58] The recommendations included: the development of an abstinence-based curriculum, increasing parental awareness and involvement around the AIDS issue, and continuation of the AAC's work.

Over the next few months, three members of the AAC, Jane Alexander, Mary Sanders, and Dorothy Nedrick, went on to develop the AAC's HIV/AIDS curriculum based upon the recommendations made by the three subcommittees. Chris Valley recalled, "They [the Beta School administration] really wanted the curriculum to be in place for the next year. It was June and they needed to get all of this pulled together."[59] Alexander went on to add,

That summer we took all of that stuff and wrote up the curriculum as directed by the group [the AAC]. We worked all summer. We didn't write it from scratch. We didn't reinvent the wheel. We used the Red Cross curriculum. They told us what to do and we rewrote the information for age-appropriate reading levels. We had it by grades all printed up and we went over each grade as a group to make any changes that needed to be made.[60]

This action was met with complaints by some of the members of the AAC who had expressed an interest in working on this subcommittee.[61]

Mary McPherson stated, "Both Elaine and I volunteered to be on the subcommittee to work on the curriculum over the summer. We were never called."[62]

When asked for her assessment of the situation, Kane replied, "When I was handed this completed curriculum, I was rather shocked to say the least." She added, "Assistant Superintendent Moore assured all of us that he wanted this [curriculum] to be a piece that everybody had input in. He wanted everybody to be involved."[63] McPherson surmised, "From what I understand, they [the AIDS Advisory Committee group] did not meet. Jane Alexander and maybe one other person in the school system completed the curriculum and we were presented with a completed curriculum in October."[64] Beta School Committee member Maureen Casey recalled,

I can tell you a rumor, that [the original AIDS] curriculum was developed over the course of the summer by two or three people. Had the complexion of this group [subcommittee] been different it would have turned out differently. Because I think in some respects, the [whole] group was railroaded.[65]

The exclusion of McPherson and Kane from the curriculum development subcommittee may have been attributed to unintentional confusion over the roles of educators and parents on the AAC. When asked her thoughts of the curriculum development subcommittee selection process, Chris Valley stated, "I didn't feel it was done in any way to keep them out. They [the AAC members] had their input. They had some framework to work with. It was the teachers' job to sit down and write it. And then they'd come back in the Fall so we could all critique what the teachers had worked on."[66] However, it seems more plausible that scarce resources in the form of time and funding motivated the actions of those who formed the curriculum development subcommittee. When I asked Jane Alexander for her explanation of the situation, she commented,

They [Kane and McPherson] weren't excluded. The subcommittees came up with recommendations that were clearly defined. If there were questions regarding these recommendations we could call people. I would only have done this as a last resort because I didn't want to bother people during the summer.[67]

Elaine Kane added: "From what I understand, this curriculum had to be completed by January '93. And as we found out later, it had something to do with grant money."[68]

Whatever the case may have been, this exclusionary action set the stage for future conflict among AAC group members. For example, when I asked Alexander to assess the interactions among group members in the first months, she stated:

For the first year it felt really good to have the controversy. In fact, I was pleased that they [McPherson and Kane] were on the Committee, because I felt that we wouldn't get anymore. This would be the ultimate of any controversy that we'd get and wouldn't it be ideal to get that settled in an advisory committee. So it felt pretty good to me, because there were times that it was just a matter of using a different word.[69]

Elaine Kane agreed: "At first the questions were welcomed."[70] Alexander's assessment of group dynamics during the second year was dramatically different. She stated,

What they [Kane and McPherson] did under the guise of being concerned Christian parents was to totally confuse and delay the process. It was a two year delay. They literally caused confusion and caused a lot of delays by arguing over semantics and what was grade appropriate.[71]

Emergence of Conflict

There appeared to be little if any conflict among Alpha's Student Committee on Sexual Awareness. However, when Beta's AAC members reconvened in fall 1992 to discuss the draft curriculum, conflict emerged. Kane recalled, "As we went through it [the curriculum] there were many more questions. . . . Asking questions became a burden, it became very upsetting to the Chairwoman."[72] McPherson's statement was even more revealing. She added, "So when September came, we picked apart the curriculum bit by bit. It really dragged things out. . . . We did give them a hard time."[73] AAC member Alice Dowling agreed: "Their format was to just disagree. They did not really have conceptual opinions of their own. So we realized, they're just here to disrupt and delay, cause a riot and leave. They did very well."[74]

Initially, conflict centered on specific issues of content. According to Kane, "There was some controversy in the first grade [curriculum] around germs and blood and we had a big discussion about [infected] blood and frightening children."[75] Another issue emerged in the fourth-grade curriculum about the topic of HIV/AIDS prevention. Bowman recalled,

When we were talking about what was going to be taught in the fourth grade, I remember we had this big fight about whether we should mention condoms. That's when things started getting testy because there would be discussion about condoms as an effective method in preventing the spread of HIV. And some of the people on the Committee got really upset that this would go against their religion. They felt public schools had no business saying this especially when it was assumed that so many people were Catholic in the town. [76]

As conflict on the committee escalated, it became personal in nature. Dowling shared the following story:

We were talking about birth control and someone brought up a personal example, talking about something that happened at home. She [Nagel] was really opening up her heart to talk about how difficult it was to find birth control pills in her daughter's room. I was sitting there as a parent. I could see her heart was breaking. We were all sitting there listening when a woman reacted to the story by making the comment, "Well obviously, she hasn't gotten what she needed and that's the whole problem." The room was silent.[77]

Nagel continued, "She ended up coming to me and apologizing afterwards, but at that point it meant nothing and I clearly knew at that point who she was."[78] "I told her to go home and look up the word Christian in the dictionary," added Dowling.[79] When I asked McPherson to comment on the situation, she responded, "I saw this as a dramatic incident, a melodramatic point to deal with an objective issue. It was the issue at hand I felt strongly about. I went over and apologized to her. She [Nagel] didn't choose to accept my apology."[80]

Conflict among AAC members was attributed to a variety of causes. Alexander felt conflict was generated by group members who felt they were losing power within the group. She stated,

So what I think was happening is that these people [Kane and McPherson] now knew they were losing their power. They had power the first year because we really did listen to them. But once it [the curriculum] was written, they were really trying to delay and it became very obvious.[81]

From the perspectives of McPherson and Kane, conflict emerged out of their resentment of being excluded from the curriculum development subcommittee. As Alexander has already mentioned, there was little incident in the AAC's first year. However, conflict emerged in the AAC's second year after the curriculum had been written. Additionally, conflict may have resulted from individual differences regarding the AAC's role. While School Committee members and more politically savvy parents viewed the AAC's role as advisory in nature, parents such as Kane and McPherson felt that once the proposed curriculum made it to the School Committee it would be implemented in the school curriculum and would be mandatory.

There were numerous ways in which conflict (and potential conflict) was handled—not mediated[82]—that further exacerbated tensions on the AAC. These techniques included: the use of positional authority to quell controversy, use of intimidation tactics, changing the curriculum review process, resignation, and majority rule.

On occasion, the positional authority of school administrators was used to deal with potential conflict. In one example, the assistant superintendent made the following opening remarks to the AAC membership on the state guidelines presented in *Comprehensive Curriculum Guidelines on HIV/AIDS for Grades K–12*: "I'm sure nobody has any problem with anything in here."[83] This technique was also evident at the AAC's March 1993 meeting. Assistant Superintendent Moore expressed concern about the number of Beta residents opposed to the inclusion of condoms in the AIDS curriculum. He stated, "This issue could splinter the community and be disruptive to the school system. It may be best to err on the side of caution. This problem is best solved in the family and not in the schools. I would like to see 'condom use' eliminated from the curriculum." Within a month and after another appeal from the assistant superintendent, the entire session on condom use was eliminated from the AIDS curriculum.[84]

The use of intimidation tactics among group members was another way in which conflict was dealt with on the AAC. Mary McPherson shared an experience. She stated,

You have to understand I have never been on a public committee. I was way out of my comfort zone. When I read a copy of the state guidelines, I found many things that jumped out at me as a problem. When I raised these concerns on the AAC, I felt my opinion was questioned. I was frequently made to feel isolated. I was told, "You're the only one who has these concerns."[85]

Elaine Kane went on to add,

I used to bring stuff to the Committee to read. It got to the point that every time I put my hand up, Jane Alexander would say, "What's the question now Elaine." It was a whole different tone when certain people would speak. One person's views in particular were held up because she was a nurse and her husband was a doctor. I thought she must have been someone important.[86]

Jane Alexander shared another story:

We had a couple of high school students on the Advisory Committee and they [McPherson and Kane] started to attack them. The mother in me just stopped them. I was a little bit older than they were and I was able to treat them like they were children. I did that on purpose. That wasn't natural. I told them, "I'll have none of that in this room." I must have reminded them of their parents because they tended to behave more.[87]

Conflict among AAC members was also dealt with by changing the curriculum review process. During fall 1992, the AAC met as a group to review the HIV/AIDS curriculum. While group members appeared to be upset that they had to pick apart the high school curriculum: "Come December," McPherson stated,

We were told, "We're not interested in nit picky things. We need to get through the entire high school curriculum by January." Here was this whole high school curriculum to be reviewed by us. We were then instructed, "If you have any problems with the high school curriculum submit it in writing by January 6th." We [Kane and I] thought that was ridiculous because we thought the Committee was supposed to be doing that work. . . . The point was that this program needed to be a done deal some time in January to get the grant money.[88]

Kane recalled, "I was very concerned that the AAC had taken a different turn and was not following the format that we had agreed upon when we first started."[89]

For Joe Graziano, the frustration of fighting for AIDS education pushed him to resign from the AAC in December. He wrote in his letter of resignation, "I became involved because of my personal experience with this horrifying disease. I hoped that I would be able to prevent even one person from becoming infected with AIDS." But he said squabbling over the issues of condoms and the discussion of sexuality made him feel powerless in the face of the disease that was devastating his family. He ended his letter by writing: "My son was not ready to die. But he wasted away. After you see life disappear in front of you, it's hard to argue over moral issues."[90]

In a letter to the editor of the *Beta Forum* another AAC member, Susan Flanagan, discussed her thoughts on how the group handled conflict. She wrote:

All viewpoints were well represented, from the ultra-conservative to the ultra-liberal, most of us being somewhere in the middle. . . . To suggest that this curriculum will corrupt the morals of our children or encourage them to engage in dangerous behavior is simply foolish. I will admit I was not in favor of everything that ended up in the curriculum but it did reflect the consensus of the Committee.[91]

As I reviewed the voting patterns of the AAC during its second year, many votes were 14–2, 15–2, 16–2. In most instances, Kane and McPherson, who would go on to form the CPCB, voted consistently against measures adopted by the larger group. These votes illustrate that the curriculum reflected the majority voice on the Committee, not necessarily the consensus of the group. One result of this conflict was the fragmentation of group members into two camps. Dominants[92] within the group rallied around supporting the work of the AIDS curriculum development subcommittee. Dowling remembered, "It was pretty interesting because I think Ellen [Nagel] went into this Committee thinking, 'Wait a minute, I'm not going to agree with that one [Dowling] over there.' "[93] Nagel added, "The more outspoken Elaine [Kane] became, the more we realized how together we were. She caused our group to really solidify."[94] Subdominant[95] members of the AAC included Elaine Kane and Mary McPherson. Chris Valley recalled,

Whenever there were votes it seemed that there were always two people who were voting against things. I felt they were looking for things to make issues of rather than attempting to come together. Everybody else was pulling together and these two people were always opposed.[96]

The entrenchment of the two groups was evident as AAC member Shirley Bowman described events in the last few months of the AAC. She stated, "By March, April, May there was a lot of fighting. It was very frustrating. Elaine [Kane] and Mary [McPherson] were voting no against everything. They weren't budging."[97]

While the dominants had power based on the positional authority of the assistant superintendent and Chairperson Alexander and the sheer number of AAC members who supported the work of the curriculum development subcommittee, Kane and McPherson as subdominant members of the AAC tried to strengthen their power by increasing their critical mass by enlisting outside support within the Beta community. This was revealed in comments made by Elaine Kane when she stated, "I started telling people what was going on in the AAC and my concerns. People were shocked. They wanted to know how this [group] could have gone on for months and they knew nothing about it."[98]

BUILDING EXTERNAL RELATIONS: COMMUNITY OUTREACH

Both Alpha's Student Committee on Sexual Awareness and Beta's AIDS Advisory Committee conducted outreach activities to build community support for their respective initiatives. Members of the Student Committee on Sexual Awareness developed relationships with members from both inside and outside the community. Collaborating with faculty, parents, school administrators, peers, and outside experts helped the students accomplish their goal of making condoms available at school. Beta school administrators and the AAC attempted to build relationships within the Beta community. This included expanding the AAC membership to include high school students and working with the Parent-Teacher Organizations (PTOs) in each of Beta's schools.

Alpha students solicited the support of faculty members. For example, they met with Bill Parker, an Alpha South High School history teacher. One afternoon Parker and Fleming discussed their concerns about Alpha South students having unprotected sex. In the conversation, Parker told Fleming, "The best way for change to occur is to come from the people who are most affected." Parker went on to add, "You can have enormous power if you choose to exercise it, particularly in one collective voice." He continued,

We [Mark and I] decided that a petition would be the way to go. A week later, he brought a friend of his, Regina Sidell, and the three of us sat down and wrote up a petition. Mark brought a few samples to me that said, "We demand the school system provide condoms to all students." I responded, "Well, we need to phrase this in a way that is a little more thoughtful. I think by just asking for condoms it is not going to go very far. We need to think about why we need condoms, and what would be the best way of going about doing this."[99]

The student group developed a petition that was circulated among students, faculty, and parents.[100]

The students also obtained support from parents inside and outside the community. For example, it was Sidell's mother who suggested that the students use the resources within the town to their advantage. Through Fleming's father the students came in contact with Beverly Wiggins,[101] the director of the Center for Prevention, who provided the group with information and strategy on how to deal with school committees. Fleming stated,

We met with her [Wiggins] several times. And she pretty much showed us the ins and outs of how to deal with school committees. She has a lot of experience. She helped us with our plan. We were originally planning on handing out condoms at school. She gave us the rundown. We never actually ended up doing the whole plan of distributing the condoms in school. We did petitions.[102]

In addition, the students came in contact with other parents in the community when they went to speak to the Alpha South PTA. Sidell stated,

We went to the PTA and spoke to them. Actually, they reached out to us. We didn't know who these people were. I didn't understand what they did before this. I was getting calls from people I've never met before. People saying, "Hey, we've been hearing what's going on, do you want help? Can we talk? Let's meet. I have ideas."[103]

The students also developed relationships with school administrators. Initially, it was Vanderbilt, the Alpha South High School principal who mentioned the importance of having School Committee support. Sidell stated, "This is the reason why we first dabbled in the School Committee." She added, "We were happy that Dr. Vanderbilt went out of his way to make sure that we knew he supported us. . . . That really helped us with the meetings. So we really didn't feel like we were fighting the whole community."[104]

The students received support from both parents and school administrators. In November 1991, student group members requested that the School Committee docket the issue of condom availability and expanded sex education for a public meeting. Cindy Newman, an Alpha parent and co-chairwoman of the Alpha South Health Task Force and Natalie Dixon, then Health Education specialist for Alpha schools provided assistance. Sidell commented, "There is an open forum time set aside to speak. We went like idiots with xeroxed packets to hand out. We wrote speeches and they [Newman and Dixon] said, 'Hey you've got two minutes to talk.' Natalie, I thought she was a godsend."[105]

She continued, "When I first spoke to Cindy [Newman] I had no idea what she could offer. I was just excited that here was a woman active in the parent community that supported me. She was willing to put in the time. We did count on them a lot."[106]

The students were successful in getting the issue of AIDS education and condom availability docketed for the January 1992 meeting.

The students also developed relationships with their peers from Alpha North. These relationships were important, according to Fleming, "Because we had all this stuff going on by ourselves." These relationships were solidified between the January 13 and 27 School Committee meetings.[107]

Fleming added, "We met with him [Lawson] and a whole bunch of students at Alpha North. We gave them the rundown of what we were doing and some ideas for their petition. We told them if they were going to do petitions, these were the rules to follow."[108] Within three days, Jamie Sinclair and John Kurtis, co-presidents of Committee on the Prevention of AIDS, organized students to collect over 1,000 signatures at Alpha North.[109]

During that week the student groups also conducted various awareness activities within school and the community. Within schools, students hung posters and distributed envelopes with lifesavers (instead of condoms) with a message on contraception. Within the community, the students co-sponsored a rally outside City Hall to support condom availability. They passed out over 400 condoms.[110] Sidell commented on the reasons behind the rally, "One, we wanted to get in our fight and two, we wanted to let the public be aware of how serious we were, and what better place to do that than in front of City Hall?"[111]

These relationships were critical to the students in that they provided much-needed support, a broader vision, opportunities to formulate strategy, and a connectedness to a larger network of individuals. In terms of support, students spoke of the importance of "just being reminded that we could do it. And what we were doing was important."[112] In another example, Fleming recalled the importance of support from peers, "If you work with people the right way," he stated, "they're going to be there for you. Like when we hooked up with the kids from Alpha North."[113]

Initially, the students were interested in condom distribution. This was reflected in their draft petition. However, after conversations with Parker, the students concluded that not much was available to them in terms of sexuality education. As a result, they created a broader vision that called for the expansion of sexuality education in the schools.[114]

With regard to strategy, students and adults discussed how the issue would be framed and presented, and protocol at meetings. In these discussions students considered the language used in discussing the issue. Sidell said, "They taught us the difference between distribution and availability and that changed our whole campaign. Because condom distribution is much more imposing than condom availability."[115]

Through their collaboration with adults, students also learned the importance of presenting facts.[116] Sidell recalled, "They helped us create a foundation. They helped us do the research. We wanted to convey to other adults that we knew what was going on. The point we wanted to get across was it's not a religious issue and it's not a political issue, it's an issue of safety."[117]

Fleming discussed how Newman "gave us good information" and background information "on the people we were dealing with."[118] The students also learned about protocol at public meetings. According to Fleming, "[Wiggins] showed us the ins and outs of dealing with a School Committee."[119] Sidell commented, "We didn't know what the system was. We didn't understand." She recounted the moments before a School Committee meeting: "They [Dixon and Newman] were familiar with the methods. They said, 'This is what's going to happen. You're gonna sit here. They're going to give you this much time to speak. These are the things you need to accent.' They were coaching us."[120]

The relationships with other community members also provided the students with the opportunity to create alliances.[121] Sidell stated, "They [the adults] had a lot of connections that we couldn't get because we were students. They had access to the parental network. We didn't." She added, "We did count on them a lot for bridging the two communities, the parent and student communities. We took advantage of that as much as possible."[122] Both Sidell and Fleming also discussed the importance of their relationships with Patrick Lawson and their peers from Alpha North.

The AAC sought to build relationships within the Beta community. This included expanding the AAC membership to include high school students and working with the Parent-Teacher Organizations (PTOs) in each of Beta's schools. AAC member Chris Valley, a Beta High School teacher, was asked to identify and invite two students from her classes to serve on the AAC. Joanne Zena and David Yost, a high junior and senior, respectively, sat on the AAC as student representatives.[123]

The AAC also established relations with each school's Parent-Teacher Organizations (PTOs). According to Assistant Superintendent Moore, "Parent education regarding AIDS was seen as a priority. Working through each school's PTO is recommended."[124] Shirley Bowman explained how this was accomplished: "There was supposed to be a representative from every school who would then go back to their own PTO meeting to report out about the work of the AAC. I think this happened at some schools and not others."[125] Chris Valley confirmed this was part of the administration's plan to educate the community. She added that she was not sure whether all parents were bringing this information back to their respective PTOs, and was also concerned about the consistency of the message being presented. She further commented, "As I look back, we should've given out minutes to be read at each school."[126] AAC members also discussed the idea of developing a list of resource materials and a handbook for parents as a means of providing information and answering questions that might arise.[127] This information was provided to parents at an Information Night in March 1993.

Aside from the information a small number of parents received through PTO meetings, the first attempts by the AAC to reach out to the larger Beta community were held more than one year after the group's formation. In these two instances the goal of these sessions was to update and inform community members on the AAC's progress.[128] Beta parent Linda Whitmire stated, "The AAC was meeting for eighteen months, supposedly a community committee and I never heard a word about it. I never knew it existed until I read they were ready to present the curriculum."[129]

According to Beta High School teacher Mary Sanders, the goal of the Parent Information Night was to inform high school parents of the progress of the AAC. Beta's clergy were also informed of the AAC's progress. Jane Alexander shared the following: "Once a year we bring together Beta's religious community [through Beta's Alliance Against Drugs]. There were close to forty ministers and priests there and they are formidable in the community. So we tried to get as many as we can in our club."[130]

In both community presentations, AAC members did not appear to be interested in obtaining community input or approval on the AAC's work since there was no formal or informal assessment of community members' views on the proposed HIV/AIDS curriculum. At the AAC's April meeting, Sanders summed up the Parent Information Night by stating: "Parents were comfortable with the information presented."[131] Mary Custer, a Beta parent who attended this event, had a different perspective on the workshop. She commented,

I got a letter and I called a few people that I knew who would be probably interested in going. We went. There were about twelve people there. I think that meeting was initially called to dispel some of the fears and rumors going around. But she [Sanders] really didn't say anything to do that. It was kind of like, "We're having this meeting. You don't have to worry. We're going to be putting on this curriculum. And you can trust us because we know what's best for the kids. We have never steered you wrong before. . . ." She also made some outrageous statements. We came out of there with our heads spinning.[132]

The lack of community outreach to solicit community input and support for the proposed HIV/AIDS education curriculum may have been related to the views held by the AAC's leadership. Some AAC members felt Beta parents wanted this type of curriculum in place in the schools.[133]

Valerie Devine commented, "Being on the Committee, I think Shirley [Bowman] was thinking, 'No problem.' Jane [Alexander] was thinking, 'No problem. We'll get it through.' They very underestimated the other group's organizational power."[134]

It is clear that AAC membership and outreach did not extend far enough within the Beta community. One educator commented, "I think I would've liked to see more teachers involved in the AAC. Teachers were not aware that this Committee was taking place."[135] Another educator, Jim Gray, who had previously directed Beta's Health and Human Development program expressed an interest to be on the AAC. He commented, "I wish I were on that Committee. I said to Jane, 'I have been doing this for ten years and nobody has asked me to even get on the AAC. Why?' I was just curious." He paused and responded, "I never did get an answer."[136] His previous experience and insights might have been beneficial to the AAC. "In hindsight," Elaine Kane recalled, "Maybe more people should have been involved with the development of the curriculum. Maybe there should have been more [community] updates."[137]

Due to the manner in which the AAC operated, it appears that it missed important opportunities to build relationships and obtain input from Beta community members. As a result, AAC members such as Elaine Kane and Mary McPherson formed the Concerned Parents and Citizens of Beta (CPCB) with other Beta parents who felt their views were not being heard by the AAC or the Beta school administration. Kane stated, "Word got out of what we were doing in the community and more and more people started calling the School Department trying to find out about the AAC and the AIDS curriculum. We eventually got parents' input."[138]

In summary, in Alpha it was a group of students who brought the need for an expanded sexuality education program to the community's attention. Through collaboration with adults both inside and outside the community, the student groups' proposed action evolved from a one-day "condom distribution day" at Alpha South High School to a city-wide student petition before the School Committee. In Beta, a group of school administrators brought the need for an HIV/AIDS education program to the attention of the PTOs. Through collaboration with parents, the AAC was developed with the goal to recommend to the School Committee, curriculum components for a K–12 HIV/AIDS education program with accompanying resource, reference, and media materials. The AAC's inability to achieve this goal as seen in the School Committee's 4–3 vote not to adopt its proposed curriculum recommendations was based upon the AAC's internal organizational characteristics and neglect in developing relationships with those who would support its efforts within the larger Beta community.

INITIATION OF ACTION

According to Sower et al., there are three conditions for initiating action which are important in determining the probability that the proposed action will move from initiation to legitimation. The conditions include: the prestige and authority held by the initiators within the community, the ability to gain access to others whose approval is necessary for the fulfillment of the group's goals, and the extent to which the proposed action is compatible with the existing conceptions of "community welfare."[139]

Prestige

This first condition, prestige, which is related to who the initiators are, examines the relationship between the identity of the initiators in the community structure and the possibility of favorable acceptance by the community at large. In general, initiation of an idea or action by persons holding positions of higher prestige or authority would seem more likely of acceptance than the same idea or action coming from those holding lesser positions. The student groups in Alpha did not hold positions of higher prestige or authority when compared to adults in the community. Willie (1987) would define the student group members as subdominant.[140] This student group's subdominant status was evident when it tried to get on the School Committee's docket. Sidell recalled,

We called up a woman we were told was in charge of [making the appointments]. She was so mean to us. We had to call back three times, 'cause we got hung up on and were being put on hold. We weren't treated with respect. She said, "We have this docket and we can put you wherever we want. So we can do this tomorrow or we can do it next year."[141]

The students also were reminded of their subdominant status when they made their first presentation before the School Committee. Sidell reflected, "They didn't take us seriously. They just kept looking at their watches. They weren't listening to what we were saying. We were in tears afterwards. I kept saying, 'Why am I doing this? Why can't we just be radicals?' "[142]

In Beta, those who initiated the call for the development of an HIV/AIDS curriculum were members of the Beta school administration: the superintendent, assistant superintendent, and health and human development specialist. With the development of the AAC, parents representing the PTOs' from all of Beta's public schools were also involved in the creation of the school-based HIV/AIDS curriculum. With the collective influence these individuals wielded and the access they had to resources within the community, it appeared that there would be little opposition to the AAC's recommendations. This was reflected in the sentiments of one AAC member who stated, "I was expecting there to be some opposition [in the community] but I also expected the School Committee to be reasonable and believe us because we knew a lot of them. A lot of us on the Committee were very active in our own PTOs."[143]

Gaining Access

While the Alpha student group may have initially lacked prestige, they gained acceptance based on their access to dominant adult groups in the community who possessed prestige and authority.[144] The students informed Sylvia Healey, president of the Alpha South PTA, about their initial experience with the School Committee. "Afterwards," Sidell stated, "we did get apologies."[145] In analyzing their next steps, it was apparent that the students continued to identify and develop relationships with individuals inside and outside the community that would help further their cause. Each of these individuals was an important resource to the students. When I asked Parker to reflect on his relationship with the students, he stated,

I wanted to make sure that their ideas had a chance to succeed. And I felt if they just focused on condoms they would weaken their chances of getting it through. I felt it [initial draft] wouldn't work. They agreed. We didn't argue at all. We talked and they actually became excited. They said, "Wow, this could be more than just condoms. Why don't we say we want condoms as part of a more comprehensive sex ed. package ?"[146]

Through their collaboration with adults from inside and outside the community, the students were able to develop a strategy that would enable them to present their concerns to the School Committee as a public health issue impacting the welfare of all students in the community.

Community Welfare

The next condition is concerned with whether the proposed action is compatible with the existing conceptions of "community welfare."[147] Students at both high schools felt justified in calling on adults to make condoms available in the city's two high schools. Their determination came from a variety of sources including published results of sexual activity and practice among their peers, the lack of adequate human sexuality education in school, awareness of the incidence of STDs among adolescents, and actions of their peers in neighboring communities. During the School Committee's first Open Forum on condom availability, Amelia Freiss, an Alpha South student, appealed to the adults in the audience with her plea, "If teenagers and children are our future, we have to keep them alive."[148–150]

Through their persistence the larger community eventually heard the student voices. One School Committee member reflected on the impact of the students' actions. She recalled, "It was impressive listening to their passion. The kids spoke directly from their experiences. They created an honest and effective dialogue. They kept prodding us."[151]

On January 27, at the School Committee's second Open Forum on the issue, students presented a petition to the Alpha School Committee with over 1,600 student and faculty signatures supporting condom availability in the city's high schools. Through their actions and public statements, the students demonstrated their unity. Kurtis stated, "Though abstinence is the only sure way to prevent AIDS, the majority of teenagers do participate in sexual activities."[152] Fleming pleaded, "We are the children and we are asking for your help. If you focus on the extraneous arguments then you are playing with people's lives."[153, 154] It was evident that students, teachers and parents from both schools were concerned about this issue.[155]

In a 7–1 vote the School Committee approved a measure to make condoms available to students at Alpha's two high schools. Sonya Schultz, School Committee chairwoman, recalled that evening: "This was student initiated. If it were not for the students' request, I don't think you would have seen this kind of vote. They were asking for help and doing it in the most appropriate way possible."[156]

While the Beta administration and the AAC may have initially held prestige within the Beta *school* community, they neglected to outreach to the *larger* community. Linda Whitmire, a Beta parent who later became the spokesperson for Concerned Parents and Citizens of Beta (CPCB) (the leading parent group opposed to the AAC's HIV/AIDS curriculum), never heard a word about the AAC.[157] These sentiments were also reflected in the voices of other Beta parents. These comments illustrate that the AAC did not develop a plan/articulate their reasons to justify their proposed action as "good" for the welfare of the larger Beta community. Therefore, the AAC did not have other community groups come forward to function as legitimizing agencies in support of the proposed HIV/AIDS curriculum. As a result, the school administration and the AAC were not able to successfully deal with those who opposed this initiative.

This oversight may have been attributed to the AAC's leadership and composition. As mentioned previously, Beta school administrators believed that most Beta residents supported some type of sexuality education curriculum. Other members with leadership roles on the AAC saw the adoption of an K–12 HIV/AIDS curriculum as inevitable. In one example, Assistant Superintendent Moore said to AAC members, "Now, let's face it, we're going to have to face this. There's going to be a whole sexual curriculum that's going to be in place in Beta within two years and there's really not much we can do about it."[158]

With regard to the AAC's composition, unanimously the membership supported some type of school-based HIV/AIDS education program in Beta. An overwhelming majority (90%) of the AAC membership supported the HIV/AIDS curriculum developed by the AAC. This was reflected in AAC's May 1993 vote to approve its proposed curriculum. This support was also illustrated in the comments made by Jackie Jones, an elementary school nurse who served on the Committee. She said, "To us the [curriculum] plan just showed common sense."[159] Another AAC member, Nan Parker commented, "We just felt like there was such a need for it [the AIDS curriculum], why wouldn't it go through?"[160] As a result of the views held by many AAC members and its leadership, the AAC did not consider obtaining broader community support for its work. Unlike in other communities where school administrators, teachers, and other community members were assessed on their views for the need and content of a AIDS education curriculum, AAC members did not assess the views of a broader constituency. This group went on to develop a K–12 HIV/AIDS education curriculum it felt met the needs of Beta residents.

This lack of outreach to the larger community prevented the school administration, the AAC, and other leaders within Beta from publicly supporting the need for an HIV/AIDS curriculum in light of the statewide statistics documenting the incidence of HIV/AIDS infection among Massachusetts adolescents. In addition, the lack of organized public dialogue during the creation of the HIV/AIDS curriculum prevented the Beta community as a whole from defining its view of the existing conceptions of "community welfare" with regard to health promotion and disease prevention.

In Alpha, a group of students—the initiating set—brought the need for an expanded sexuality education program to the community's attention. Through collaboration with adults both inside and outside the community, the student groups' proposed action evolved from a one-day "condom distribution day" at Alpha South High School to a city-wide student petition before the School Committee. Sidell stated, "Looking back, we did nothing that we thought we were going to do."[161] Their success was based upon their internal organizational characteristics and the external relationships they developed. Their initial goal and objectives were modified as a result of the external relationships they developed with respected adults inside and outside the community. Through these alliances, adults provided support. In addition, these relationships also provided the students with an understanding of Alpha's political system. This collaborative effort enabled the students to develop a level of prestige and credibility in the community with which to voice their public health message. This collaboration also provided adults with the opportunity to overcome their previous failed attempts to implement a sexuality education curriculum in Alpha's schools. The interrelationships that emerged during the initiation stage were an example of how adults as a dominant group and youth as a subdominant group worked together in a complementary fashion toward fulfillment of their mutual goals.

When the Alpha School Committee voted 7–1 in favor of condom availability and then charged the school administration with forming a Task Force to explore the components of a comprehensive health education curriculum, the students achieved their goals. They also realized the adults had to follow through. This is evident when Fleming commented, "We went to a couple of meetings. It just seemed like the adults knew what they wanted. That didn't bother me. I'd worked with a good majority of them, and I knew what they stood for. I knew things were OK even if I wasn't there. We did our piece."[162, 163]

In Beta, a group of school administrators—the initiating set—brought the need for an HIV/AIDS education program to the attention of the Parent-Teacher Organizations. Through collaboration with parents, the AAC was developed with the goal to recommend to the School Committee curriculum components for a K–12 HIV/AIDS education program with accompanying resource, reference, and media materials.[164] The AAC's inability to achieve this goal as seen in the School Committee's 4–3 vote not to adopt its proposed curriculum recommendations was based upon the AAC's internal organizational characteristics and neglect in developing relationships with those who would support its efforts within the larger Beta community. With regard to the AAC's internal organization, Beta school administrators did not relinquish their leadership role to members of the group. As such, much of the work of the AAC was directed by the assistant superintendent and the chairperson who had a clear stake in seeing that an HIV/AIDS education curriculum be developed in a timely fashion. This was evident in how the goals and objectives of this group were determined. While the AAC had a clear goal and objectives, it appeared that the group's goal and objectives were dictated by the school administration. While all members of the group supported the development and implementation of a school-based HIV/AIDS education program, group members differed in their opinions on the objectives to be used to attain this goal. Over time, conflict emerged within the group around the exclusionary nature of the AAC's curriculum development subcommittee and the curriculum it subsequently developed. Over the next year, this conflict further created rifts among members on the AAC. This conflict also spread to the larger community as those opposed to the curriculum subcommittee's work actively solicited the support of other community members. Because the AAC neglected to conduct any type of public dialogue or information campaign that would demonstrate to the larger community the need for such a program in Beta's schools, no organized groups came forward to legitimize its efforts. As such, when misinformation about the proposed curriculum spread like wildfire in the community, Beta school administrators and the AAC were helpless. According to School Committee member Maureen

Casey, "A lot of information being disseminated to the community was second hand. It became tarnished, exploited." This was due in large part to the fact that there was not enough accurate information being provided to the larger community through the school administration, the AAC, or the Beta School Committee.[165]

Interestingly, in the early stages of this debate, Beta students did not have a voice. In retrospect, Beta parent Valerie Devine commented, "We didn't give students enough opportunities to express their views."[166] The lack of collaboration among adults within the Beta community and the lack of collaboration between adults and youth hindered the implementation of an HIV/AIDS curriculum in Beta's schools. In addition, the interrelationships that emerged among adults opposed to the curriculum during the initiation stage was an example of how adults representing a subdominant voice were able to attain a critical mass within the community to attain their goal of preventing the implementation of the HIV/AIDS curriculum developed by the AAC.

NOTES

1. C. V. Willie, *Theories of Human Social Action* (Dix Hills, NY: General Hall, Inc., 1994), p. 57.

2. C. Sower, J. Holland, K. Tiedke, and W. Freeman, *Community Involvement* (New York: The Free Press, 1957), p. 68.

3. Ibid., pp. 64–71.

4. M. Azzato, "Sex Education Programs Criticized," *Alpha Graphic*, 3/18/87, p. 8.

5. Alexander Interview, 6/15/95.

6. The group which becomes the initial sponsor of community action is labeled the "initiating set." By and large, the members must be local residents. It is very difficult if not impossible for nonresidents to become an initiating set for local community action. In Sower, Holland, Tiedke, and Freeman, *Community Involvement*, p. 68.

7. Sidell Interview, 12/22/94.

8. A random survey of students conducted by the Alpha South High School newspaper, the *Advocate*, found that 18% of freshmen, 27% of sophomores, 45% of juniors, and 48% of seniors described themselves as sexually active and one-fourth of all sexually active students used no birth control. Results of student survey in the *Advocate*, 9/30/91.

9. In a related article in the *Advocate*, entitled "Cambridge Leads the Way in Condom Distribution," the authors mention the outreach work of a group of peer leaders at Cambridge Rindge and Latin High School who had handed out envelopes containing condoms with instructions and information about AIDS prevention. In R. Wand, B. Stern, and D. Mirsky, "Cambridge Leads the Way in Condom Availability," *Advocate*, 9/30/91.

10. Fleming Interview, 12/7/94.

11. P. Mahoney and R. Telegen, "School Committee Votes to Make Condoms Available," *The Capsule*, 1/31/92, p. 3.

12. Sidell Interview, 12/2/94.

13. In the initiation stage, the group first needs to develop an internal organization between persons of common interests. It is through a convergence of interest arising out of the values, beliefs, and relationships of the larger community that a group is formed which is concerned with the initiation of a specific action. The relationships between the persons whose interests converge are such that there is a basis for internal organization. In Sower, et al., *Community Involvement*, p. 67.

14. Schultz Interview, 8/29/93.

15. *AIDS Advisory Committee Report*, Beta Public Schools, June 1993.

16. "Mike [Moore] and I had been meeting routinely," stated Alexander. "It had become a district-wide concern that we needed to address the health education issue. We had developed a survey for all faculty and I recommended in a report to the school administration that health education was fragmented and didn't have a sequence. We also didn't address contemporary health issues." In Alexander Interview, 6/15/95.

17. Valley Interview, 1/15/96.

18. Ponds Interview, 1/15/96.

19. Casey Interview, 11/3/95.

20. Ibid.

21. Alexander Interview, 6/15/95.

22. Valley Interview, 1/15/96.

23. McPherson Interview, 1/8/96.

24. Ponds Interview, 1/15/96.

25. Dowling Interview, 10/27/95.

26. Kane Interview, 12/3/95.

27. Nagel Interview, 10/27/95.

28. Bowman Interview, 10/6/95.

29. Pagano Interview, 10/27/95.

30. Nagel Interview, 10/27/95.

31. Porter Interview, 10/27/95.

32. Pagano Interview, 10/27/95.

33. Nagel Interview, 10/27/95.

34. Sower, Holland, Tiedke, and Freeman, *Community Involvement*, p. 69.

35. Sociologist Max Weber (1925) characterized those formal organizations that dominate modern societies as bureaucracies: rationally created formal organizations that are based on hierarchical authority and explicit rules of procedure. In T. J. Sullivan and K. S. Thompson, *Social Problems: Divergent Perspectives* (New York: John Wiley and Sons, 1984), p. 110.

36. Fleming Interview, 12/7/94.

37. Sidell Interview, 12/22/94.

38. *AIDS Advisory Committee Minutes*, 2/2/92.

39. Kane Interview, 12/3/95.

40. *AIDS Advisory Committee Minutes*, 10/7/92.

41. Ibid., 2/12/92.

42. Dowling Interview, 10/27/95.

43. Sidell Interview, 12/22/94.

44. Fleming Interview, 12/7/94.

45. Sidell Interview, 12/22/94.

46. Fleming Interview, 12/7/94.

47. Healey Interview, 8/19/94.

48. Sidell Interview, 12/22/94.

49. Sower et al. write, "If, however, the opposition is so great that they can not see how the goal can possibly be achieved, they will. . . . not continue as an initiating set for community action, for the goal will not be objectively achievable. If they do not see the possibility of success, they could continue as a discussion or protest group." In Sower et al., *Community Involvement*, p. 70.

50. Sidell Interview, 12/22/94.

51. *AIDS Advisory Committee Minutes*, 3/11/92.

52. Bowman Interview, 10/6/95.

53. Kane Interview, 12/3/95.

54. Valley Interview, 1/15/96.

55. *AIDS Advisory Committee Minutes*, 4/8/92.

56. Ibid.

57. The findings included:

Elementary: Kindergarten–Grade 3

• to teach at least two sessions in each grade that focused on health and wellness, sleep, exercise, and nutrition;

• to discuss illness, germs and diseases;

• to learn how diseases are spread through coughing, sneezing, and blood;

• to discuss prevention by washing hands and the use of tissues.

• With regard to AIDS, students would learn how AIDS is and isn't passed and how to be compassionate for people with the disease.

Grades 4 and 5

• to reinforce concepts covered in previous grades;

• to teach basic information about human sexuality;

• to teach basic first-aid procedures;

• to discuss the physiology of the reproductive, circulatory, and other internal systems;

• to present information on HIV/AIDS and AIDS prevention, including how to avoid contracting HIV through sexual abstinence and not sharing needles, for drugs, tattooing, or ear piercing.

Middle School: Grades 6–8

• infuse concepts of HIV/AIDS into the QUEST Life Skills program;

• stress sexual abstinence in the curriculum;

• removal of video, *Answers for Young* from the seventh-grade curriculum due to the poor quality of the film;

• use of current eighth-grade video, *Understanding AIDS* in the seventh grade and identify an additional video to be shown to the eighth-grade classes;

• invite an outside speaker to come in and talk with parents;

• make information available to parents, possibly through the development of a handbook. It was also suggested that this may be the appropriate place for a parent consent form.

High School: Grades 9–12

- In addition to the *Learn and Live* curriculum currently being used, other curricula could be used to supplement the lessons. These included: *Preventing Sexually Related Disease: Choosing Abstinence, Preventing AIDS, Teaching AIDS*; *DiGrassi Health Curriculum–AIDS Module*; *Peer Leadership: Preventing AIDS*;

- Special programs could also be offered including:
  —a person or group of persons with AIDS talking with students.
  —school-wide assembly for students providing them with information in a theater format.
  —an AIDS Awareness or Health Fitness Day. (*Source*: *AIDS Advisory Committee Minutes*, 5/20/92.)

58. Ibid.
59. Valley Interview, 1/15/96.
60. Alexander Interview, 6/15/95.
61. Kane Interview, 12/3/95.
62. McPherson Interview, 1/8/96.
63. Kane Interview, 12/3/95.
64. McPherson Interview, 1/8/96.
65. Casey Interview, 11/3/95.
66. Valley Interview, 1/15/96.
67. Alexander Interview, 7/23/96.
68. Kane Interview, 12/3/95.
69. *Alpha School Committee Minutes*, 6/15/92, pp. 5, 6.
70. Kane Interview, 12/3/95.
71. Alexander Interview, 6/15/95.
72. Kane Interview, 12/3/95.
73. McPherson Interview, 1/8/96.
74. Dowling Interview, 10/27/95.
75. Kane Interview, 12/3/95
76. Bowman Interview, 10/6/95.
77. Dowling Interview, 10/27/95.
78. Nagel Interview, 10/27/95.
79. Dowling Interview, 10/27/95.
80. McPherson Interview, 1/8/96.
81. Alexander Interview, 6/15/95.
82. Another feature of community action is mediation or intercession. It has no specific sequential ordering, no special place in time. Mediating activity may be required in any or all stages of the process of community action. There is always the possibility that two or more parts of a social system may reach an impasse. They may become nonfunctional. They cannot agree. They can go no further. Therefore, they jeopardize the welfare of the total community by their inability to resolve existing differences. Willie, *Theories of Human Social Action*, p. 59.
83. *AIDS Advisory Committee Minutes*, 3/30/93.
84. *AIDS Advisory Committee Minutes*, 4/14/93.
85. McPherson Interview, 1/8/96.
86. Kane Interview, 12/3/95.
87. Alexander Interview, 6/15/95.
88. McPherson Interview, 1/8/96.

89. Kane Interview, 12/3/95.

90. Graziano letter, December 1992.

91. S. Flanagan, "One Extreme Viewpoint Has Prevailed," *Beta Forum*, 7/14/93, p. 10.

92. Dominant status is not an intrinsic property of the white population and subdominant status is not an intrinsic property of the black population. Whites, blacks, or other population groups are dominants when their members collectively control disproportionate resources, have the authority to choose action strategies, and have the organizational capacity to commit resources for the implementation of such choices. In C. V. Willie, *Effective Education* (Dix Hills, NY: General Hall, 1987), p. 41.

93. Dowling Interview, 10/27/95.

94. Nagel Interview, 10/27/95.

95. Willie, *Effective Education*, p. 41.

96. Valley Interview, 1/15/96.

97. Bowman Interview, 10/6/95.

98. Kane Interview, 12/3/95.

99. Parker Interview, 8/12/94.

100. Mahoney and Telegen, "School Committee Votes to Make Condoms Available," p. 3.

101. Early on, members of the initiating set relied on technical assistance provided by outside individuals who had a history of working with school committees. Beverly Wiggins and Kevin Crane co-authored "Condom Availability in a Small Town: Lessons Learned from Falmouth, Massachusetts," *SIECUS Report*, October/November 1992. This article outlines suggestions for holding public hearings on condom availability. In addition, these students obtained some of their initial ideas from what their peers had accomplished at a nearby high school. Students also received training through participation at AIDS Action's Teen AIDS Conference.

102. Fleming Interview, 12/7/94.

103. Sidell Interview, 12/22/94.

104. Ibid.

105. Ibid.

106. Ibid.

107. Ibid.

108. Fleming Interview, 12/7/94.

109. *Tab*, 2/4/92, p. 1.

110. Mahoney and Telegen, "School Committee Votes to Make Condoms Available," p. 1.

111. Sidell Interview, 12/22/94.

112. Ibid.

113. Fleming Interview, 12/7/94.

114. Student Petition, 1991.

115. Sidell Interview, 12/22/94.

116. Fleming Interview, 12/7/94.

117. Sidell Interview, 12/22/94.

118. Fleming Interview, 12/7/94.

119. Ibid.

120. Sidell Interview, 12/22/94.

121. Sower, Holland, Tiedke, and Freeman, *Community Involvement*, p. 68.

122. Sidell Interview, 12/22/94.

123. Vincent Interview, 1/15/96.

124. *AIDS Advisory Committee Minutes*, 2/12/92.

125. Bowman Interview, 10/6/95.

126. Valley Interview, 1/15/96.

127. *AIDS Advisory Committee Minutes*, 5/20/92.

128. Casey Interview, 11/3/95.

129. Whitmire Interview, 12/8/95.

130. Alexander Interview, 6/15/95.

131. *AIDS Advisory Committee Minutes*, 3/30/93.

132. Custer Interview, 12/3/95.

133. Alexander Interview, 6/15/95.

134. Devine Interview, 10/27/95.

135. Valley Interview, 1/15/96.

136. Gray Interview, 12/8/95.

137. Kane Interview, 12/3/95.

138. Ibid.

139. Sower, Holland, Tiedke, and Freeman, *Community Involvement*, pp. 64–71.

140. Willie, *Effective Education*, p. 41.

141. Sidell Interview, 12/22/94.

142. Ibid.

143. Bowman Interview, 10/6/95.

144. Sower, Holland, Tiedke, and Freeman, *Community Involvement*, p. 71.

145. Sidell Interview, 12/22/94.

146. Parker Interview, 8/12/94.

147. Sower, Holland, Tiedke, and Freeman, *Community Involvement*, pp. 64–70.

148. Alpha School Committee Minutes, 1/13/92, p. 14.

149. Ibid., p. 9.

150. Sidell also spoke at the Open Forum. She stated, "A very low percentage of children can communicate with their parents on sensitive subjects such as sex. Therefore, the schools need to be the alternative place for these types of issues [to be discussed]." In *Alpha School Committee Minutes*, 1/27/92, p. 5.

151. Eisen Interview, 8/24/93.

152. Mahoney and Telegen, "School Committee Votes to Make Condoms Available," p. 1.

153. *Alpha School Committee Minutes*, 1/27/92, p. 4.

154. Ibid., p. 9.

155. Sidell Interview, 12/22/94.

156. R. Lear, "Sex Ed Debate Heats Up," *Tab*, 1/21/92, pp. 1, 6, and 12.

157. Whitmire Interview, 12/8/95.

158. Kane Interview, 12/3/95.

159. S. Patton, "Anti-AIDS Education Fighters Reach Out," *The Patriot Ledger*, 6/23/93, p. 1.

160. Parker Interview, 10/27/95.

161. Sidell Interview, 12/22/94.

162. Fleming Interview, 12/7/94.

163. Sidell also reflected back on her experiences. She stated, "The first year we were involved, we went to the meetings, but it was kind of ridiculous for us to go. I mean, I think we did it just to be fair. They had two representatives from South and two from North, but really it was out of our hands." Sidell Interview, 12/22/94.

164. AIDS Advisory Committee Minutes, 2/12/92.

165. Casey presentation, Harvard Graduate School of Education, 4/22/96.

166. Devine presentation, Harvard Graduate School of Education, 4/22/96.

CHAPTER 5

Obtaining Community Support for Health and Sexuality Education Programs

INTRODUCTION

The second stage of community action process—the *legitimation stage*—involves getting approval for the proposed action from persons and groups in the community.[1] A fundamental process of events in this stage is the expansion of the initiating set into the "sponsoring set" by the growing involvement of persons and organizations that function as legitimizing agencies. The sponsoring set has three primary tasks: to justify the proposed action as "good" for the welfare of the community, to gain support from the appropriate "legitimizers" for the action, and to be able to deal with any possible opposition.[2] This analysis of the legitimation stage is subdivided into the following three chapters. Chapter 5, is an analysis of how the sponsoring sets obtained community support. Chapter 6, examines the emergence of community voices opposed to the respective sexuality education initiatives in Alpha and Beta. Chapter 7 is an analysis of how individuals and community groups counteracted opposition.

EXPANDING HEALTH AND SEXUALITY EDUCATION

On January 27, 1992, the Alpha School Committee addressed the health education curriculum issue. It charged the school administration to form a Task Force to explore the components of a comprehensive health curriculum.[3] Daniel Hawthorne, a School Committee member, asked that the administration make every effort possible to involve people from the community. School Committee chairperson Sonya Schultz added that people who addressed the Committee about these issues could be asked to volunteer.[4] This expansion of the original "initiating set" to include members of the community in a more formal structure known as the Health Education Task Force—the sponsoring set—was an important development in the community decision-making process in Alpha.

With the defeat of the AAC's proposed HIV/AIDS education curriculum, and the emergence of the grassroots organization Community Advocates for Responsible Education (CARE), came an organized call from parents in Beta for the development of a school-based *comprehensive* K–12 health education program. CARE members were interested in presenting HIV/AIDS information within the framework of comprehensive health education. Up to this point, Beta school administrators, the School Committee, and other community members had focused their efforts on the development of an HIV/AIDS specific education program. At about this same time, Beta school administrators were also interested in receiving state funding through the state Department of Education's Health Protection Grant. One of the requirements for funding was the creation of a community advisory committee. On March 28, 1994, the Beta School Committee appointed a 36-member committee. This action formalized the creation of the "sponsoring set." Due to the resounding defeat experienced by proponents of the HIV/AIDS education programs in the past, the HAC membership knew how important it would be to get community approval for a proposed K–12 comprehensive health education program.

Benefits to Community Welfare

In Alpha, the Task Force[5] surveyed school teachers, administrators, parents, and students. Results from the surveys verified the need for an expanded sexuality education program. In Beta, after two attempts to adopt HIV/AIDS education programs, school administrators worked with HAC members to conduct a community-wide assessment to develop a comprehensive K–12 health education program. Results from the survey demonstrated overwhelming support for such a program.

Initially, the Task Force's subcommittee[6] surveyed teachers and administrators. Dixon stated, "One of the early tasks we undertook was to identify what programs were already in place in the system that related to sexuality and HIV/AIDS education. To accomplish this we developed a survey and sent it to all K–12 professional staff."[7] Once responses from teachers and administrators were collated and analyzed, several patterns emerged. Highlights included:

- emotional and social growth skills permeated all curriculum areas in grades K–8;
- current events articles and student inquiry were common mechanisms for discussing AIDS and STDs;

- information about human physiology and disease prevention were covered in ninth/tenth-grade biology courses.

In addition, many staff noted that they wanted support in dealing with these issues. Others expressed concern about the importance of these topics and the lack of time to teach them.[8]

Task Force curriculum subcommittee members also realized the important role of parents. In October 1992, they met with parents at six of Alpha's nineteen schools to assess their attitudes and concerns. One hundred sixty parents completed questionnaires on sexuality education topics. The results included:

- parents overwhelmingly supported a comprehensive sex education program;
- parents wanted to be informed of curriculum topics and requested parent workshops;
- most parents supported teaching students in all grades, age-appropriate material about sex, health, and AIDS.[9]

In October 1992, the Task Force's curriculum subcommittee also conducted a survey of a representative sample of eighth and ninth graders about their knowledge, attitudes, behaviors, and needs.[10] However, the school administration never completed the analysis of these data. Therefore, these results have never officially been reported or utilized. Interestingly, this curriculum, which was targeted to students, had been developed without much student input.

Teachers were again surveyed in March 1993 for the purpose of gaining their perspectives about students' needs and behaviors. Dixon commented, "There were a range of viewpoints on what was appropriate to teach students. However, the majority of teachers echoed the need for thorough information at the ninth grade level. Some teachers even questioned whether this was too late."[11]

When the results from the initial teacher/administrator survey were analyzed, Dixon commented, "Gaps in Alpha's program were obvious and glaring."[12] Results from the parent and second teacher surveys provided additional evidence to verify the need for an expanded sexuality education program in the Alpha's schools.

Initially, there were no organized efforts by individuals or community groups in Beta to justify the need and benefits of the AAC's proposed HIV/AIDS curriculum, and the later the *Free Teens* program. This phenomenon may be partly explained by the beliefs held by school administrators and the AAC leadership, who felt most Beta residents supported some type of sexuality education curriculum. Jane Alexander, the AAC's chairperson, reflected back on her experience: "[It's important] to know your community. Make sure you're not going off and developing a program without surveying your community. I think any town should expect this. You need to do your homework."[13-15]

On March 28, the Beta School Committee appointed a 36-member HAC to focus its efforts on the development of a comprehensive health education curriculum. According to Beta School Committee member Jean Anderson, the goal of the HAC was to develop recommendations for a health curriculum. This would be accomplished by hiring a person to conduct a community assessment about what was needed in a K–12 comprehensive health curriculum and by developing a curriculum based on those needs.[16]

With regard to community welfare, HAC member and former AAC member Shirley Bowman stated, "We [the HAC] had to educate the community that we had no health education in the schools. But it was a fine line to stay pro–public schools when you're saying the public schools aren't doing their job. Our [the HAC's] message was that public schools needed some help."[17] One way in which the HAC membership educated the general community was to raise awareness around the need for comprehensive health education rather than present the shortcomings of Beta's present health education program. At one of the HAC's initial meetings in June 1994, former health education director Jim Gray presented findings from the *Massachusetts 1993 Youth Risk Behavior Survey*. This study, which was commissioned by the Massachusetts Department of Education, presented findings from a survey of nearly 3,000 high school students from 39 cities and towns in the Commonwealth of Massachusetts on adolescent sexual activity, education, and practice.[18]

Additionally, HAC members worked with the Beta High School PTO to sponsor an AIDS Awareness program for Beta residents in April 1994. The goal of the program was to provide medical/physiological information about AIDS and information on the transmission and prevention of the disease. Before the event, Jane Alexander commented, "It is hoped that the evening will enable parents to feel more knowledgeable and comfortable talking with their children about AIDS and teaching them to act responsibly, morally, and sensibly."[19]

Obtaining Approval

Another task of the sponsoring set is to obtain the support of respected groups and organizations. To accomplish this task, Sower et al. state, "the proposed action requires the approval of some community members and the active sponsorship of others who are in a position to influence action."[20] Through the early work of the Alpha Task Force it became apparent that the majority of those surveyed supported some type of school-based sexuality education program. In Beta, there was no organized effort by the school administration, the AAC membership, nor other community-based groups to obtain community support and approval for the

AAC's proposed HIV/AIDS education plan.[21] With regard to the *Free Teens* program, Beta residents would have three weeks to review and comment on the program after a public viewing. Interestingly, school officials decided not to hold public hearings on the proposed curriculum. After two failed attempts, the HAC solicited community input on the need and development of a comprehensive health education curriculum.

After approximately ten months of data collection and soliciting community support, the Task Alpha Force presented its recommendations to the School Committee in January 1993. Its main recommendation was to pilot test a sexuality education program at the ninth-grade level and eventually implement age-appropriate materials for all grades. Other recommendations were in the areas of program staffing, in-service training, and materials.[22, 23]

At this meeting individuals representing community groups publicly verbalized their support of the Task Force. In particular, Fern Mendon, co-president of Alpha PTA Council stated, "We unanimously support : (1) the process for developing the curriculum; and 2) the work of the Task Force in the implementation of a city-wide health education curriculum to meet the needs of Alpha's children."[24]

In another example, Rick Dillon, from Alpha's Substance Abuse AIDS Coalition, stated, "Condom availability should remain intact, but only in the presence of a comprehensive program involving parents and the community."[25] Alpha students also endorsed the Task Force's work. This was illustrated by a petition presented to the School Committee signed by 1,630 students or approximately two-thirds of the Alpha High School student population calling for an expanded sexuality education program. Student support was also evident in an editorial in the Alpha High School student newspaper *The Capsule*.[26] At the conclusion of this meeting, the School Committee voted unanimously to support the Task Force's recommendations concerning the human sexuality HIV/AIDS curriculum.

Over the next few months, other individuals and community groups emerged to voice or reaffirm their support of the Task Force. These included parents, the Alpha Clergy Association, Supporters of Student Health Education in Alpha (SSHEA), the Alpha Teachers Association, and other organizations serving Alpha residents. The media also supported sexuality education in the schools. For example, in one editorial in the *Alpha Graphic*, entitled "Sex Education is Needed," the author writes, "Listen to the students. It's not enough just to teach them about the basics anymore. Students should be trusted with as much information as available, taught in a frank and honest atmosphere."[27]

Parents had other opportunities to provide their input. Public meetings on the pilot curriculum were conducted by the Task Force between February and April 1993. A third meeting was held for the Parent Advisory Committee for Special Education. The purpose of these meetings was to present the proposed goals, objectives, and content of the ninth-grade course and to obtain their responses. Following the presentation, parents were asked to comment on the proposed course in writing using the Parent Perspective Form.[28] Approximately 190 parents attended these forums and 77 completed the form. These written perspectives were summarized in a report to the School Committee. An excerpt from the conclusion read:

Many parents stressed the urgent nature of such a curriculum and suggested ways to expand the program. . . . The need to emphasize the positive aspects of abstinence was of concern to at least one-third of all responding parents. The selection of teachers was the next most commonly discussed topic.[29]

The mobilization efforts of supporters and opponents of the Task Force's efforts culminated at the May 10, 1993 School Committee meeting. Over 600 people filled Bell Junior High auditorium to voice their positions and hear the Task Force's final recommendations. Of approximately 70 speakers, 56 voiced their support.[30] State Senator Lisa Pell (D-Alpha), who recognized the School Committee's leadership role, commented: "We cannot stand idly by while our children make serious decisions without understanding the nature of their choices. This program will ensure that they have accurate information and a respect for themselves and others."[31] David Berkeley, an Alpha parent who opposed the curriculum stated, "Teachers should not be teaching these types of subjects which belong at home."[32]

After four hours of public testimony, the Health Education Task Force submitted its final recommendations. In a 9–0 vote, School Committee members approved "the report from the Health Education Task Force, including the proposed outline for the ninth grade human sexuality course."

This meeting provided a forum for members of the community and the School Committee to legitimize the process and the work of the Task Force. The overwhelming community support and the unanimous School Committee vote formalized the collaboration between the Task Force and school administrators as they implemented the ninth-grade pilot program.

In Beta, proponents of the AAC's HIV/AIDS education program did not build alliances with enough individuals and community groups who could have provided support and approval for this initiative. Even though some individual parents and students[33] came forward during the June 14 and 21, 1993 public hearings, more than one-half of the 600 people who attended these meetings were opposed to the AAC's proposal. Some of the opposition to the proposed curriculum centered on curriculum content and age-appropriateness of the material.[34] Other parents expressed concern about school's usurping parental rights and crossing moral boundaries.[35] Still other parents felt schools should stick to reading, writing, and arithmetic.[36] One Beta parent, Gina Nolan, recommended developing a new AIDS curriculum: "I am not opposed to an AIDS curriculum. I am opposed to this one. Let's not rewrite this one. Let's get a new one."[37]

After nearly ten hours of public debate, the Beta School Committee voted 4–3 to reject Superintendent Kurtz's request to revise the proposed plan, saying it could not be salvaged. "We need to start at the beginning," said School Committee member Patricia Dorman. "I see no hope for this curriculum."[38] Committee members Maureen Casey, Dan Craig, and Chairman Joseph Ponds also voted to reject the plan. Maureen Casey recalled her position,

No one had opposition to teaching the biological facts of AIDS. The problem came when the line was crossed from science to morals. I could quote you an example in the seventh grade curriculum: "Some adults would like you to believe that sex outside marriage is wrong." Well, you're damn right I do.[39]

Chairman Joseph Ponds voiced his opposition to the plan with the comment:

There were some items that were too graphic at an early age. Even proponents said at the time, "We'll just take it out." And I have a real problem with that. This is not a menu that is a la carte. This should be a comprehensive program that meshes together.[40]

Paul Andros, Karen White, and Jean Anderson supported the AIDS curriculum, but asked for revisions.[41]

Members then voted in favor of a motion to have the superintendent present a procedure at the next School Committee meeting for the development of an AIDS curriculum for the Beta schools.[42]

After the public hearing, Elaine Kane commented on the vote: "I hope this sends a clear message to the school department that parents want a say in their children's education. They want to be involved. A lot of good people with solid values came out and found each other."[43] The previous day Jane Alexander, AAC chairwoman, defended the AAC's work in an interview with *The Boston Globe*. She stated,

It [the proposed curriculum] is not to promote promiscuous behavior. It talks about what puts a person at risk and how to avoid risk. Abstinence is one of the issues covered thoroughly. This is just a proposal, it is not formal school policy yet. I would expect the School Committee and community to make modifications. They may choose to reject it. But with AIDS having the impact that it is having in our society, a curriculum like this is something that should at least be out there for debate and I expect it to be emotional.[44]

Superintendent Peter Kurtz recalled that it was the largest turnout for a school meeting since he had taken his job two years before. He acknowledged that AIDS education is a tough issue for the schools but said he is determined to tackle it. He said, "AIDS is not a new topic and will not go away. At a minimum we have the responsibility to teach students what AIDS is and how it's acquired and what they can do to avoid it. As a community there should be some common ground that we can reach on this."[45]

Some community members were shocked about the outcome. Nan Parker, an AAC member, commented, "I would say, we were all very surprised, because we just felt like there was such a need for it."[46] Others expressed dismay: "Students want AIDS education and a lot of us think it's sad we have to wait," wrote Beta High School junior Billy Walsh. "There's definitely a need for more awareness."[47] Beta High School sophomore Brian Harrison wrote, "Ignorance leads to chaos. Protection whether in the form of education, abstinence or a condom is our only vaccine today. Education is not advocating sex or promiscuity, it is mentioning the hard truth."[48]

Superintendent Kurtz was also shocked by the intense sentiment against the proposal. He also alluded to how difficult it would be to develop an AIDS curriculum that would satisfy all community members. He stated,

There is a core of about nine or ten people who are extremely vocal and developing a formidable following. It will be a challenge to develop an AIDS education plan that will satisfy the parents' opposition group. It's frustrating to be at this point. Getting anything done seems like it will be a battle.[49]

Patricia Dorman, a member of the Beta School Committee stated, "If we held the public hearings before we had a curriculum, we'd be a lot better off. AIDS education should reflect the community."[50, 51]

Over the next six months, Beta school administrators reviewed a variety of HIV/AIDS curricula. Four curricula were provided by the Concerned Parents and Citizens of Beta.[52]

At the Beta School Committee's January 24, 1994 meeting, Superintendent Kurtz proposed an HIV/AIDS curriculum which reflected the guidelines established by the School Committee.[53] This curriculum included two lessons in grade 7 on medical facts on AIDS information and prevention and three lessons in grade 9 from the *Free Teens* program on delaying sexual intimacy.[54–56] "To truly appreciate and understand the program proposed for 9th grade," Dr. Kurtz stated, "It is important to have the material presented in a fashion similar to how students would receive it."[57] As such, a public viewing of the program was scheduled for January 31 at East Middle School.

Interestingly, school officials decided not to hold public hearings on the proposed curriculum. This was done, "in an effort to avoid a repeat of hearings held in June."[58] Beta residents would have three weeks to review the program and submit written comments on the curriculum to the school administration offices.[59] Many Beta residents expressed support for the superintendent's proposal. "I think you have hit a home run with this [program] and I applaud your efforts," said Beta police Sergeant Pat Donovan.[60] Public support for this program appeared to be evident to Superintendent Kurtz. When interviewed by *The Patriot Ledger* he stated, "I can't see many, if any parents objecting to the material as it was presented [at the Forum]."[61]

As school administrators presented their proposal for an HIV/AIDS education program for Beta schools they again circumvented an important part of the community decision-making process. They selected a curriculum without obtaining community-wide input. While school administrators may have obtained approval from some community members including the CPCB, they overlooked the sentiments of other Beta parents including CARE members. Shirley Bowman, a Beta parent and CARE member recalled:

We heard rumors that there was going to be this *Free Teens* program. So we got hold of it, and we looked at it and decided as a group that we really didn't like it. So we went in to him [Dr. Kurtz] and presented him a list of reasons why we didn't like the curriculum. And he said, "Well, I really like it. Just wait until the presenter comes [on January 31]."

She continued,

So I was really ripping. I didn't like the guidelines for the *Free Teens* program. And even Jane Alexander was saying, "It'll be O.K. It's O.K. It's not bad, we can take some of the slides out." When I read it, I thought it was derogatory and had a real subtle message that the only way to live was in a married, male/female situation.[62]

Another Beta parent and CARE member, Nan Porter felt that the "[*Free Teens*] program would have been O.K., if you could remove" various sections. However, it was made quite clear by Heather Thalen, regional coordinator of *Free Teens*, during the January 31 presentation, that the program could not be altered in any way.[63]

Parents who wanted teenagers to learn that condoms could reduce the spread of HIV/AIDS asked school administrators to offer an alternative to the abstinence-only *Free Teens* curriculum. "We need to offer another program for those children who are not abstaining now," said CARE member Ellen Nagel. "We don't agree with an abstinence-only program. It does not stress in addition to abstinence, that if you are sexually active, how you should protect yourself."[64] Members of CARE provided Dr. Kurtz with an alternative AIDS education course entitled *Preventing AIDS*.[65] "We're asking him [Kurtz] to treat *Free Teens* and this alternative [*Preventing AIDS*] program equally," said Valerie Devine of CARE. "We're also asking him to hold public hearings on both of them.[66]

Thomas Hampton, a local Beta activist and CPCB member, predicted the school administration's actions would lead to eventual conflict. He stated,

He [Dr. Kurtz] eventually recommended *Free Teens*. He picked that out without even consulting the other side. He made a mistake because given the controversy that was going on between the two groups, CPCB and CARE, he should have said, "How can I take a program from them [CPCB] because that will make the other side mad."[67]

This conflict came to a head on February 17, 1994, when *The Patriot Ledger* ran a cover story entitled "Rev. Moon linked to AIDS course." The intent of this article was to expose *Free Teens* author Ronald Peter's ties to Reverend Sun Myung Moon's Unification Church.

Following a series of news reports over the next few days that raised additional concerns about the curriculum's content, Dr. Kurtz formally withdrew his recommendation for School Committee approval of the ninth-grade program. He commented, "Given the level of [Peter's] involvement with the Unification Church and the concerns that have been raised, I don't feel the *Free Teens* program can be effective."[68] Beta School Committee chairman Joseph Ponds felt the *Free Teens* program met school officials' goals. However, he said, "The problem is perception. So often in public policy as in politics, the perception becomes the reality. If it's seen as a biased program, obviously we are going to have extreme difficulty getting the support for it."[69]

Kurtz's action to withdraw the program marked the second time in eight months that Beta school administrators had been unsuccessful in building broad community support for a school-based HIV/AIDS education program. At the same meeting the School Committee voted to approve the implementation of the grade 7 program in the fall of 1994. Information and materials for this program would come from a publication entitled *AIDS: What Teens Need To Know*, published by the Weekly Reader Corporation.[70] Later in the meeting, the School Committee voted 5–2 to have a committee of professional educators develop an age-appropriate, information-based unit of instruction on AIDS for ninth-grade students at Beta High School.[71] After the vote, School Committee member Dorothy Nedrick said it was time for the Beta community to come together. She commented, "We need to identify our priorities, educate our children on preventing this disease. Rather than fighting, we need to find common ground to begin working toward that goal."[72, 73]

One month later at the Health Advisory Council's (HAC) initial meeting, members discussed the need for obtaining community input around the development of a comprehensive health education program. One method which was supported by the HAC membership was a community-wide assessment.[74] At the HAC's May meeting, John Baker, an outside consultant with Community Health Resources, presented a plan to the group. Following a group discussion about the feasibility, logistics, timeline, and funding for such a study, the committee voted unanimously to study the opinions of students, parents, faculty, and other community members regarding the health education needs of Beta students.[75-77]

Over the next few months, Council members discussed a list of 30 potential topic areas, including nutrition, mental health, hygiene, drug use and abuse, first aid, human sexuality, and AIDS, to be included within the questionnaire. Additionally, the survey was designed to determine: (1) the percentage of respondents that supported the instruction/discussion of each health education topic listed in the survey; and (2) the grade level at which respondents felt instruction/discussion of each health topic should begin.[78]

Analysis of the survey data revealed that the majority of community members surveyed supported some type of comprehensive health education for grades K–12.[79-81] Some of the concerns raised over a comprehensive health education curriculum revolved around issues of age-appropriateness of materials, the teaching of values, and the need for parental involvement in the development of the program. One Beta parent wrote, "Sexuality is a difficult issue for most parents and many choose denial. . . . I think this information should be introduced gradually at age-appropriate intervals."[82] Another parent responded, "I feel it is very important to teach health material in a factual, physiological way. Content should be sent home to parents so they can teach/discuss the moral aspects of the topics. I do not think the educational system should impose upon families by discussing morals."[83] Another Beta parent stated, "I would like materials available to parents."[84]

Commenting on the survey results, Superintendent Kurtz stated, "The results of the survey provide a clear direction for the school system in terms of providing health education to the students."[85] Beta School Committee chairperson Jean Anderson added, "When the results of the survey came back, they simply said exactly what we knew all along, but now we had it in black and white to prove it."[86] In an interview, Health and Human Development specialist Jane Alexander remembered how the survey results motivated her to remove a discussion of HIV/AIDS from the fourth- and fifth-grade curricula:

The reason I took HIV/AIDS out of the 4th/5th grade curriculum was not because it wasn't good. It was wonderful. I hated taking it out. But if you do a survey and they [the majority of parents] didn't want sexual intercourse to be talked about until middle school it was better to pull it out. After all, you can't talk about AIDS if you don't use the word sexual intercourse. Not with any honesty. So it was better to pull it out.[87]

Based on the survey results, the HAC voted to recommend to the School Committee that a comprehensive K–12 health education curriculum be developed and adopted by the 1995–1996 school year.[88] On March 27, the HAC presented the survey results to the School Committee.

With the release of the results of the survey, it appeared that the time was at hand for the Beta Public Schools to move forward with the development and implementation of a comprehensive health education program.[89] Other Beta community members also publicly supported a school-based comprehensive health education program. One parent wrote in the *Beta Forum*, "In my opinion Beta is woefully behind every other community in the area. It's about time given the results of the town survey for the schools that we develop such a curriculum and get on with it. It's what people want."[90] Another Beta resident commented, "Education is one of our greatest gifts that we can give our children. It's imperative that our children be taught with up-to-date and factual information in schools about sex."[91] A former Beta High School student said,

I am embarrassed and ashamed of the town of Beta. Before I graduated [from Beta High School] I had one abortion and two STDs. . . . Wake up Beta! Teens are having sex whether you like it or not. We need a sex curriculum. Face reality. Your kids are having sex and they need this information desperately.[92]

Alexander concluded: "Parents of public school students have been given a voice with which to participate in the design of the health education curriculum."

The success of the HAC's proposed action was related to the internal organization of the group. When I asked Alexander about how the group functioned she commented,

As chairperson I ran good meetings. I was able to get the agenda taken care of because we ran [the HAC] by Robert's Rules of Order with majority vote and citizen participation taken under advisement. Any conflict we had was related to the health education curriculum subcommittee presenting to the larger [HAC] group. However, there wasn't the angriness we saw in the past. We [the HAC members] played by the *rules*.[93]

Interestingly, no members of CPCB or any other organized opposition group participated as voting members of the HAC.

The second stage of community action process—the *legitimation stage*—involves getting approval for the proposed action from persons and groups in the community. To accomplish this task, Sower et al. states "the proposed action requires the approval of some community members and the active sponsorship of others who are in a position to influence action." In Alpha, the Task Force surveyed school teachers, administrators, parents, and students. Results from the surveys verified the need for an expanded sexuality education program. After approximately ten months of data collection and soliciting community support, the Task Force presented its recommendations to the School Committee in meetings in January and June 1993. These meetings provided a forum for members of the community and the School Committee to legitimize the process and the work of the Task Force. The overwhelming community support and the unanimous School Committee vote formalized the collaboration between the Task Force and school administrators as they implemented the ninth-grade pilot program. In Beta, proponents of the AAC's HIV/AIDS education program did not build alliances with enough individuals and community groups who could have provided support and approval for their proposal. Even though some individual parents and students came forward during the June 14 and 21, 1993 public hearings, more than one-half of the 600 people who attended these meetings were opposed to the AAC's proposal. After two failed attempts at trying to adopt HIV/AIDS education programs, Beta school administrators worked with HAC members to conduct a community-wide assessment to develop a comprehensive K–12 health education program. Results from the survey demonstrated overwhelming community support for such a program.

NOTES

1. C. Sower, J. Holland, K. Tiedke, and W. Freeman, *Community Involvement* (New York: The Free Press, 1957), p. 96.

2. Ibid., pp. 99–114.

3. *Alpha School Committee Minutes*, 1/27/92, pp. 12–14.

4. Ibid., pp. 10–14.

5. In February 1992, Alpha assistant superintendent Paul Redman sent an invitation letter to interested students, school personnel, and community members to join the Task Force. This group, which began meeting in March 1992, was comprised of 50 community residents. Redman stated, "We wanted to include people from broad perspectives, so that we could have some dialogue." In their initial meetings, Task Force members subdivided into four subcommittees; curriculum, school environment, community resources, and health services.

6. In my research, I focused on the curriculum subcommittee. Initially, this subcommittee developed a set of short-term goals which included gathering information, the review of current curriculum offerings, and developing a scope and sequence for the curriculum. The long-term goal was to recommend a comprehensive K-12 health education curriculum. It was in fulfilling their short-term goals that this subcommittee was able to convince the larger Task Force membership, the School Committee, and the community at large that they were working on behalf of the welfare of the community.

7. N. Dixon, *Educating for Life: Implementing Sexuality and HIV/AIDS Education in the Alpha Schools* (Master's Thesis, Cambridge, MA: Cambridge College, 1993), p. 37.

8. Alpha Health Education Task Force, *Report and Recommendations*, December 1992.

9. Other results from the parent questionnaire included:

• While almost all parents were comfortable with students in grades 4–6 learning about reproductive anatomy and puberty, a small number did not want their children taught specifics about sexual physiology and behavior;

• A majority of parents did not want information about sexual orientation given to children in grades K-3. A smaller number did not want this topic discussed in grades 4–6. Parents of older children supported teaching about this topic;

• Many parents urged that the physical, emotional, and spiritual aspects of sex be integrated into the curriculum;

• Many parents wanted the topic of personal responsibility addressed in relationships and abstinence as the healthier choice to be emphasized in the curriculum;

• Parents were also concerned about the expertise of the teacher. (*Source*: Alpha Health Education Task Force, *Report and Recommendations*.)

10. *Alpha School Committee Minutes*, 5/26/92, p. 10.

11. Dixon Interview, 6/30/95.

12. Dixon, *Educating for Life: Implementing Sexuality and HIV/AIDS Education in the Alpha Schools*, p. 38.

13. Alexander Interview, 6/15/95.

14. Over the next few weeks, notices about the HAC's formation went out to elementary and middle school parents. Announcements were also made at PTO meetings and carried in the local newspaper and cable station. According to School Committee member Maureen Casey, "It [the HAC] was open to anyone who wanted to join. They [the school administration] wanted a large cross-section of the community." The members of this group represented school administrators, educators, parents, students, health care professionals, human services providers, and clergy. In *Beta School Committee Minutes*, 3/94, and Casey Interview, 11/3/95.

15. J. W. Ferro, "AIDS Course Put in Hands of Local Teachers," *Beta Forum*, 3/2/94, pp. 1, 20.

16. R. Aicardi, "Limiting Health Panel to 36 Stirs Flap," *The Patriot Ledger*, 6/8/94, pp. 1, 22.

17. Bowman Interview, 10/6/95.

18. See Chapter 1, note 47.

19. "Beta High PTO to Sponsor AIDS Awareness," *Beta Forum* 4/5/95, p. 3.

20. Sower, Holland, Tiedke, and Freeman, *Community Involvement*, p. 99.

21. Casey Interview, 11/3/95.

22. According to draft materials presented by the Task Force, the curriculum will be based on "core values." The values are broken down into values for the health education curriculum and the human sexuality curriculum. Included in the values for the health education curriculum are: respect, responsibility, honesty, and trustworthiness. The core values of the human sexuality curriculum include: self-worth, sexuality, abstinence, decision-making, sexual behavior, and relationships. In *Draft Materials*, 1992.

23. *Report and Recommendations*, December 1992.

24. *Alpha School Committee Minutes*, 1/11/93, p. 4.

25. Ibid., p. 5.

26 The editorial read, "Our position remains that students should delay sexual intercourse, but if they choose not to, it is our responsibility to provide students with this information to assist them in their decision making." G. Weiss and K. Saxon, "Condom Program a Success," *The Capsule*, 6/4/92, p. 2.

27. Editorial, "Sex Education Is Needed," *Alpha Graphic*, 3/4/93, p. 1.

28. Dixon, *Educating for Life: Implementing Sexuality and HIV/AIDS Education in the Alpha Schools*, pp. 71–74.

29. Health Education Task Force, 1993.

30. These individuals represented groups such as Alpha Teacher's Association, Alpha Substance Abuse/AIDS Coalition, Alpha Human Rights Commission, Alpha School Nurses Association, the Unitarian Society of Alpha, Second Church of Alpha, Temple Emanuel, Gay and Lesbian Advocate Defenders (GLAD). *Alpha School Committee Minutes*, 5/10/93.

31. Ibid., p. 7.

32. Ibid., p. 13.

33. Some people in the audience voiced strong support for the proposed AIDS curriculum. Beta parent Joe Anderson stated, "I support this curriculum because we have an opportunity to teach our children at all ages about this dreadful disease. This is not like drugs and alcohol where you have a second chance." In J. W. Ferro, "AIDS Curriculum under Fire," *Beta Forum*, 6/16/93, p. 22. Other parents supported the program because the curriculum would deal with the issue of denial by creating awareness about AIDS. Kathy Bartow, a nurse and Beta parent said, "A lot of parents aren't willing to talk about AIDS. My children have to be taught about AIDS and they have to start early." In S. Patton, "Debate on AIDS Heated," *The Patriot Ledger*, 6/15/93, p. 1. Another Beta parent, Susan Sullivan, agreed: "Ignorance does not insure protection. Kids should learn these lessons from professionals not from other kids on the playground." In Ferro, "AIDS Curriculum under Fire," p. 22. One of the only young people to speak during the public hearing was a 20-year-old college student. "Kids won't spend their entire lives in Beta," said Mark Anderson. "They could end up anywhere in the world and they need education to protect themselves." In Ferro, "AIDS Curriculum under Fire," p. 22.

Several high school students and teachers urged the School Committee to approve the plan, saying all pupils won't follow advice to abstain from sex. In S. Patton, "Beta Rejects Curriculum on AIDS," *The Patriot Ledger*, 6/22/93, p. 16. "The fact is that many teens feel invincible," said Chris Christansen, a Beta High School junior. "Abstinence isn't attractive to many teens. Isn't it your moral duty to save the lives of as many teens as possible?" Another Beta High School student, Ann Murphy, commented, "We all have to put away our phobias and fears. This is about our lives. Abstinence is great, but it's not a realistic goal for a lot of kids. We have to realize many kids are having sex, and unprotected sex. You can't just leave it up to parents, because many don't talk about sex. We students deserve to be told the truth about the disease." In R. Aicardi, "AIDS Curriculum—Back to Ground Zero," *Beta Forum*, 6/23/93, p. 24. A member of the AAC who devised the AIDS curriculum defended the group's motivation. "The only agenda I had was that I care about your children," said Chris Valley, a Beta High School teacher and AAC member. "I'm concerned that in 10 years we're going to be hearing about

Beta students dying of AIDS." In S. Patton, "Anti-AIDS Education Fighters Reach Out," *The Patriot Ledger*, 6/23/93, p. 1.

34. With regard to the explicitness of the AIDS curriculum content, parents objected to what they considered graphic language, including "body fluids" and references to needles. Elaine Kane, CPCB member and mother of five children, stated, "I am not against AIDS education, but I am against this curriculum. There are so many other programs out there that are not so explicit. This approach does not uphold morals and values and only promotes sex." In A. Reid, "Beta Schools Air AIDS Plan," *The Boston Globe*, 6/20/93, p. 1. Another Beta parent, Mary Williams, agreed: "I have thoroughly reviewed the proposed AIDS curriculum for the Beta Public Schools. It is my opinion that this curriculum is far too explicit to be presented to our children." In Ferro, "AIDS Curriculum under Fire," p. 22.

Mary Custer, a CPCB member and mother of five children in Beta schools, said the curriculum's discussion of safe sex practices incorrectly assumed that students are sexually active. In A. Reid, "Foes of Teaching on AIDS Test Clout," *The Boston Globe*, 6/27/93, p. 1. Some students agreed. One former Beta High School student, Sharon Whitmire, stated,

I am a virgin. I plan to stay that way until I marry. Throughout the years of junior high, high school and beyond I have experienced everything from holding hands at a school dance to being alone in a dorm/apartment. I know and understand the pressures of today's teens, for I am one. . . . I am here to sort of testify that when taught and expected to wait teens CAN and WILL wait. (*Source*: Copy of Sharon Whitmire testimony.)

Other parents were concerned about the age-appropriateness of the curriculum content. One Beta parent, William Conner, pleaded with the Committee: "My children still have boogey men in their closets and monsters under their beds. We don't need to introduce them to death and disease. We shouldn't throw fear into them." In S. Patton, "Debate on AIDS Heated," *The Patriot Ledger*, 6/15/93, p. 1. Another Beta parent, Brenda Burns, who has eight children, disagreed with the curriculum. Discussion of sexuality, intercourse, and the proper use of condoms, she said, "is not abstinence-based and is immoral for young kids. There should be a program on AIDS but this goes too far." In Reid, "Beta Schools Air AIDS Plan," p. 1. Tom Hampton, a CPCB member, also addressed the School Committee. He asked, "I want to know how giving kindergarten children who still believe in Santa and the tooth fairy this information will stop the spread of AIDS." In Ferro, "AIDS Curriculum under Fire," p. 22.

35. Still other parents opposed the proposed curriculum because they felt such education was to be done within the home and not the school. Brenda Burns commented, "Only parents have the right to teach their children about AIDS. Teachers should teach my children to read." In Reid, "Beta Schools Air AIDS Plan," p. 1. Another Beta parent said, "There is a very real danger of usurping parental rights here. The kids are relating to peers and teachers who don't appear to hold my moral values." Another parent expressed his sentiment: "Everytime you turn a page in the curriculum, there's an undermining of parental authority and values." In Ferro, "AIDS Curriculum under Fire," p. 22.

36. Patton, "Debate on AIDS Heated," p. 1.

37. Ferro, "AIDS Curriculum under Fire," p. 22.

38. Patton, "Beta Rejects Curriculum on AIDS," p. 16.

39. Casey Interview, 11/3/95.

40. Patton, "Anti-AIDS Education Fighters Reach Out," p. 1.

41. Aicardi, "AIDS Curriculum—Back to Ground Zero," pp. 1, 24.

42. At the Alpha School Committee's June 28 meeting, Dr. Kurtz proposed that the School Committee establish the following parameters around the development of an AIDS education program in Beta schools. The recommendations included:

• The parent is the primary teacher of the student. A parent information/training component relative to HIV/AIDS education would allow for coordinated efforts between home and school.

• The provision of medically sound information about AIDS, how it is acquired, and how it can be avoided.

• Sexual abstinence and non-intravenous drug use should be stressed as two sure ways to avoid contracting the virus.

• Referencing the transmission of HIV/AIDS virus through sexual contact should be limited to middle and high school levels. (*Source: Alpha School Committee Minutes*, 6/28/93, p. 1.)

The School Committee voted unanimously to support the superintendent's proposed recommendations.

43. Aicardi, "AIDS Curriculum—Back to Ground Zero," pp. 1, 24.

44. Reid, "Beta Schools Air AIDS Plan," p. 1.

45. Ibid.

46. Parker Interview, 8/12/94.

47. Patton, "Anti-AIDS Education Fighters Reach Out," p. 1.

48. B. Harrison, "Ignorance Leads to Chaos," *Beta Forum*, 6/30/93, p. 10.

49. Reid, "Foes of Teaching on AIDS Test Clout," p. 1.

50. Patton, "Beta Seeks Compromise on AIDS Curriculum," pp. 1,19.

51. *Alpha School Committee Minutes*, 6/21/93.

52. Kane Interview, 12/3/95.

53. *Alpha School Committee Minutes*, 1/24/93.

54. *Free-Teens* is an abstinence-based sexuality education curriculum. Abstinence-based education refers to sexuality education programs which emphasize the benefits of postponing sexual involvement and refraining from intercourse; such programs also include information about non-coital sexual behavior and contraception. *Alpha School Committee Minutes*, 1/24/93.

55. M. Goldberg, "Kurtz to Detail AIDS Curriculum Monday Night." *Beta Forum*, 1/21/94, p. 1.

56. M. Goldberg, "Parents Take Sides on AIDS Education," *Beta Forum*, 1/26/94, pp. 1, 14.

57. *Alpha School Committee Minutes*, 1/24/94, p. 2.

58. M. Goldberg, "New Lessons Proposed for Beta," *The Patriot Ledger*, 2/17/94, p. 9.

59. Ibid.

60. M. Goldberg, "Both Sides Willing to Try Superintendent's Proposal," *The Patriot Ledger*, 1/25/94, p. 6.

61. M. Goldberg, "Former Foes Accept Class Program," *The Patriot Ledger*, 2/1/94, p. 1.

62. Bowman Interview, 10/6/95.

63. Goldberg, "Former Foes Accept Class Program," p. 1.

64. M. Goldberg, "Parents to Ask for Condom Option," *The Patriot Ledger*, 2/7/94, p. 9.

65. This risk reduction curriculum stresses sexual abstinence while telling students who have sex to use condoms. Additionally, the curriculum teaches decision-making skills and has students discuss postponing sex and the risks involved with sexual activity. In Goldberg, "New Lessons Proposed for Beta," p. 9; and J. Seltz, "Lesson Plans," *The Patriot Ledger*, 2/19–20/94, p. 1

66. Goldberg, "New Lessons Proposed for Beta," p. 9.

67. Hampton Interview, 12/1/95.

68. M. Goldberg, "Beta to Drop AIDS Course," *The Patriot Ledger*, 2/19–20/94, pp. 1, 10. In a later interview Kurtz commented, "As we began to see that there wasn't the flexibility in the program it [*Free Teens*] wasn't appropriate for us." In Kurtz Interview, 7/23/96.

69. Ibid., pp. 1, 10.

70. *Alpha School Committee Minutes*, 2/28/94, p. 3.

71. Ibid., p. 6.

72. *Alpha School Committee Minutes*, 2/22/94, p. 4.

73. J. W. Ferro, "AIDS Course Put in Hands of Local Teachers," *Beta Forum*, 3/2/94, pp. 1, 20.

74. *Health Advisory Committee Minutes*, 4/13/94, p. 1.

75. *Health Advisory Committee Minutes*, 5/11/94.

76. J. C. Perez, "Schools Seek Parents' Views on Topics for Health Lessons," *The Patriot Ledger*, 10/13/94, p. 8C.

77. M. Goldberg, "Survey Will Seek Health Course Views," *The Patriot Ledger*, 6/16/94, p. 7C.

78. *Report of the Health Education Needs of the Beta Public Schools*, 2/95.

79. In a *Report of the Health Education Needs of the Beta Public Schools*, issued in February 1995, analysis of the survey data revealed that the majority of parents, professional staff, students, and community members surveyed supported some type of comprehensive health education for grades K–12.

• Among parents, there was strong support for a family life and sexuality education program in the school system, especially in the middle and high schools.

• Approximately 90% of parents favored some form of health education, including topics on sex education and HIV/AIDS education.

• 30% of parents felt AIDS instruction should begin in elementary schools, while 45% of parents felt such instruction should begin in middle schools.

• Among professional staff, there was strong support for instruction on: personal care (98%), food and nutrition (97%), alcohol, tobacco, and other dug use/abuse (94%), and self-esteem issues (90%), in middle and high schools.

• Approximately 80% of professional staff favored some form of health education including the topics of sex education (82%) and HIV/AIDS education (80%).

• 51% of professional staff said AIDS instruction should begin in middle schools compared to 29% in high school.

• Among students, there was strong support for alcohol education (90%), CPR training (90%), HIV/AIDS education (87%) in the school system, especially in the middle and high schools.

- Interestingly, 60% of students surveyed favored some type of family life and sexuality education program in the middle and high school.
- 57% of students said HIV/AIDS instruction should begin in middle schools.
- Among community leaders, there was strong support for healthy eating practices (100%), self-esteem issues (100%), pregnancy prevention (100%), and HIV/AIDS education (100%) in the school system, especially in the middle and high schools.
- 63% of community leaders surveyed felt AIDS instruction should begin in middle schools. (*Source*: *Report of the Health Education Needs of the Beta Public Schools*, 2/95.)

80. Ibid., 2/95.

81. Massachusetts Department of Education, Health Protection Grant, 1995–1996, p. 1.

82. *Report of the Health Education Needs of the Beta Public Schools*, 2/95, p. 10.

83. Ibid., p. 9.

84. Ibid., p. 10.

85. D. Falbo, "Survey Called Mandate for Sex Education," *Beta Forum* 3/8/95, pp. 1, 24. In a later interview Superintendent Kurtz stated, "The [results of the] survey was a clear message. There was a high rate of return and parents said, 'Yes!' we want health education and these are the areas we want addressed." He concluded, "Parents realized they've a role in educating their children." In Kurtz Interview, 7/23/96.

86. Anderson Interview, 12/1/95.

87. Alexander Interview, 6/15/95.

88. D. Falbo, "Sex Ed Sparks More Heated Debate," *Beta Forum*, 4/26/95, pp. 1, 12.

89. "Time to Move Forward," *Beta Forum*, 3/15/95, p. 11.

90. "What People Want," *Beta Forum*, 3/29/95, p. 11.

91. "Education Imperative," *Beta Forum*, 6/21/95, p. 11.

92. "Embarrassed, Too," *Beta Forum*, 5/3/95, p. 11.

93. Alexander Interviews, 6/15/95 and 7/23/96.

CHAPTER 6

Opposition to Health and Sexuality Education Programs

OPPOSITION

Along with community support for school-based comprehensive health education programs, there were individuals and community groups in Alpha and Beta opposed to such an idea. Their opposition was based upon fundamental differences about who has control over what is taught to children/ adolescents, the purpose of schools, and curriculum instruction and content. Some Alpha and Beta residents were moved to action by requesting to join the Task Force/AIDS Advisory Council with the hope of influencing the curriculum development process. Others demonstrated their opposition by exiting. They accomplished this by removing their children from the pilot program or from the public schools, or by remaining publicly silent on the subject. Still others expressed their dissatisfaction by voicing their opposition at public meetings and through the media.[1, 2] Some of these individuals went on to form community-based parent groups. In Alpha, parents formed Alpha Citizens for Public Education (ACPE) and in Beta, parents formalized their opposition through the creation of the Concerned Parents and Citizens of Beta (CPCB). In comparing the effectiveness of these two groups, the initial success of CPCB was related to both the group's internal characteristics and its ability to capitalize on the AAC's inability to create community support for its initiative. ACPE's lack of clear goals and objectives and its inability to create alliances with other community groups prevented it from developing broad-based community support for its initiative.

Adults disagreed about who should control what was taught to children and adolescents. In response to the Alpha School Committee vote to expand sexuality education within the schools, Alpha parent Edward Simon wrote in the *Alpha Graphic*, "We submit that the Alpha schools abrogate to themselves those facets of child development which are the exclusive right and responsibility of parents. . . . The Alpha schools are teaching immorality."[3] A Beta parent commented on the debate waging in her town: "Sexuality should be taught exclusively in the home by parents who love their children and are willing to impart their good sense and values in such an important an area of development. Children's sexual behavior and attitudes should never be taught in a public school setting." [4] CPCB members wrote a letter to the editor of the *Beta Forum* in which they stated, "We disapprove of social programs in our schools because of the lack of consensus regarding teaching philosophies and values. We believe this undermines the parents' role as primary teachers of the children and subordinates the academic purpose of schools."[5] Alice Dowling, an AAC member, provided her own account of the opposition's motivations. She said, "They [the parents] won't have control. You're taking away their parent power and they won't allow that."[6]

Opposition to school-based comprehensive health education programs was also related to the community members' beliefs about the proper academic role of the school. In another letter to the *Beta Forum* editor, CPCB members wrote: "We believe the purpose of schools is academics, not redefining or clarifying values, not introducing deviant sexual activity, not explaining how to take illegal drugs safely, and not providing social services."[7] Rob Kiley, an Alpha parent and ACPE member, expressed concern about the future direction of Alpha schools: "As a rule I support the schools. I'm just concerned they are getting themselves sidetracked. The schools are losing sight of what their primary goal is. They have to be very careful about what areas they go into and what impact it will have on the educational curriculum."[8]

Opposition to the program was also based upon curriculum instruction and content. CPCB members challenged the teaching philosophy behind the proposed comprehensive health education curriculum. In a letter to the editor of the *Beta Forum*, CPCB members wrote,

The ninth-grade health curriculum is based, as usual, on a non-directive decision-making teaching model. The evidence is overwhelming that the kids who are exposed to this so-called teaching technique indulge in harmful behavior more than kids who have no program at all. Parents take responsibility for educating your own children.[9]

A month later, they commented,

We do not believe that a "non-directive" teaching approach works because it lacks authoritative teaching. Drug (and sex) education should teach objective dangers;

there is something to be learned not explored. Teachers should authoritatively teach, not act as facilitators of students who share their feelings void of "right and wrong" answers. We do not support this decision-making teaching approach to health education.[10]

In reflecting back on the curriculum debate, one CARE member explained:

Their [CPCB] theory is how can you give these children a curriculum that has no right or wrong. [Their argument is that] we are giving them a curriculum and we're telling them "Here's a situation, what do you think you'd do?" Lots of people feel that these children are inexperienced and may not know what to do. I can understand what they're saying. You hope parents have addressed this at home.[11]

Another CARE member concluded, "I think it's [the issue] about critical thinking."[12]

Community members in both Alpha and Beta also challenged content aspects of the proposed health education curricula. Alpha parent and ACPE co-director Leslie Hale was concerned about how sexual abstinence would be taught. "Abstinence is presented not as a value, virtue or way of life, but as a means of contraception," Hale stated. As for condoms, she cited their failure rate: "When the rubber hits the road during sexual intercourse, that rubber breaks or slips one in six times. They don't tell young people about this danger. They're going to send students to their graves with their condoms on. May God forgive them."[13]

Commenting on the ninth-grade course guidelines at an Open Forum, Alpha parent and ACPE co-director Brian Carr said the guidelines include graphic descriptions of homosexual lovemaking and advocacy of safe sex as opposed to abstinence. He continued, "I'm concerned about the very controversial and sensitive subjects that are being brought into the primary grade level. This isn't geography or arithmetic or spelling."[14] Opponents in Beta had similar concerns. CPCB spokesperson Linda Whitmire commented in an interview: "Somewhere along the line we crossed over from a medical information issue into a moral values issue and that is the quicksand we have been stuck in too long."[15] Beta School Committee member Maureen Casey agreed: "This curriculum crossed the line of science and got into the line of morals and that's where I think that there was this volcanic explosion. Somewhere we crossed over the line."[16] In a later interview Whitmire added:

You just don't know what comes under health these days. When I think of health, I think of nutrition, cardiopulmonary resuscitation, first aid and exercise. But that is not what health means today. Today it can mean anything from traditional health to pregnancy counseling to suicide prevention, especially social services. Those are the issues I don't favor [in a health course].[17]

Those opposed to the proposed health education curriculum offered advice on future programs. One Beta community resident commented, "Schools should not teach our children anything unless they can teach them total abstinence. Anything other than that would not be healthy for our children in a time when sexually transmitted diseases and pregnancy are so rampant among our youth."[18]

DEMONSTRATING OPPOSITION

Individuals and community groups in both communities demonstrated their opposition in various ways. Some individuals requested to join the Task Force/AAC with the hopes of influencing the curriculum development process. Alpha residents Susan Simon and Rob Pike requested to join the Task Force. Simon, who held different views from the majority of the Task Force members, was interested in bringing "her voice" to the table. She commented, "I actually got invited on the Task Force because of cigarette money. They had to make sure the Task Force represented the community. And they really didn't have the conservative voice."[19]

In Beta, Elaine Kane and Mary McPherson volunteered to serve on the AAC. Other residents demonstrated their opposition by choosing to exit from the process. Some parents removed their children from the pilot program or from the public schools altogether. Alpha parent and ACPE spokesperson Mary Citron recalled, "My kids know [about sex]. My son said, 'Mom, can I opt out of sex ed?' I said, 'It's up to you.' And he said, 'I really don't want to take it Mom.' He knows what he needs to know."[20]

Alpha parent Marion McKinley, who removed her three children from Alpha schools, stated: "[I'm] appalled parents want this kind of information given to their children in their [parents'] absence. There's no way I'm going to buy into a system that's fostering that. . . . I'm paying tax dollars for a school system I cannot use."[21]

In Beta, two CPCB members removed their children from the Beta Public Schools. Kane stated, "My husband and I removed our children from the Beta Public Schools at great expense."[22]

Other Alpha residents remained publicly silent on the issue. One Alpha School Committee member stated, "The public forums were not the place . . . a climate that people felt comfortable expressing their reservations with the curriculum."[23] Another Alpha School Committee member recalled, "People stopped me in the street, in the supermarket saying they were very uncomfortable with the dichotomy, that they had some questions about what a health program should look like. But they were not comfortable speaking up."[24]

Sonya Schultz had her thoughts on why some residents remained silent. She commented, "There are people with legitimate concerns who have not expressed them because they fear being connected with that demagoguery. What they [the opposition] succeeded in doing was shutting off debate."[25]

Sylvia Healey, an original member of the Task Force's curriculum sub-committee, was more vehement. She stated, "Those who didn't support sex ed got drowned out. That's why it was important that Rob and Susan were on the Task Force. You don't have to be a crazed fanatic to have reservations about the sex ed curriculum."[26]

Other individuals and community groups verbalized their opposition at public forums and in the media. One of the first public opportunities for Alpha residents to voice their concerns over the health and sexuality curriculum was at the School Committee's Open Forum in January 1993. Of the twenty-two individuals who addressed the School Committee, eight individuals opposed to the development of the curriculum had the opportunity to present their opinions.[27] Linda Hale, an Alpha parent, was instrumental in organizing the opposition. She stated, "We did get twenty to thirty bodies to that meeting."[28] The events at this meeting were significant because many of those who opposed the plan later became the "core group" of Alpha Citizens for Public Education (ACPE). In its first few months, membership, according to Carr, had grown from "100 to 250 members."[29]

One of the first signs of parent discontent over Beta's HIV/AIDS curriculum was expressed to the school administration in the winter of 1993. Assistant Superintendent Moore shared these concerns at the AAC's March 1993 meeting. He mentioned that Beta parents had expressed to him concerns about closed AAC meetings and the expediency with which the AAC developed and wished to implement an HIV/AIDS curriculum. He went on to add, "We need to present ourselves as a Committee. I hope that we can have this curriculum implemented. This program has the potential of dividing the community and our work may not reach fruition."[30]

As Kane and McPherson reached out to adults in the Beta community, more parents wanted to voice their concerns to the AAC. "We met for two years and we didn't have any problems," said Alexander.[31] Approximately 50 parents came to the AAC's April meeting. Tensions ran high. Custer recalled: "When I walked into the room, there were girls there that I had been very close with. They asked, 'What are *you* doing here?' And that's when I got nervous. I responded, 'Don't I have a right to come into this room? I have kids in this school.' "[32]

Many of the parents in attendance told the AAC that in order for them to support the curriculum it must be "abstinence-based." One Beta parent commented, "A 100 percent way to avoid contracting AIDS is to refrain from having sex."[33] After the meeting, Elaine Kane, an AAC member who opposed the curriculum, was quoted in the paper as saying: "Parents are beginning to wake up. And there's a lot of concern that this is just the beginning. Gay and lesbian awareness could be next."[34]

Emergence of ACPE and CPCB

ACPE and CPCB members publicly expressed their opposition to the proposed health education curricula in their respective towns. Over time these groups would demonstrate their opposition by providing school administrators with alternative abstinence-based curricula, namely, the *Free Teens* program, question the selection and legitimacy of the Task Force/ Health Advisory Council, take on the school administration's "opt in/opt out" policies, conduct community forums, and ultimately run a slate of candidates in their respective School Committee elections.

Both ACPE and CPCB members provided school administrators with alternative, abstinence-based curricula, namely, the *Free Teens* program. ACPE co-founder Linda Hale met with Alpha school administrators Paul Redman and Natalie Dixon in mid-1992 to discuss the ninth-grade curriculum. Dixon recalled,

[Hale] wanted to show us [Redman and me] materials on AIDS prevention. At the time we met with her, we asked whether we could alter or use parts of the curriculum *[Free Teens]*. Because we were looking at what's out there, we were able to say, "Hey, if we can't change it and if we have to go to New York for training and couldn't come back and be trainers in our system, it doesn't work well."[35]

According to Hale,

I presented to them [Redman and Dixon] an abstinence-based program. It is not an abstinence-only program. It does devote 3–4 slides to condom use. It's a two hour slide show developed by a friend of mine Richard Peters. What they told me was that they liked parts of it, they didn't like other parts of it, and could they get permission to use parts they liked. Richard's policy on that is no. When you buy the curriculum you buy the philosophy. You can't take ten slides of it and plug it into [another] program. They wouldn't take the program.[36]

After the defeat of the AAC's proposed HIV/AIDS curriculum, CPCB members approached the Beta school administration. According to CPCB member Elaine Kane: "We wanted to offer an alternative [curriculum]."[37]

CPCB member Carolyn Banner added, "We gave them [Kurtz, Moore, Alexander] all these curricula. They looked at them. They're the ones that picked *Free Teens*."[38] Kane concluded, "We still think it's [*Free Teens*] a good curriculum. Whatever it's connection. From everything we saw it was excellent. It gave the facts and it let kids know the consequences of their actions."[39]

ACPE and CPCB members also questioned the selection and legitimacy of the Task Force/HAC. ACPE members expressed frustration because they felt they had been "shut out" of the Task Force. Specifically, Bob Carr,

ACPE co-director, was angry that members of his group were not asked to join.[40–42]

Hale's frustrations grew because she had been told that she would be kept informed about the Task Force's work. She added, "They never kept me informed."[43] A year later when three individuals were added to the Task Force it appeared [to Hale] that, "requests were not honored in the order received."[44] Apparently, she had not been informed that two of the newly appointed members had requested to serve the previous year and the other member, like other school personnel, did not have to submit a formal request.

In an *Alpha Graphic* article, "Group Set to Fight Sex Ed," Dixon responded to some of ACPE's accusations. She commented, "It doesn't make sense that they think the process is closed. We're taking the time to get a lot of input."[45] The Task Force worked for ten months collecting community input. However, for some who wanted to participate *on* the Task Force, it seemed that the process was closed. For example, Rob Pike shared his initial experience. He said,

I found out early on . . . they were looking for a Task Force. So I'm thinking, I'm a concerned parent. I wrote a letter to the Director. Nothing happened. Started to hear that the Task Force was formed. I said, "But wait a minute, I haven't heard anything. How come I didn't get on?" What was sent back was a condescending message that I was this parent and that people on the Task Force were educators and people highly involved in sex education. It was sad.[46]

With regard to membership on Beta's Health Advisory Council, Linda Whitmire shared the following story: "In one of the meetings we had with Dr. Kurtz, he was talking about the creation of the HAC and he said, 'I'd love to have you on that group Linda. I think you'd be beneficial.' So I said, 'I'd love to be on. Let me know how I can apply.' I never heard from him again."

She continued:

At a later School Committee meeting, I asked to join the HAC. They [the School Committee members] responded: "Well, you know . . . uhm." Finally Frannie Galvin, President of Beta High School's PTA said, "We're under a deadline because of the tobacco grant money." At that point the School Committee was embarrassed. Jean Anderson responded, "Well, this is an open committee. We've never refused anyone. We are still taking applications." I jumped on that the next day. Went right up to the Superintendent's Office with Carolyn [Banner] and Mary [Custer]. We sat at the next HAC meeting as part of the committee. After we made three or four votes someone on the committee asked, "These people haven't been approved by the School Committee. Are they eligible to vote on these issues?" They said, "Well, we better not do that. So they didn't take our votes anymore."[47]

Beta School Committee chairman Joseph Ponds shared his account:

We decided to form a [Health Advisory] Committee. There was a deadline. Every-one was invited. The deadline comes and goes and these people (CPCB) aren't involved. I remember the day vividly when I talked to Peter [Kurtz] and said, "What's the membership look like?" And we went down the list and I said, "Where's so and so?" He responded, "Haven't heard from them." "Well, what are you going to do?" I asked. His response, "Well, we offered it and that's it!" Then Linda [Whitmire] comes along. Someone says in the sake of fairness and so it doesn't get all mucked up again, "Let's put her on." In hindsight, I think we were reaching out too much.[48]

In an interview, School Committee member Maureen Casey provided her assessment of the situation:

And of course the question that any intelligent person would ask is, "Why didn't they join it before?" Some people did say, they didn't see it. Well, if they didn't see it, then they have to be deaf, dumb, and blind, because it was advertised in the *Forum*, it was advertised on cable, and in the parent newsletter. They would have had to had their head in the sand not to have been aware.[49]

On June 6, 1994, on the recommendation of Dr. Kurtz, the Beta School Committee voted 6–1 to close out membership on the HAC. This vote changed Kurtz's initial offer, shutting the door to Whitmire and seven oth-ers who wanted to join the HAC.[50] After the vote, Kurtz commented, "I know there were some expectations that more people could join the coun-cil," Kurtz said. "I apologize for that. There wasn't the expectation that this many people would come forward. . . . I am concerned that this many people would interrupt the continuity of the committee's work."[51] In a later interview, Kurtz recalled,

We were up into large numbers [on the HAC]. They [Whitmire and the seven others] were never appointed. I only told them I would recommend them. One person was one thing. Two, three, four was another. Now the Committee was larger than expected. I called them and told them I wasn't going to recommend them. I told them circumstances had changed. What started out as one or two people was now eight. I told them they could come to the [HAC] meetings. They were open to the public.[52]

Maureen Casey, the dissenting vote, said school officials who pledged to allow more members on the HAC felt the School Committee should let the eight community members join the Council before closing it to new mem-bers. CPCB member Elaine Kane believed the School Committee acted on ideology, not numbers. She said, "I'm very disappointed. You're turning [people] away because they don't get along with your thinking. This is a deliberate attempt to keep people off [the HAC]. You are discriminating."[53] Meanwhile, there were four or five people who never showed up to HAC meetings.[54]

ACPE and CPCB members had legitimate complaints with school administrators on the selection of Task Force and HAC memberships. Most individuals I interviewed thought the selection process was inclusive. In a letter to the community, Alpha school superintendent Ivan Brown reiterated the school administration's commitment to inclusion.[55, 56] Beta School Committee chairperson Jean Anderson discussed the open format of HAC meetings.[57]

Granted, Alpha's Task Force was in existence one year before any formalized opposition arose. However, public records suggested that the process was not inclusive. With regard to Task Force membership, Sonya Schultz asked the school administration on January 13, 1992 to consider including School Committee members, as well as individuals who addressed the Committee. Of the twenty-five individuals who spoke that evening, eight of the seventeen people (47%) supporting condom availability were asked to sit on the Task Force. None of the eight individuals who opposed the program was asked. Furthermore, in reviewing the 50 names of the initial Task Force, I could not identify one individual who was opposed to the development of the curriculum. In a review of subcommittees' membership issued three months later, all 32 members supported a comprehensive health education curriculum. It was not until a year later that three more individuals, two with dissenting views, were added to the curriculum subcommittee. In comparison, three of the nineteen (16%) members of Beta's AAC were opposed to submitting the HIV/AIDS curriculum to the Beta School Committee.

While individuals such as Rev. Matthew Barker would argue that "when you are charged with a task, you don't automatically reach out to the opposition,"[58] I examined other people's responses to see what I could learn. There were a variety of explanations. One may have been the result of a simple oversight or carelessness. *Tab* reporter Rhonda Lear said, "The Task Force was developed from an established parent network. It didn't occur [to the planners] that not everyone would be included."[59] CPCB member Carolyn Banner commented on the composition of the AAC, "It was very incestuous. The same people sit on all the committees in this town."[60] Another reason may have been that members who were not representatives of the school system had to submit a written request. Assistant Superintendent Redman mentioned that "members of the Task Force had to submit a request in writing."[61] There was also the possibility that there was a deliberate attempt to exclude individuals from the Task Force. This is evident in Riley's comments, "We wanted people who were going to participate in the process, not obstruct the process. And so, there were people, I know, who were turned down."[62]

Simon reiterated this point. She stated, "One reason I think they didn't invite people like Bob [Carr]. . . . They didn't have anything to discuss. Where I don't think I was saying that."[63] There may be a variety of explanations for this oversight; however, it was also obvious, in talking with Hale, that she "never got a clear story as to why she was turned down."[64] Interestingly, as the Beta school administration formed the HAC, CARE member and Beta parent Valerie Devine recalled, "They put out this blanket invitation to anyone who wanted to join this committee. But they were also saying in the background, 'Jane [Alexander] could you call this person. See if she wants to be on the committee.' He [Kurtz] told us he wanted to get both sides together."[65]

With such a sensitive issue before the community it seems as though planners in both Alpha and Beta would have been more attentive to selection process procedures. As planners became more aware of the diversity of views held by community members, they seemed to realize their mistake. Redman commented, "When the group finally came together, when you looked at the spectrum of opinions and views it did not include as much on the conservative end. I think the issue of providing the balance should have been more apparent to us initially."[66]

Strategies Employed by ACPE and CPCB

In Alpha and Beta, ACPE and CPCB questioned the legitimacy of their respective community advisory councils. Alpha citizens filed a complaint with the Middlesex County District Attorney's Office alleging that the Task Force violated Massachusetts' Open Meeting Laws. CPCB members filed similar complaints in 1993 and 1994 with the Norfolk County District Attorney's Office. CPCB co-founder and member Carolyn Banner discussed the motivation behind the initial action: "We did file and try to overturn what the [AIDS Advisory] Committee was doing. It wasn't an open process. In a last ditch effort, we tried to halt them until more people could get involved."[67-69] In 1994, two weeks after the HAC voted to accept the results of a survey on health education and to recommend that the School Committee establish a comprehensive K–12 health education curriculum, a group of eight Beta citizens filed a second complaint.[70, 71] Within one week, Assistant District Attorney John Carlson responded. Jane Alexander concluded, "[After] we got the letter from the DA everything was fine and dandy. [The letter read] we may, in the interest of courtesy, want to think better about quorums. We had to go down to the Town Hall and swear in, which we all did. At meetings I took the notes and we were back in business."[72]

ACPE and CPCB members also opposed their respective school administration's "opt in/opt out" policies concerning the comprehensive health education curricula. After the Alpha School Committee adopted the Task

Force's recommendations, Superintendent Brown stated, "Parents have the option to have their child opt out." Carr took issue with school officials. Because the program was designed to be integrated into other curricula it would be impossible for parents to exempt their children from it.[73, 74] Sandra Riley, a School Committee member, rejected these criticisms by saying the sexuality education curriculum would be distinct from the regular curriculum.[75] However, Alpha resident Sherman Parker addressed this point in a letter to Riley. He wrote, "I have seen the grant application for this program. It specifically states that the program is to be 'integrated' and 'mandatory.' "[76]

Later in the fall, Carr discussed the option of developing an "opt in" policy.[77] Despite ACPE's criticisms the "opt out" policy remained.

In Beta, a group of parents questioned the "opt out" policy of the original HIV/AIDS curriculum in June 1993. This issue surfaced again in the spring of 1994 when the Beta school administration discussed the implementation of the ninth-grade health education curriculum for the following academic year.

In his comments at a Beta School Committee meeting, Dr. Kurtz stated, "The health course will be mandatory for ninth graders and carries two credits but passing the course is not a requirement for graduation."[78] Later in the meeting, in responding to a question from Linda Whitmire, Kurtz told parents that they could remove their child from any portion of the health education class without penalty. Two weeks later, CPCB wrote in the *Beta Forum*:

We find the status of this course precarious. According to Dr. Kurtz, it [the ninth grade curriculum] is mandatory, yet students can opt out and it is not required for graduation "in 1995." In keeping with Dr. Kurtz's primary objective of parents as the primary educators, we question why parents are not given the respect to determine the need of their own children for such a course on an elective basis. Since you will be voting on this curriculum, we ask that you consider these points.[79]

Another community resident asked in the "Sound-Off" section of the *Beta Forum*:

The Committee has said that this course is mandatory but not required. Does anyone know what "mandatory but not required" means? Perhaps the committee would consider writing a little handbook to help all of us uneducated parents understand more clearly what it means when it says something.[80]

Whitmire was even more cynical. She commented, "Even though they give you this supposed option of opting out, it's a joke. You know they really pressure you into taking it. The ones that don't go are oddballs."[81] Reverend James Russo, pastor at St. Timothy's Catholic Church, offered another view: "Offering a [health education] program is not optional. Something needs to be offered. Whether you accept or reject it that's a freedom that needs to be respected. Nobody is being forced. Parental consent needs to be given."[82]

ACPE and CPCB members generated community awareness for and against their cause by conducting community forums. ACPE hosted, "What's Wrong with Sex Education Anyway?" in March 1993. The event was billed as a "Symposium [that] will address issues related to both the ideology and the ethics of sex education."[83] Speakers such as anti-pornography activist Judith Rice discussed how material being used for sex education and AIDS prevention is based on fraudulent information about sexual development, homosexuality, and AIDS. She said, "Homosexual sex is "anal sodomy that rips . . . tears apart. This isn't pleasant lovemaking below the belt. Only they're [the students] being told this is love. We should weep for our children because who would teach our children that is love?"[84]

Immediately after the forum, however, Carr apologized for "some of the tactics" panelists used to denounce school plans to teach students about condom use, homosexual behavior, sex, and AIDS. "We didn't want to put people down," said Carr. "I feel bad and want to apologize to those who may have been offended."[85]

CPCB hosted two Information Nights in June 1993. "These meetings," according to Mary McPherson, "were held in June a week before the School Committee vote. It was purposively done that way."[86] Kane added, "We put together the two information nights [on this issue] for parents because there was only one copy of the curriculum in each school for every parent to look at. We were sure that once they saw what the School Department wanted to implement they would not like it. As our civic duty and as parents, we decided to inform the people that couldn't be at those meetings."[87] Elaine Kane opened the first of the two Information Nights with the comments:

We're not opposed to AIDS education. We're only opposed to this particular curriculum. As parents we encourage compassion in our children to all people affected with any disease. We do not feel the need to focus on the suffering of any one disease or the any other afflictions that children will encounter in their lives.[88]

According to McPherson, the purpose of these meetings was threefold: (1) to make people aware of what was in the HIV/AIDS curriculum, (2) to make people aware that we were targeted by Planned Parenthood and SIE-CUS, and (3) to make people aware that the AIDS curriculum was basically a gay curriculum.[89] More than 150 Beta residents listened to a critique of the AIDS curriculum and its accompanying resources. In addition, attendees had the opportunity to view "The Gay Agenda" and "Sex Respect."[90, 91]

Whitmire summed up the evening: "People were aghast when they came and found out what was in the curriculum." She went on to tell the following story:

I passed out a short version of my critique. I got up there and talked about oral sex. This was verbatim from the curriculum. . . . When I came to some of the graphic stuff, one of the elderly women in the front row said, "Oh, don't say that out loud. It's very vulgar!" I responded, "I'm going to say it out loud because this is what's going to be taught to your children in school. If you can't hear this here, why would this be a good thing to put in school?" I think that was very effective.[92]

CPCB members felt that these Information Nights enlightened community members and "got people to attend the School Committee's public hearings."[93, 94]

ACPE and CPCB members also became involved in their respective School Committee elections by running or endorsing a slate of candidates. Early on, ACPE considered running candidates for School Committee.[95] By late summer, they outlined their platform which called for spending less time on "social programs" and more time on academics. Carr stated, "There is a trend by the administration and faculty to divert ever larger portions of the school day to social engineering experiments. These range from mandatory homosexuality sensitivity assemblies to 'multicultural' classes."[96]

Alex Libow, executive secretary of the Alpha Election Commission, recalled, "There hasn't been this much interest in the School Committee in over twenty years."[97] ACPE endorsed several candidates, all of whom were unsuccessful in their bids for a School Committee seat.

In the 1994 and 1995 School Committee elections, CPCB developed and mailed out a newsletter to Beta residents—*The Grassroots Forum*—endorsing particular candidates for the School Committee elections. In the 1994 edition, CPCB endorsed the candidacies of Maureen Casey, John Custer, and Lorraine Donovan.[98] Additionally, the newsletter discussed the limitations of other School Committee candidates.

Opponents to Beta's school-based health curriculum also formed a political action committee (PAC). In March 1994, Tom Hampton, a local activist who believed schools should teach teenagers that sexual abstinence is the only way to stop the spread of AIDS, formed the town's first political action committee called RAVE (Restore American Values in Education). This committee raised money to support School Committee candidates who shared Hampton's views. "It's reaching the point where we're close to moral bankruptcy in this country," he said. "I want to reverse this trend, and a good place to start is the local level at the grass roots. I'm concerned that the kids get the proper values." Hampton said he got the idea of starting RAVE after reading about a Randolph man who formed his own

PAC for local elections.[99] Three days before the election, RAVE ran paid ads in the *Beta Forum* and *The Patriot Ledger* that urged Beta voters to know where the candidates stood on various issues including health/AIDS education.[100] ACPE became a PAC shortly before the 1993 School Committee elections.

Other activities conducted by those opposed to a comprehensive health education curriculum included the use of the television and newsprint media[101] to raise community awareness for their position. The CPCB also conducted a series of community outreach activities.[102, 103] Each of these activities was meant to raise community awareness and opposition to the proposed health education plans.

COMPARING THE EFFECTIVENESS OF ACPE AND CPCB

In comparing the effectiveness of ACPE and CPCB, the initial success of CPCB was related to both the group's internal characteristics and its ability to capitalize on the AAC's inability to create community support for its initiative. Having the opportunity to interview five CPCB members, I learned that the internal characteristics of CPCB were part of the reason why they were initially successful in defeating the AAC's proposed HIV/AIDS education curriculum. Formalized community opposition to the AIDS curriculum was seen in the formation of the Concerned Parents and Citizens of Beta (CPCB) in May 1993. Members of this group described themselves as predominantly middle class and conservative and viewed their mission as preservation of family values in Beta.[104] "Elaine [Kane] and Mary [McPherson]," said CPCB member Tom Hampton, "were both on the AAC. They were opposed to the AIDS curriculum plan. They got the ball rolling and brought people together."[105] Kane added, "We were just a bunch of parents who felt a certain way. We decided to get together and talk about what we were going to do. We knew we had to inform parents of what was exactly in that curriculum."[106] Linda Whitmire, who became the CPCB's spokesperson, added, "We wanted to show the School Committee that we didn't want this [AIDS] curriculum."[107] Health and Human Development specialist Jane Alexander added,

They met in kitchens in Beta. If the town was as committed to health education as these people were committed to their cause, we could wipe it [AIDS] out. They were organized and committed. I mean they were very, very formidable. They were successful. They did delay action a long, long time.[108]

The common bond among members of the CPCB was their genuine concern for the physical, academic, and moral health of their children. Their goal, as stated in *The Patriot Ledger*, read: "It is our belief that sexual promiscuity and drug abuse are inherently dangerous to our children.

Therefore, our goal is to educate our children to what is best for them, not to accommodate behavior that we know is dangerous."[109] To accomplish their goal, CPCB members sought to influence the content of the AAC's proposed HIV/AIDS education curriculum. While the group agreed there should be some education about the spread of AIDS in a school-based curriculum, they also believed there should be an absolute emphasis on sexual abstinence instead of condom usage and explicit discussions of risky sexual behavior.[110] Kane, who emerged as the CPCB's leader, commented, "Somebody or some group has to speak out for upholding morals and values, and we want to be heard."[111]

In comparison, the internal characteristics of ACPE were part of the reason why they were not successful. Mary Citron, ACPE spokesperson, confirmed this point: "But we were just flailing around and we didn't have directions, money, organization. We were just sort of reacting all the time."[112] It was evident that ACPE did not have clear goals and objectives. In response to a question about what he hoped his group would accomplish, ACPE co-founder Carr replied, "Well, we didn't really know."[113] The lack of clear goals prevented the group from developing a plan which would have formalized the relationships among group members. As a result, individual actions drove the group. Hale stated, "Bob immediately took it upon himself to be the media spokesperson. . . . This was the beginning of my frustration with Bob, because in my opinion he made ACPE a one-man show."[114] Carr's belief that he was in charge is also exemplified in his recollection of ACPE's forum: "*I* let Linda run the Q&A session to start with and then *I* took it over."[115] ACPE members maintained individual goals. They did not develop common goals. Hale discussed futile attempts to address this issue:

When I brought up the issue with ACPE members, that I felt we needed to have by-laws . . . to have protocol, as a group, concerning the delegation of responsibility to different people, formation of committees, and agreement about decision-making, it just became, it just became. . . .[116]

The impact of ACPE's inability to develop common goals was evident in an observation made by Mark Sawyer, Committee '93 spokesperson. He wrote, "While we hear what ACPE is against, it is not clear what it is for. If they could demonstrate that there is clear thinking behind what they are for, they'd gain more adherents and more respect."[117] The fact that ACPE did not develop common goals—a charter—may have been the result of Carr's lack of experience with group development. Hale recalled,

I don't think Bob has had any consciousness about how to organize a group. And when I said to Bob, "You need to make these decisions about what is the ACPE platform, what do we agree on and not agree on, what do we want to say to the media, this needs to be decided according to protocol with a group of people." He said that takes too much time.[118]

ACPE members continued to operate independently. As such, they were unable to build upon each other's strengths—combining Hale's grassroots community organization skills and Carr's media proficiency.

To achieve their goal of influencing the content of AIDS education in Beta, CPCB members raised some procedural concerns regarding the creation of the AIDS Advisory Council and development of the initial HIV/AIDS curriculum. While initial group membership did not exceed more than a handful of Beta residents, CPCB members were also successful in garnering support for their position by hosting a series of community outreach activities that raised community awareness about the proposed HIV/AIDS education plan. These activities helped to build alliances with individuals and groups within the community. This is reflected in Elaine Kane's statement: "Word got out more and more of what we were dealing with in the community. We did have parents start coming to the [AAC] meetings."[119] These community outreach activities created important alliances within the Beta community. Meanwhile, the AAC was not conducting this type of community outreach.

Opponents of the AAC's proposed HIV/AIDS education curriculum also created alliances with individuals outside the community. One resident alluded to the training and support CPCB members received: "From my understanding there were very high profile people here from Washington who came up here and trained people from CPCB."[120] When I asked CPCB members about these trainings, Carolyn Banner responded, "Everyone thinks we had a map for this. According to a plan."[121] CPCB member Mary Custer added, "It was really a comedy of errors. We were operating on a wing and a prayer."[122] Elaine Kane confirmed these sentiments in her interview. She commented, "We missed the boat on quite a few things just from being inexperienced. Really, truly just being parents and trying to muddle through, we did really well."[123]

However, early on, members of Concerned Parents and Citizens of Beta (CPCB) did seek advice and information from outside experts. Elaine Kane recalled,

I picked up the [Boston] *Herald* one day before I really got into this. Before I knew anybody or had any support. I felt totally alone. Then I saw in the paper this man [Bob Carr] in Alpha opposing this sex ed program. So, I called information and got his phone number. I called him on the phone and told him I was on the AAC. And he gave me information on what it was going to be like.[124]

According to Beta activist Tom Hampton, at a later point, Carr "came down and filled us in on what happened in Alpha."[125] With regard to internal organization, one of the first things the group was advised on was to designate a spokesperson. CPCB spokesperson Linda Whitmire stated, "We were just a bunch of people at first. There were a lot of different people saying different things for the group [CPCB]. We felt we had to be cautious about who was speaking to the press. One of the things we were advised on by someone from *The Pilot* was having one spokesperson."[126] CPCB member Tom Hampton added, "We decided that Linda [Whitmire] would be the spokesperson because she was well spoken and she expressed her thoughts well."[127]

ACPE did not develop external relationships with groups within the community that could have provided them with both guidance and a greater level of credibility. Hale stated, "I feel, looking back, that it would have been better for Bob and me if we amassed a greater understanding of how the system operated. . . . We could have locked arms with parents across the community who were experiencing similar frustrations."[128] Without having the prestige that other individuals and groups held in Alpha and without creating alliances with community members who could lend their approval to their cause, members of ACPE operated more like a protest group than a group interested in changing the norms and practices of the community.

By contrast, members of Alpha Citizens for Public Education (ACPE) did ally themselves with outside experts. Hale tried to get the school administration to adopt an abstinence-based curriculum developed by Richard Peters, who was a member of her church, the Unification Church. Hale and Carr used WAZE through their connection with Jeannine Greer to promote upcoming ACPE events. It was through this contact that Carr became acquainted with others who were involved in similar work. In July 1993, Carr attended meetings hosted by Pilgrim Family Institute in Lexington, Massachusetts. Participants discussed "grassroots organizing" strategies. When asked to comment, Carr replied, "The only thing the Pilgrim Family Institute has done is provide an opportunity to bring all these disparate groups together."[129] The Pilgrim Family Institute has since relocated to Alpha and has changed its name to the Massachusetts Family Institute (MFI). MFI is one of many groups that comprise the Interfaith Coalition, a greater Boston conservative ecumenical group founded by Carr in 1994. Their current effort has been to work with Massachusetts legislators in sponsoring Bill H1817 which would require parental approval before "morally or religiously sensitive" subjects—including homosexuality—could be discussed in public school classrooms. In June 1993, Hale organized a conference in Bridgeport, Connecticut with Mildred James, a faculty member at Boston University's School of Medicine and a board member of the World Medical Health Foundation.[130] This conference was specifically directed to school committees, town and city officials, and parents in the New England region who were interested in outreach.[131]

CPCB members were initially successful in *maintaining* the norms and practices of the Beta community because they operated as a group with a common goal and mission. Additionally, they were able to build upon each member's strengths to educate the larger Beta community about their position and their opposition to the proposed HIV/AIDS education curriculum when the AAC remained relatively silent. Jane Alexander commented, "They literally disabled all of our credibility. They made sure to let everybody know who didn't know anything about health, which were a lot of people in Beta [their side]."[132] By creating alliances with community members who could lend their approval to their cause, CPCB members initially attained a level of prestige that allowed them to successfully vocalize their opposition to the proposed AIDS curriculum and then have the opportunity to recommend an alternative health education to Beta's superintendent.

It was not until after the emergence of Community Advocates for Responsible Education (CARE) and the defeat of the *Free Teens* curriculum that CPCB members began to act more like a protest group by objecting to the selection of the HAC's membership and challenging the legitimacy of this group by requesting a review of its meeting practices through Massachusetts' Open Meeting Law. Such actions which appeared to delay the development of a school-based comprehensive K–12 health education program began to be met with disfavor in the community. This was reflected in the sentiments of Beta residents who called in to the Sound-Off section of the *Beta Forum*. One citizen commented, "I'm tired of hearing about the Concerned Parents group. I feel they do not represent every concerned parent in Beta, nor does every concerned parent share their views."[133]

Another resident called in to say:

The Concerned Parents and Citizens of Beta appear to be happy that an AIDS education curriculum had been stalled again, and it seems that this year's agenda will be to try to delay it even further. It's about time, given the results of the town survey, for schools to develop such a curriculum and get on with it.[134]

MEDIATION

While there was much activity in the public arena, the discussion and development of Alpha's *Health and Sexuality* curriculum occurred in more private settings. This environment, unlike the public arena, was a place where individuals could engage in dialogue. Even though people held divergent views, the commonality that bound them together in this effort was their mutual concern for the students. Dixon remembered: "The curriculum that is in place is a result of an enormous amount of group work. And when we came to places where we agreed to change this and do that, it was joyful on a profound level. The commonality was the concern for students."[135]

The interactions among subcommittee members, between the dominant voices who supported the ninth-grade curriculum and the subdominant voices who had some reservations, again, demonstrated the outcome of a complementary relation between dominant and subdominant groups in society. The subcommittee successfully achieved its goal of creating a curriculum that incorporated the best thinking from all of its members.

NOTES

1. In A. O. Hirschmann's *Exit, Voice and Loyalty, Responses to Decline in Firms, Organizations and States*, the author discusses three ways in which management can determine the performance of its respective firm or organization. The first measure is seen when customers stop buying the firm's products or employees leave the organization. This is known as the exit option. The second measure, identified as the voice option, is when the firm's customers or the organization's members express their dissatisfaction to the management. The third measure, known as loyalty, is defined by the consumer's and/or employee's special attachment to the organization. In A. O. Hirschmann, *Exit, Voice and Loyalty, Responses to Decline in Firms, Organizations and States* (Cambridge, MA: Harvard University Press, 1970), pp. 4–80.

2. In *The Governing of Men*, Alexander Leighton discusses three universal kinds of behavior with which individuals react to authority when subject to forces of stress. These behaviors included cooperation, withdrawal and aggression. In A. Leighton, *The Governing of Men* (Princeton, NJ: Princeton University Press, 1945), pp. 263–274.

3. E. A. Simon, "Alpha Schools Would Be Spreading Gospel of Immorality," *Alpha Graphic*, 1/27/93, p. 13.

4. "Teach About Sex in the Home," *Beta Forum*, 6/1/94, p. 11.

5. Concerned Parents/Citizens of Beta (letter), *Beta Forum*, 3/30/94, p. 10.

6. Dowling Interview, 12/3/95.

7. Concerned Parents/Citizens of Beta (letter), "Concerned Parents Setting Record Straight," *Beta Forum*, 5/11/94, p. 10.

8. Kiley Interview, 8/28/93.

9. Concerned Parents/Citizens of Beta (letter), "Concerned Parents Setting Record Straight," p. 10.

10. Concerned Parents/Citizens of Beta (letter), "Finding Status of Health Course Precarious," *Beta Forum*, 6/15/94, p. 10.

11. Bartow Interview, 10/27/95.

12. O'Neff, Carol Interview, 10/27/95.

13. B. English, "Facts of Life Can't Be Hidden," *The Boston Globe*, 2/10/93, p. 21.

14. J. Sullivan, "Foes Get Early Start against Alpha Sex Education," *The Boston Globe*, 1/17/93, p. 30.

15. J. W. Ferro, "AIDS Course Put in Hands of Local Teachers," *Beta Forum*, 3/2/94, pp. 1, 20.

16. Other comments included: "I think this goes beyond the issue of morality. It's a known fact how you can get AIDS, but if we're going to sweep this under

the rug [by not telling adolescents] this is crazy. This is the real problem. I think a lot of people don't want to admit to the fact that 54% of kids between the ages of 14 and 19 are having sex. I just hope that something is done and we get some kind of curriculum that's not watered down or wishy-washy. Hopefully, we'll at least prevent some teenagers from contracting AIDS." In Riding Interview, 12/11/95; and Casey Interview, 11/3/95.

17. M. Goldberg, "School Committee Makes Proposed Health Texts Available," *The Patriot Ledger*, 5/24/94, p. 6C.

18. "Teach Abstinence," *Beta Forum*, 6/15/94, p. 11.

19. Jean Fish, a co-chair of the Task Force's curriculum subcommittee, informed the School Committee that in order for Alpha to meet the guidelines for $300,000 in possible state funding, the Task Force would have to be renamed and its composition slightly revised. This funding was made available when Massachusetts voters passed a referendum in November 1992 creating the Tobacco Control and Comprehensive Health Education programs. In *Alpha School Committee Minutes*, 5/10/93; and Simon Interview, 8/24/94.

20. Citron Interview, 9/16/94.

21. L. Pappano, "Alpha Sex-Ed Exodus Begins: A Few Angry Parents Will Send Their Children to Private Schools," *The Boston Globe*, 7/18/93, p. 1.

22. Kane Interview, 12/3/95.

23. Eisen Interview, 8/24/94.

24. Levy Interview, 8/26/94.

25. Schultz Interview, 12/3/94.

26. Healey Interview, 8/19/94.

27. *Alpha School Committee Minutes*, 1/11/93, pp. 2–23.

28. Hale Interview, 8/24/94.

29. R. Lear, "Politics of Sex Education: National Right-Wing Ties Alleged as Fight Enters Voting Booth," *Tab*, 6/29/93, p. 10.

30. *AIDS Advisory Committee Minutes*, 3/3/93

31. Alexander Interview, 6/15/95.

32. Custer Interview, 12/5/95.

33. *AIDS Advisory Committee Minutes*, 5/24/94.

34. On May 24, the AAC presented its report and curriculum to the Beta School Committee. The report included the following recommendations:

- The Council does not recommend that condoms be distributed to students in the Beta school system.

- The Council recommends that parental permission be given for student participation in the HIV/AIDS curriculum at grades K–8 and that such permission at the high school level be given for each separate session.

- The Council recommends that a parent handbook on HIV/AIDS be prepared and distributed including a description of the approved curriculum by grade level.

- The Council recommends that evening HIV/AIDS programs be conducted separately for parents of elementary, middle, and high school children.

- The Council recommends that the entire Council continue to review the approved curriculum in light of new print and nonprint resources.

The Beta School Committee voted to accept the report, not endorse the recommendations. The report and the proposed HIV/AIDS curriculum would be discussed at a public forum of the School Committee meeting on June 14 with a second meeting, if necessary scheduled on June 21.

Some of the 50 people at this meeting opposed the curriculum plan. Public discussion on the sensitive subject, they said, should be postponed until further information is available. Carolyn Banner, a Beta parent, said, "I'm opposed to the June 14 date. We need a lot more time." Other parents in the community voiced their opinions. One said, "I will not sit back and blindly trust our educators. It seems to me that they have to prove the validity of the program they propose and ensure that it's not a social experiment to our children." In S. Patton, "Parents against Lessons on AIDS Plan 2 Meetings," *The Patriot Ledger*, 6/4/93, p. 11.

35. Dixon Interview, 10/7/94.

36. Hale Interview, 8/24/94.

37. Kane Interview, 12/3/95.

38. Banner Interview, 12/3/95.

39. Kane Interview, 12/3/95.

40. B. Carr (letter), *The Boston Globe*, 10/31/93, p. 5.

41. M. Houston and R. Lear, "Officials Fear Religious Right Targeting Schools," *Tab*, 3/23/93, p. 8.

42. Hale Interview, 8/24/94.

43. Ibid.

44. Ibid.

45. S. Lyons, "Group Set to Fight Sex Ed,"*Alpha Graphic*, 3/25/93, p. 20.

46. Pike Interview, 11/9/94.

47. Whitmire Interview, 12/8/95.

48. Ponds Interview, 1/15/96.

49. Casey Interview, 11/3/95.

50. M. Goldberg, "Board Retains Size of Health Council," *The Patriot Ledger*, 6/7/94, p. 1.

51. *Alpha School Committee Minutes*, 6/6/94.

52. Kurtz Interview, 7/23/96.

53. Goldberg, "Board Retains Size of Health Council," p. 1

54. Whitmire Interview, 12/8/95.

55. Part of Brown's letter read,

The parents and staff members of the Task Force and the School Committee will continue to make every effort to assure that interested members of the community are fully informed about curriculum plans and have opportunities to comment. Parent meetings will be held in the coming weeks as part of the planning process for the ninth grade curriculum. Information concerning these and other meetings will come through the local schools. It is our expectation that the development of the K–12 health education curriculum will be done in a thoughtful and reasonable way and will consider the views of Alpha parents. In addition, should citizens of Alpha want to provide input in this process, they can do so in one of two ways by writing (1) the Task Force or (2) the School Committee. (*Source*: Brown Letter, 2/2/93.)

56. I. Brown, Viewpoint: "Input Needed on Health Curriculum for Schools," *Tab*, 2/16/93, p. 16.

57. Goldberg, "Board Retains Size of Health Council," p. 1.

58. Barker Interview, 1/12/95.

59. Lear Interview, 9/19/94.

60. Banner Interview, 12/5/95.

61. R. Lear, "PAC Groups Enter Political Arena," *Tab*, 8/31/93, p. 1.

62. Riley Interview, 9/7/93.

63. Simon Interview, 8/24/93.

64. Hale Interview, 8/24/93.

65. Devine Interview, 10/27/95.

66. Redman Interview, 10/7/94.

67. Banner Interview, 12/5/95.

68. S. Patton, "Beta Proposes Early Start on AIDS Ed," *The Patriot Ledger*, 5/27/93, p. 1.

69. Patton, "Parents against Lessons on AIDS Plan 2 Meetings," p. 11.

70. This complaint signed by CPCB members sought to invalidate the HAC's March 6 vote. In the letter they write:

We, the undersigned taxpayers of Beta, allege that the Health Advisory Council (HAC), a governmental body appointed by the Beta Public School Committee, has violated several provisions of the Open Meeting Law. The meetings were defective in terms of quorums present; the process of deliberating and voting was flawed; and the committee failed to carry out the provisions for maintaining public records. We believe the HAC to be a "governmental body" and is therefore, subject to the provisions of the Open Meeting Law. (*Source*: CPCB letter, 3/20/95.)

Due to the complaint, the School Committee avoided direct consideration of the HAC's recommendations. However, they voted 6–1 to accept the results of the health survey. School Committee member Maureen Casey, who cast the dissenting vote, commented: "I think it was inappropriate for the committee to move forward while there is a cloud over the Council's vote." In D. Falbo, "Complaint Is Filed against Health Council," *Beta Forum*, 3/29/95, p. 22.

71. With regard to the HAC's Open Meetings, school Superintendent Dr. Kurtz sought legal counsel from the town and the district attorney. In a letter dated March 27, 1995, Beta Town Counsel Andrew Shea wrote:

Your questions are directed to membership of the Council, whether it is a "governmental body" under the Open Meeting Law, what constitutes a "quorum," and what are the consequences of votes taken by the Council in the absence of a quorum.

OPINION

• The Advisory Council established under Ch. 71, Sect. 31 is a "governmental body" within the meaning of the Open Meeting Law.

• As such, all meetings must be duly posted and open to the public unless executive session is permitted in accordance with the statutory requirements.

• A quorum is defined by Sect. 23A of Ch. 39 as being a "simple majority of a governmental body unless otherwise defined by constitution, charter, rule or law applicable to such governing body."

• The number required to constitute a quorum is based on the official membership itself, regardless of the existence of actual vacancies. In my opinion, therefore, a quorum of the Council consists of 19 members being present at a duly called meeting.

• If a quorum is present, and in the absence of other by-laws, actions will be by vote of a majority of the members present at the meeting and voting. (*Source*: Shea Letter, 3/27/95.)

72. Alexander Interview, 6/15/95.

73. R. Lear, "Sex Education Counterview," *Tab*, 3/30/93, p. 13.

74. Lyons, "Group Set to Fight Sex Ed," p. 20.

75. M. Houston and R. Lear, "Struggle over Sex Education: Officials Fear Religious Right Targeting Schools," *Tab*, 3/31/93, p. 8.

76. S. Parker (letter), "Rizzo Is Wrong," *Alpha Graphic*, 4/22/93, p. 17.

77. B. Carr (letter), *The Boston Globe*, 10/31/93, p. 5.

78. Goldberg, "School Committee Makes Proposed Health Texts Available," p. 1.

79. Concerned Parents/Citizens of Beta (letter), "Finding Status of Health Course Precarious," *Beta Forum*, 6/15/94, p. 10.

80. "Let's Get This Straight," *Beta Forum*, 6/29/94, p. 11.

81. Whitmire Interview, 12/8/95.

82. Russo Interview, 1/5/96.

83. ACPE Invitation Letter, 3/16/93.

84. R. Lear, "Fever Pitch at Forum," *Tab*, 4/6/93, p. 1.

85. Ibid.

86. McPherson Interview, 1/8/96.

87. Kane Interview, 12/5/95.

88. Community Forum Videotape, 6/7/93.

89. McPherson Interview, 1/8/96.

90. Patton, "Parents against Lessons on AIDS Plan 2 Meetings," p. 11.

91. K. Michalski, "AIDS Proposal Opposed," *The Patriot Ledger*, 6/8/93, p. 10.

92. Whitmire Interview, 1/8/96.

93. Kane Interview, 12/5/95.

94. CPCB members also hosted a community-wide AIDS Information Night in August 1993. Dr. Janet Lapey, a Milton physician, presented an overview of the medical aspects of AIDS and its impact on society. Nancy Sutton, executive director of Family First in Medfield, Massachusetts, who has been "involved in assisting parents and concerned groups in organizing to stop comprehensive sex ed programs and Project 10 programs in public schools," discussed the impact of the Massachusetts Education Reform Act on Beta schools with participants. In *Community AIDS Information Night Agenda*, 8/23/93; and J. Hart, "Battle Lines Being Drawn on Classroom Sex Education," *The Boston Globe*, 8/28/93, p. 1. Sutton urged attendees to establish a rapport with school officials and work for a compromise on an AIDS curriculum. "You have to show them you are not irrational and not the unreasonable enemy," Sutton said. She also suggested starting a parent newsletter if school officials were unresponsive, and filing lawsuits if necessary. In AIDS Information Night Videotape, 8/23/93; and S. Patton, "Battle over AIDS Education Resumes," *The Patriot Ledger*, 9/1/93, p. 12.

95. M. Houston and R. Lear, "Officials Fear Religious Right Targeting Schools," *Tab*, 3/23/93, p. 8.

96. L. Pappano, "Sex-Ed Foes Set Alpha Platform: Group Seeks to Address Other Issues," *The Boston Globe*, 8/29/93, p. 1.

97. Ibid.

98. Concerned Parents/Citizens of Beta, *The Grassroots Forum*, Spring 1994.

99. "Beta Fund Backs Teaching of Abstinence," *The Patriot Ledger*, Spring 1993, pp. 1, 7.

100. Hampton Interview, 12/1/95.

101. In the early stages of the debate, individuals opposed to the health education curricula appeared on a local cable television program called "Meet Your Neighbor" to discuss their point of view. According to program host and Beta resident Alice Dana: "They [CPCB] wanted the publicity" (In Dana Interview, 1/12/96). In a review of letters to the editor of the *Beta Forum*, it was found that there were dozens of letters written by individuals and/or groups opposed to the health curriculum during the period from April 1993 to June 1995. The vast majority of these letters were written by members of the CPCB. Additionally, opponents to the curriculum also voiced their opinions in the "Sound-Off" section of the *Beta Forum*. During the height of the debate a large number of the calls published in the paper were from individuals opposed to the health curriculum.

102. CPCB members collected signatures from over 300 parents opposed to the AIDS curriculum. In R. Aicardi, "AIDS Curriculum—Back to Ground Zero," *The Patriot Ledger*, 6/23/93, p. 24; and A. Reid, "Foes of Teaching on AIDS Test Clout." *The Boston Globe*, 6/27/93, p. 1. Hampton discussed this strategy:

One of the first things we did was we went out and got signatures from people who were opposed to it [AIDS curriculum]. We went to the supermarkets and asked people if they were opposed to explicit sex education in schools. And a lot of people responded, "Yeah, I don't want that stuff in our schools." So they signed the petition. We invited them to the School Committee hearings. (*Source*: Hampton Interview, 12/1/95.)

103. In Alpha, opponents of the curriculum asked religious institutions to print the following in their respective church bulletins:

Did you know that Alpha, with your tax dollars is planning on teaching sex ed. K-12? Would you like to know what is going to be taught? Would you like to have a say? A group of parents is seeking more parent ideas. (*Source*: ACPE Documents.)

The CPCB was also successful in getting its message printed in local church bulletins. Kane recalled, "We went to the clergy because we felt for sure the priests would back us as Catholics. The response from some was to put an announcement in their church's bulletin that urged parents to resist the plan." In Kane Interview and S. Patton, "Beta rejects curriculum on AIDS," *The Patriot Ledger*, 6/22/93, p. 16. At St. Helen's Church the following appeared in the parish bulletin, a weekly newsletter available to the all parishioners: "Safe sex is neither safe nor moral. To call this program 'risk reduction' is misleading. The risk is still present. The moral implications are not reduced." In CPCB's *The Grassroots Forum*, Spring 1994.

104. Reid, "Foes of Teaching on AIDS Test Clout," p. 1.
105. Hampton Interview, 12/1/95.
106. Kane Interview, 12/5/95.
107. Whitmire Interview, 12/8/95.
108. Alexander Interview, 6/15/95.
109. S. Patton, "Battle over AIDS Education Resumes," p. 12.
110. Reid, "Foes of Teaching on AIDS Test Clout," p. 1.
111. Kane Interview, 12/5/95.
112. Citron Interview, 9/16/94.
113. Carr Interview, 8/18/94.
114. Hale Interview, 8/24/94.
115. Carr Interview, 8/18/94.

116. Hale Interview, 8/24/94.

117. M. J. Sales, "ACPE out of Touch with Kid's Futures," *Tab*, 8/17/93, p. 16.

118. Hale interview, 8/24/94.

119. Kane Interview, 12/5/95.

120. Alexander Interview, 12/5/95.

121. Banner Interview, 12/5/95.

122. Custer Interview, 12/5/95.

123. Kane Interview, 12/5/95.

124. Ibid.

125. Hampton Interview, 12/1/95.

126. Whitmire Interview, 12/8/95.

127. Hampton Interview, 12/1/95.

128. Hale Interview, 8/24/94.

129. S. Lyons, "Sex Ed Clash Flares," *Alpha Graphic*, 7/1/93, p. 26.

130. The World Medical Health Foundation, an organization based in Washington, DC, sponsors the *Free-Teen* program, an abstinence-based sexuality education program.

131. R. Lear, "Politics of Sex Education," *Tab*, 6/29/93, p. 1.

132. Alexander Interview, 6/15/95.

133. "Another View of Concerned Parents," *Beta Forum*, 2/2/94, p.11.

134. "What People Want," *Beta Forum*, 3/29/95, p. 11.

135. Dixon Interview, 10/7/94.

CHAPTER 7

Neutralizing Opposition

NEUTRALIZING OPPOSITION

The actions of individuals and community groups in both Alpha and Beta demonstrated that full endorsement of the proposed health education curricula was not possible. Sower and his associates believe that the opposition groups can be neutralized. For example, some individuals opposed to the proposed school-based curriculum decided to voice their opposition by participating on the Task Force or the HAC. Other parents opposed to this initiative removed their children from the pilot programs or removed them from the schools altogether. For other parents, such as ACPE and CPCB members, they decided to be more public in their opposition to the initiative and less willing to work within the established decision-making structure. Schultz recalled the actions of ACPE: "They came prepared to shut us down . . . you could tell by the tone, the demands and the shouting out. I had a choice of taking control of the meeting or letting it go crazy."[1]

According to Sower et al.'s theory, this type of opposition must be counteracted or the action process may be endangered.[2] This was illustrated when the Beta School Committee did not adopt the AAC's HIV/AIDS education proposal.

As a result of the AAC's inability to create external relationships with community-based groups and institutions within Beta, there was no broad base of support among community groups who might legitimize the AAC's proposed curriculum. In fact, when opposition arose it was addressed by individuals. In one instance, Jane Alexander responded,

I'm a little appalled at the negative attitude I'm seeing. As a public school I feel we have an obligation to provide information on timely issues, such as AIDS. We can't close our eyes to the problem. Other towns are way ahead of us in their programs on AIDS. We have a responsibility to move forward.[3] Our task is to teach prevention without condoning sexual activity.[4]

In another instance, the editor of the *Beta Forum* did speak out in favor of the AIDS curriculum in an editorial:

Today there is a terrible epidemic. It is called AIDS. Again it is time for parents and schools to reinforce each other in warning our children. . . . In the end there will not be total agreement. But the curriculum is the hard work of honorable people who have the best interest of our children in mind. It is an excellent curriculum. . . . These schools are not trying to usurp parents' responsibility as the moral guardians of their children.[5]

However, after writing the editorial, the editor experienced the worst week of her life. "They literally scared the daylights out of her," recalled Alexander.[6]

Superintendent Kurtz also addressed some parental concerns.[7] In the last months of the AAC's work he publicly announced that the Beta School Committee would not adopt an AIDS curriculum without first obtaining parental input.[8] Additionally, in an attempt to dispel the belief that the AAC operated secretly in "closed meetings," Kurtz announced that copies of AAC minutes would be made available in all Beta schools, the school administration office, and at the main branch of the Thayer Public Library. He commented, "Part of Beta's reputation is that there's nothing done behind closed doors. We want the community to be behind what we do."[9, 10]

As opposition to the HIV/AIDS curriculum became louder, no organized groups or institutions defended the AAC's work, not even the AAC's membership itself. This was evident in the comments made by Beta High School student Ann Murphy: "There were a lot of people that supported me after the fact, but I almost felt like saying to those people, 'Thank you, but where were you when I was standing up there [at the public hearing] and people were yelling at me. None of you spoke up.' "[11]

When I asked AAC member Shirley Bowman to comment on this lack of public support for the AAC's proposal, she responded, "I wasn't standing up and saying, 'I work on that AAC.' Are you nuts? I mean they [the CPCB] had swayed the crowd. They had turned them against the curriculum. It was too scary. By the end of the night they had successfully intimidated everyone on the Committee."[12]

AAC member Ellen Nagel provided another explanation. She recalled,

We had been told by [Assistant Superintendent] Moore not to stand up and speak at the public hearing. We were told not to defend it. It wasn't our place to defend the curriculum. So we assumed Jane [Alexander] would defend the curriculum. Or

Dr. Kurtz would defend it. Someone. No one defended it. None of the Committee spoke. So it looked like it was just rolled right over.[13]

Elaine Kane confirmed this view: "They were asked not to get up by the Superintendent and the Assistant Superintendent. No one said anything to me or to Mary. In other words we were on the other side."[14]

AAC member Chris Valley explained the administration's strategy. She said, "The Superintendent was very much afraid that we were going to be attacked personally and he didn't want that to happen." However, she added,

As people asked questions, nobody was answering their questions. These questions could have been answered by people on the AAC. We should have been up front as a Committee to answer questions. People were concerned. . . . They were frightened about their children. I felt that we could've stopped some of what was going on. I mean people were getting up and speaking against compassion, speaking against teaching children to wash their hands. It was bizarre.[15]

A Beta community member who attended the public hearings recalled, "I remember being amazed that, as someone who had nothing to do with the Committee, I was asking myself, 'Why aren't these guys getting up and talking.' "[16] Supporters of the AIDS curriculum conceded that they were surprised by the level of organization against the AAC's proposal. When I asked Dr. Kurtz for an explanation of this strategy, he stated, "The AAC which was a broad-based group had done its job. Now it was up to the School Committee to hold public hearings. The purpose of these hearings was to get input from the public and utilize this information to revise the curriculum." He concluded by stating, "I probably wouldn't put a topic like this out for public debate again. I saw the discussion as a distraction to the primary purpose of education."[17]

Over time, many residents and community groups in both Alpha and Beta demonstrated support of the curricula by counteracting ACPE and CPCB activities. These strategies included: generating community awareness; dispelling misinformation by providing information through media campaigns and public forums; supporting candidates for political office; and linking ACPE and CPCB with other conservative groups. In Beta there was also the emergence of an organized student voice.

Following the Alpha School Committee's January 1993 meeting, local residents generated community awareness by conducting a letter-writing campaign. The purpose of this campaign, according to Alpha activist Hannah Golden, was "to get lots of letters to the School Committee supporting the sex ed program and to inform people of what was going on in Alpha."[18] In a short period of time, over 3,000 letters were mailed to Alpha residents from organizations supporting sexuality education. Golden also reached out to Alpha clergy. She commented, "The clergy would be critical in this process. I gave copies of materials to Rabbi Wexler, Vice-president of the Alpha Clergy Association."[19] Information was then passed on to other clergy within the community.[20]

Other individuals and groups emerged to support the Task Force's work after ACPE's forum entitled "What's Wrong with Sex Education Anyway?" Sandra Riley responded, "It was among the most horrible experiences of my life. The people were hateful, nasty, just made crude remarks."[21] In the words of Reverend Jack Andrews "it was a wake-up call."[22] Golden added, "There were differences in people's actions. Differences in people who had been versus those who hadn't been to the Forum. I was trying to wake people up . . . the religious right was in Alpha."[23] It was not until after the Beta School Committee's vote to scrap the proposed HIV/AIDS curriculum that individuals and community-based groups within Beta began to organize around the need for a school-based HIV/AIDS education curriculum. A series of newspapers that covered events in Beta carried editorials. An editorial in *The Patriot Ledger* read:

It's hard to imagine how anyone who read the AIDS curriculum proposed for use in the Beta schools would decide to scrap it completely rather than adapt it to make it more acceptable. The K-12 curriculum was not perfect but it could, and should have been amended. Opposition to teaching about AIDS in the early grades was justified. But the suggested curriculum with minor modifications could have been followed from grade 4 on.[24]

Adults within the community also expressed support and interest in a school-based HIV/AIDS curriculum. Beta parent Kathy Bartow wrote in a letter to the editor of the *Beta Forum*:

Beta performed an injustice to its students by voting down the AIDS curriculum. Dr. Kurtz's recommendation to modify the curriculum was also voted down, condemning our children to an indeterminate period of time in which they will be left uneducated on a serious health care crisis. . . . I implore our school committee members to accept an AIDS curriculum. This is an emotional issue for us all. As one student so aptly put it, "Put away the phobias and fears and teach our children."[25]

This individual support was followed by more organized efforts under the direction of Community Advocates for Responsible Education (CARE), a grassroots parent organization formed in August 1993. CARE members generated community awareness about the shortcomings of the *Free Teens* program and initiated action around the development of a comprehensive K–12 health education program for Beta's public schools. For example, Shirley Bowman, an original member of the AAC and CARE member, recalled, "We went in to meet with him [Dr. Kurtz] and said, 'We don't like this curriculum for these reasons.' We outlined a list of reasons."[26] The concerns included: outdated research findings, gender bias, inaccurate medical findings, presentation of material in a fearful/shameful manner, and the depiction of the family structure in a limited view where single parent families were either ignored or depicted as troubled.[27] CARE members also provided evidence that the development and publication of the curriculum was linked to the Unification Church.[28]

Soon thereafter, Dr. Kurtz withdrew his recommendation for School Committee approval of the ninth-grade *Free Teens* program. CARE member Nan Parker remembered, "We stopped *Free Teens*. That was the first thing we did."[29]

Up to this point, Beta community members and CARE members had supported a school-based HIV/AIDS education program. However, CARE's long-term goal was to initiate action around the development of a school-based comprehensive K–12 health education program. This vision is captured in CARE's mission statement:

We the members of CARE believe in the importance of a sequential, comprehensive, developmentally appropriate health education curriculum for students in grades K–12 enrolled in the Beta schools. We believe this curriculum must provide students with accurate information and the necessary skills to enable them to make healthy and responsible decisions throughout their lives. We believe that in order to insure the healthy future of the children of Beta, the community at all levels must embrace comprehensive health education throughout the school experience.[30, 31]

"We wanted to educate people in the community about who we were," said CARE spokesperson Kathy Bartow. "We wanted to create public awareness that there was another sentiment within the town. We also wanted to get people together to show their support [for a comprehensive health education program]."[32]

Supporters sought to dispel misinformation about the curriculum and their efforts by providing accurate information through the media, public forums, and letter-writing campaigns. Jane Alexander remembered, "I can tell you that there was an awful lot of misinformation going around."[33] Ellen Nagel, CARE spokesperson, said, "We had our facts. What they did was take our facts out of context."[34]

One way in which supporters of the health education curriculum countered this misinformation was to provide accurate information and facts on local cable television shows. Alice Dana, host of the local cable program called "Meet Your Neighbor," decided to air a show that would express the views of those who supported the AIDS education curriculum. She recalled, "[I did a show] with Shirley Bowman. She discussed her brother who died of AIDS. I wanted people to look at Shirley and say this could happen in my family. It was a very moving piece." She added, "Parents and schools should have the information to disseminate to the children.

You can't kill someone with information. You can kill someone with a lack of it. You have to get this information to kids. Their life depends on it."[35]

ACPE members ran a successful media campaign. For example, Boston news reporters attended the School Committee's January meeting at ACPE's invitation. Schultz recalled: "I'll never forget that night . . . we were walking into the room, and I noticed a Channel 4 newscaster standing in the hallway. Somebody was behind him with a camera. Well, the room was standing room only."[36]

Pam Ferguson, an ACPE member, obtained air time on Alpha's local cable access channel to show "The Gay Agenda" and "The Gay Agenda in Public Education." Other ACPE members promoted their message through the use of print and radio media. In a review of articles and letters that appeared in the *Tab* and the *Alpha Graphic* from January to May 1993, Carr and Hale wrote numerous op-ed pieces and letters to the editor. Additionally, Carr was quoted regularly in *The Boston Globe*. ACPE also used the airwaves of WAZE to invite individuals to attend public meetings to voice their opposition to the curriculum. These strategies, which were highly successful in promoting ACPE's message to residents in Alpha and in Massachusetts, evolved out of Carr's media background.[37, 38]

In response, Sheila Fenn, an educator and local video producer, developed "Response to the Gay Agenda," a panel discussion on homophobia with Alpha clergy, parents, and school activists. Fenn stated, "Whatever she [Ferguson] puts on, I will counter-program. Because I think that you should see both sides."[39] ACPE's media tactics compelled private citizens to speak out. Nadine Nadler, an Alpha resident, stated, "After weeks of following the media blitz of a small but vocal minority of Alpha parents bombarding the press with alarmingly malevolent misinformation, I feel compelled to speak out."[40] Even the local newspapers responded. An editorial in the *Alpha Graphic* a week later was entitled "No Place for Hate."[41]

Another way in which supporters countered misinformation was by hosting community forums. On April 12, 1994 the Beta High School PTO sponsored an AIDS Awareness program for Beta residents. The Second Church of Christ, like some other religious institutions in Beta, was conducting its own sexuality education program. Reverend Riding, pastor of the Congregational Church, continued, "We had done an AIDS Awareness program here at the church. Two of them. One for our young people and one for adults."[42] Interestingly, there was no concerted effort by the Beta clergy to speak publicly on the issue. Riding explained, "I think they wanted to duck it. And the fact that I've been here thirty years, I probably have more knowledge of the community than any of them. This was one of the reasons I sort of took the bull by the horns and decided we were going to do something about it."[43]

Members of Supporting Student Health Education in Alpha (SSHEA) responded by co-sponsoring a public forum with the Alpha Human Rights Commission and the Alpha Substance Abuse and AIDS Coalition entitled, "A Partnership: Sexuality Education in the Home, Schools, and Community," in October 1993. The purpose of this event was to increase awareness around HIV/AIDS and foster better communication between parents, schools, and children.

Supporters of health education also countered the opposition by writing letters and articles to the local papers. "Whenever they saw something crazy in the Sound-Off section of the *Beta Forum*," stated Alexander, "they put some article in the paper."[44] Bill O'Neff discussed the relationship he developed with the editor of the *Beta Forum*: "Cathy Collins always printed every word I asked her to, even when she didn't want to print things. I just called her and talked it out with her. She told me a couple of times: 'Bill, I'm going to put this in but they're going to call me up and tell me I'm going to hell.' "[45] Other community residents wrote letters to the local paper. In one letter, Beta resident Charles Smith wrote:

Beta is a town of families of "good old American" values and participation. Nevertheless, Beta is not an easy place to be different—different in religion, color, background, politics, experiences, persuasions. Beta tends to be a rather homogenous community, which gives it strength and stability at times, but it also leads to very parochial thinking. Nothing prepared me, however, for the rage and reaction over the AIDS curriculum. I did not just hear criticisms of the curriculum. I heard hate, venom, righteousness, religious chauvinism, intolerance. . . . Many claim they are not homophobic, but I heard and felt homosexual hatred. Much of this was said in the veil of religious convictions. . . . I urge all people of Beta, whatever your religious persuasion or feelings on the curriculum, to help stop this movement now. It will harm our community. It distorts our democratic process and it flies in the face of pluralism. Our strength is that we can disagree. . . . Let us respect the rights of others who differ. Let us have dialogue.[46]

After the defeat of the initial HIV/AIDS curriculum, another Beta resident, Harry Moss, wrote, "We in Beta need all the information we can get on this life threatening epidemic. We need an AIDS, sex and drugs education in our schools. We can't wait another 15 months."[47] Other community residents called for accurate information presented within the framework of a solid curriculum. Carol Adolini wrote, "This is not a sex issue. It is a health issue and I cannot for the life of me figure out why such an important health issue would be so ignorantly ignored or so idly left to fester, while a weak inappropriate curriculum is implemented."[48, 49]

Proponents of the health education curriculum in Alpha also sought to counter misinformation. In a local newspaper article, Alpha School Committee member Sandra Riley chastised groups like ACPE for making false accusations and not being interested in a genuine exchange of ideas and opinions.[50] During the School Committee's May meeting, Kanner accused the ACPE of failing to provide accurate information. She stated, "I just feel that it needs tremendous emphasis, the misinformation campaign that has been pushed along by opposition groups like ACPE, and how very dangerous and irresponsible their message and information is."[51] Interestingly, ACPE members also accused curriculum supporters of generating misinformation.[52]

In both communities, proponents endorsed particular community members running for School Committee. In response to ACPE's slate of School Committee candidates, members of Alpha's political establishment became active and formed Committee '93. This political action committee, comprised of activists and parents, interviewed all sixteen candidates and endorsed a slate of candidates for the November elections. "In the initial meeting," Alpha parent Martha Kaplan recalled, "there was a lot of discussion about what should be done to inform people of the candidates."[53] State Representative Daniel Colin (D-Alpha) added, "Committee '93 was interested in electing progressive School Committee candidates. We went through a process. We developed a questionnaire and conducted interviews. We then mailed out a slate card with endorsements [and] distributed it at the polls."[54] Colin felt the slate card increased the vote total of all the candidates endorsed by Committee '93.[55] SSHEA, which also became a PAC, also created a slate card of its endorsements for the election.

Proponents of the curriculum initiative in Beta formed a political action committee and developed and mailed out a slate card of candidates they supported for the School Committee elections. In April 1994, CARE became a political action committee rallying community support for School Committee candidates who supported medically accurate, reality-based sexuality education. According to CARE member Valerie Devine, "We wanted to get people elected to the School Committee who would appreciate our point of view."[56] Through funding from a private source, CARE mailed out a candidate slate card for the April School Committee elections. All five candidates it backed were elected. Jane Alexander talked about the impact of CARE's political action committee on School Committee races: "When it's time to vote, actually everybody wanted to get the CARE group endorsement when they're running for office in town."[57] Additionally, Beta citizen and lawyer David Shaw took out an advertisement in the local paper endorsing the 1995 candidates who supported the comprehensive health education curriculum.[58]

Other Beta community members publicly responded to *The Grassroots Forum*, a newsletter developed by the Concerned Parents and Citizens of Beta (CPCB). Bill O'Neff, CARE member and Social Action Committee member of Beta's Unitarian Universalist Church, wrote:

Our town election saw the introduction of a disturbing new tactic to the local political scene. During the campaign's final days we saw a sophisticated mailing by

CPCB which distorted the positions of, and attacked the character of the two winners of the School Committee race. The mailing, "a newsletter," sought to portray these two dedicated child advocates as smut peddlers and conniving usurpers of parental authority. It is certainly acceptable for CPCB to endorse candidates, it is quite another thing to promulgate lies and innuendo in an effort to undermine support for their opposition. . . . This self-important minority should read the writing on the wall. Twice the people of this community have spoken. Twice they have supported those candidates who have called for a comprehensive health curriculum.[59]

Another Beta resident commented, "We happen to be one family that received *The Grassroots Forum* in the mail days before the election but what it did was make us look at Miriam Ireland and John Long."[60] Still other community residents countered the actions of Tom Hampton's PAC, which called itself "Restoring American Values in Education." Andrew Hilton, chairman of Beta's Republican Town Committee wrote:

We all want the finest schools for our children and a morally safe environment in which they can learn and grow. But Tom Hampton wants to build a wall of bigotry around the very minds that education strives to broaden. This is not an American value. It is true that he is a member of the Republican Town Committee, but he does not represent the committee, its members or for that matter, any rationally thinking Republican we know.[61]

Another method used to counteract the activities of ACPE and CPCB was to identify its members' associations with conservative organizations. The earliest accusations made *Tab* front-page headlines: "Officials fear religious right targeting schools."[62] In his address to the School Committee in May, Melvin Caan, chairman of the State Board of Education, made a series of comments linking ACPE to the "religious right." He stated, "The material that has been distributed by ACPE is very similar to material appearing in many communities nationwide in opposition to any comprehensive health and sex education in the public schools."[63] Mary Citron, ACPE spokeswoman, charged that Caan's comments were intended to incite hatred. She said, "He came in an official capacity to increase fears based on totally untrue allegations and inferences."[64] This debate brought up difficult issues about the right to question public proceedings and the use of labels for particular groups. At the same time, it raised suspicions about a group that wanted to avoid extremist connotations when, in fact, it had drawn materials for its arguments from Christian fundamentalist literature.[65]

CPCB was also linked with conservative groups. Initially, the CPCB was associated with fundamentalist values as seen in the comments made by then Morrison School PTO president Valerie Devine, following the defeat of the initial HIV/AIDS curriculum. She stated, "We are concerned with the religious overtones and fundamentalist views that are surfacing here.

They [the CPCB] have a right to express their views, but they don't have a right to turn the School Committee into a theocracy."[66] Other proponents of the original HIV/AIDS curriculum said the debate exposed a well-organized, vocal, and conservative faction in the community that believes the only way to educate children about AIDS is to teach strict sexual abstinence.[67, 68]

About six months later, members of CARE exposed the relationship between the author of the *Free Teens* curriculum and the Unification Church. On the morning of February 27, 1994, *The Patriot Ledger* printed the following title for its lead story, "Rev. Moon linked to AIDS course."[69] CARE members Shirley Bowman and Bill O'Neff also worked with the local media to educate others about the connection between the CPCB and other national right-wing fundamentalist groups. O'Neff made the connection public in his letter to the editor of the *Beta Forum*, dated April 6, 1994.[70, 71]

In response to these accusations, CPCB co-founder Elaine Kane responded, "I was flabbergasted when I first heard about it. It just became a joke with us."[72] Ironically, as CPCB member Carolyn Banner pointed out: "It was interesting. It was actually accusations about being affiliated with them [the Christian Coalition] that actually brought us to them."[73] CPCB spokesperson Linda Whitmire felt that being identified as members of the Christian Coalition was "a way to distract from the real issue."[74]

As the debate evolved from a discussion around an HIV/AIDS education program to the development of a comprehensive health education curriculum in Beta more students became involved. Initially, only a handful of Beta students including Ann Murphy and Sharon Whitmire expressed their views. Part of the reason for this may be related to how students were publicly treated when they expressed their views on HIV/AIDS education. After a series of encounters at public meetings and in the newspapers, Ann Murphy's father Michael said his daughter had refrained from making any more comments in favor of the curriculum: "[Amy] has been the target of jeers and other nasty comments after her speech [at the School Committee's June 21 public hearing]."[75]

Over the course of the next year, however, students on both sides of the issue expressed their opinions in writing and at School Committee meetings. In one instance a student called in to the *Beta Forum* with the comment, "I'm a freshman at Beta High School. I feel it would be a good idea to have AIDS education because we need to know more about AIDS and how to prevent it."[76] Not all students were in agreement; another student stated, "I am a fifteen-year-old girl and I know that some kids won't listen no matter what. Adults should be the kind of people that kids can look up to. Adults should tell kids not to have sex until they're married. More kids will listen than they think."[77]

At the School Committee's April 26, 1994 meeting, Sarah Earl, a Beta

High School senior and School Committee student representative, spoke out in favor of a school-based health and AIDS education program in school. After distributing copies of an article about health and sex education that ran in *The Patriot Ledger*, she said, "I'm very disturbed about this article. I'm almost ashamed to live in this town. Every other community [around us] can mention condoms without having parents flip out and go totally off-the-wall insane." Another student representative to the School Committee, Kathy Williams, stated, "If all the other towns are doing this and nothing's gone wrong, we could do it too." Student representative John Bartlett asked the group what students could do to speed up the implementation of a health curriculum.[78] CARE member and Beta parent Kathy Bartow provided her account of the events around this meeting. She recalled,

They [the School Committee members] questioned [the students] whether the seniors wanted this or not or was it just talk. And the students on the School Committee said, "We'll get a list for you." By the next meeting they had a petition drawn up that most of the seniors did sign stating that they wanted AIDS education. It was a majority of the seniors.[79]

On June 5, 1995, Kathy Williams presented the School Committee with a petition signed by over one hundred Beta High School seniors. In presenting this petition she stated, "You have to think about the parents who don't teach their kids. They will graduate without being informed."[80, 81]

COMPARING THE EFFECTIVENESS OF SSHEA AND CARE

Ultimately, there was a concerted effort by individuals and community groups in both communities to counteract the activities of those opposed to school-based comprehensive health education programs. SSHEA and CARE emerged as the prominent groups in their respective communities to create community awareness and support for such initiatives.

Less than a month after ACPE's forum, a more formalized organization, Supporters of Student Health Education in Alpha (SSHEA), was created to support the Task Force's efforts.[82] SSHEA founder Sarah Kanner recalled,

I, in my almost forty years, have never witnessed such hatred and bigotry, prejudice and lies. I was overwhelmingly saddened by it [the ACPE's March Forum]. I was outraged enough to make many phone calls during the next few days and get SSHEA started. Natalie [Dixon] gave me the names of some people like Cindy Newman, Sylvia Healey and Hannah Golden. And we had a meeting at my house.

She continued,

I felt we needed to demonstrate. I felt strongly that we lived in a community that given the facts, would support the development and implementation of comprehensive sexuality education. However, if we did not mobilize that support and make our voices heard, then perhaps this small group of people who opposed it would appear to have more support and appear louder than a majority of the community.[83]

With regard to the internal organization of this 25-member group, Kanner explained,

My neighbor Kathy Smith worked on the membership drive. She lives right behind me. I was in essence the self-appointed chairperson. My other neighbor, Lori Suarez who lives next door to Kathy, was the self-appointed treasurer. This was really grassroots. Joan who lives across the street from Lorraine did the Voters Guide.[84]

SSHEA's goal was: "to demonstrate continuing, broad-based support for the development and maintenance of a sensitive and comprehensive K–12 health and human sexuality education curriculum for Alpha residents."[85] To accomplish this goal, SSHEA sponsored an evening telethon to explain the facts about the pilot program to Alpha residents. The group also gathered over 800 pledges of support. With these funds, SSHEA took out a full-page ad in the two local newspapers supporting the Task Force's efforts.[86] SSHEA also worked with other Alpha community groups to host a community forum entitled "A Partnership: Sexuality Education in the Home, Schools and Community." Additionally, SSHEA successfully recruited curriculum supporters to the School Committee's May meeting to support the Task Force's recommendations. Kanner commented: "We worked hard to get people to the meeting. . . . We put together a list and got people to start out speaking about different aspects of it [the curriculum]. It was carefully orchestrated."[87]

Beta parents from the Parent Advisory Council (PAC), Beta's PTOs, the AAC, and the school administration came together to form Community Advocates for Responsible Education (CARE) to support AIDS education in Beta schools. Health and Human Development specialist Jane Alexander recalled,

I got a group of parents together that I knew were not the silent majority, that I saw at these meetings, that were willing to get up and talk about how they thought the curriculum was good. I got Bev Wiggins from the Prevention Center to provide technical assistance and they formed a club called CARE, Community Advocates for Responsible Education [in August 1993]. I orchestrated that, and moved out, because I wanted to continue to be an educator, not the community person.[88]

According to Shirley Bowman, the initial meeting consisted of a group of people who wanted AIDS education in the Beta schools. Bowman stated,

"Some of us in CARE were on the AAC. We still wanted to see AIDS education in the schools and we wanted to support Jane Alexander's efforts. We were going to work towards that end."[89] "I was done," recalled Ellen Nagel, an original AAC member. "Then all these people came out and said, 'If you can't continue this fight, we will.' " Nagel joined 20 other Beta parents to form CARE.[90]

Over time technical assistance was provided to the group to create both some level of internal organization and a common goal. Alexander recalled, "One thing that I am proud of is the way that I was able to get other people involved in this battle. Probably the best thing that I did was to get a group of parents together and get them the technical support."[91] Technical assistance provided by outside experts shaped the internal organization of the group. According to Jane Alexander, Bev Wiggins acted as the technical assistant for CARE. She stated, "Yeah, she [Wiggins] trained them and taught them and showed them what to do."[92] Bowman added, "Bev [Wiggins] really helped us with [thinking about] how we would come together as a group with our spectrum of ideas and wishes. Bev taught us to organize this group. She helped us with a mission statement and with the goals."[93] CARE member Bill O'Neff added, "Beverly [Wiggins] suggested things like using one person [for a specific task]."[94] CARE member Linda Margola added, "Yeah, one night we talked and we picked and said, 'O.K. you can be that and you can be that.' Kathy [Bartow] was our spokesperson because she was a good talker."[95] "Val was our fearless leader," added O'Neff. "She kept us focused."[96] Technical assistance from Jane Alexander also helped shape the group's vision and allowed Beta School Committee member Jean Anderson to see her idea realized. CARE member Shirley Bowman remembered:

In October/November [1993] we were still working on an AIDS education program, because we were confused about comprehensive health education. Some people [in CARE] didn't want this talked about in the schools, others wanted AIDS education, others wanted homosexuality to be taught as normal. So we asked Jane [Alexander] to come in and give us a lecture on comprehensive health. What it was. What it means. What it entails. She came with her charts and explained it to us and explained how sexuality fit into a comprehensive health education plan. Once she explained this, we decided to support a public school initiative to develop a comprehensive health education program. That became our mission.[97]

As I studied the early stages of SSHEA's and CARE's formation, members discussed how the groups functioned. Members also "remembered definite disagreements" amongst each other.[98] These conflicts were settled in various ways. Kanner discussed how conflict was handled in one particular situation:

Hannah [Golden] came here with a lot of information about what's happening elsewhere,[99] which frankly I said, "Come on, this isn't happening here in our community. This is isolated. Stealth candidates?[100] Come on, this is Alpha?" I couldn't buy into it. I don't feel like I am in a battle to fight the Right. I think in doing what I'm doing, I need to know about the work the Radical Right is doing . . . and put it into the framework.

She continued,

It was important that we didn't sit down and talk about what Concerned Citizens of Falmouth was doing, or what Brian Carr was doing for an hour or two. We needed to take action toward a specific goal. . . . I think we had some difficulty when Hannah became very vocal about the efforts of the Religious Right and how that was happening in Alpha. And I think it became difficult for many people. I think we distanced her. SSHEA distanced ourselves from it. It was really important for us to stay mainstream, to focus on the public health problem. I think Hannah's work was really important to the effort, but it had to happen on kind of the side.[101]

Initially, when the issue of condom availability in the high school was discussed among CARE members, there was a sharp difference of opinion. According to members I interviewed, this issue had the potential of fracturing the group during its earliest days of existence. However, through dialogue, respect for each other, and a sense of understanding the group's larger vision, group members reached a consensus on CARE's position. Valerie Devine shared the following story:

Shirley [Bowman] and I saw ourselves as pretty left. Both of us believed condoms should be in the high school. Some people were also afraid of Bill [O'Neff] because they thought he would come out saying, "I don't give a shit, put condoms in [the high school]." But to keep the group cohesive and to keep our goal in mind, we had to put those [individual] feelings aside. We had to stick to our common goal which was comprehensive health education in the [Beta] schools.[102]

When I asked other CARE members how the group mediated conflict, I was given a variety of answers. Kathy Bartow felt that even though there was a difference of opinion among various group members: "We were in it for the kids."[103] Bill O'Neff added, "We had respect for each other."[104] Nan Parker felt that CARE members were able to mediate conflict through honest dialogue. She commented, "Even though we [Bill and I] disagreed probably more than any two members in the group, he was honest about how he felt. I was honest about what I felt."[105] Linda Margola remembered their more pragmatic approach: "I remember when we had differences, we had a majority vote."[106]

Both SSHEA and CARE also created and maintained relationships with individuals and groups within their respective communities. Kanner recalled SSHEA's first outreach activity:

We got together a decent amount of people to do a phone bank. Somebody volunteered their law offices and we had twenty people making [calls]. . . . We all used our elementary school phone books. Some people had the League of Women Voters [list], some people had their temple or church lists, whatever we could drum up.[107]

Within a short period of time SSHEA got the support of over 800 Alpha residents. At SSHEA's April 3, 1993 meeting, group members discussed the importance of building relationships with key individuals and groups in Alpha. Many of SSHEA's members were active in political, civic, social, and religious organizations in Alpha. As such, group members were able to reach out to community groups which included: clergy and lay leaders to whom SSHEA provided accurate information on the curriculum, key people in Alpha and on regional and state organizations who could provide financial support and speak at public engagements, lawyers who could provide legal advice, and media representatives to whom SSHEA could disseminate information packets and press releases containing accurate information on the ninth-grade pilot program.[108]

CARE members in Beta were able to initiate action around the development of a school-based comprehensive K–12 health education program because of the prestige CARE members held and alliances they created with individuals and community in Beta. CARE members established relationships with other Beta parents who sat on the Parent Advisory Council (PAC), the various school Parent-Teacher Organizations (PTOs), the original AIDS Advisory Council. CARE members were successful in these endeavors because many of them held prominent positions within these organizations. CARE members also made a point to develop a relationship with Beta school superintendent Peter Kurtz. CARE member Shirley Bowman remembered that early on in the group's existence, CARE members visited with Dr. Kurtz: "We met with him and we introduced ourselves and told him we wanted to support him in his efforts. We wanted Superintendent Kurtz to know that we were a group. That we were serious. That we had members."[109] CARE members also maintained or created relationships with Beta School Committee members. One CARE member mentioned: "Most of the proponents [of AIDS education on the School Committee] were very good friends of mine."[110] CARE spokesperson Kathy Bartow also made it a point to publicly announce the formation of CARE at the School Committee's January 21, 1994 meeting.[111] The success of CARE's outreach efforts was evident in the comments made by one Beta parent in the *Beta Forum*: "I would like to commend this group of parents for coming forward in such a volatile atmosphere. . . . I wish CARE the best. We need to hear a balanced view on this serious issue, not just the side represented by Concerned Citizens [CPCB]."[112]

Both SSHEA and CARE had clear goals and objectives and worked collaboratively with individuals within and outside their respective communities to influence the community decision-making process around the development of respective school-based comprehensive health education programs. Interestingly, in both Alpha and Beta, these community groups mobilized in reaction to various events in their respective communities— SSHEA was formed after ACPE's March 1993 forum "What's Wrong with Sex education Anyway?", and CARE was formed after the defeat of the AAC's proposal. However, over time these community groups became more proactive in their role as advocates for comprehensive K–12 school-based health education programs.

Many proposals for social change flounder and eventually fail because the initiating set bypasses the legitimation stage and attempts to move immediately from initiation to implementation. It was during the legitimation stage that both support and opposition for the comprehensive health education programs emerged. Various community groups in both communities established sufficient credibility to execute their proposals. Alpha students established credibility by obtaining over 1,000 signatures to petition the School Committee.[113] This credibility was reinforced when the School Committee approved their request for a condom availability program and then charged the school administration to create a Task Force to explore the development of an expanded educational program. In Beta, the AAC did not solicit community input and approval for its proposed HIV/AIDS education program. As a result, community groups like CPCB were successful in mounting sufficient opposition to defeat this proposal. With the emergence of CARE, however, came a unified call within the community for a comprehensive health education curriculum.

Individuals and community groups such as SSHEA and CARE publicly supported the work and recommendations of the Task Force and the Health Advisory Council, respectively. Individuals and groups opposed to the curriculum also had the opportunity to demonstrate their points of view. However, the main opposition groups, ACPE and CPCB, began to lose credibility—ACPE in response to its March forum and CPCB after the defeat of the *Free Teens* program.[114] Over time, the School Committees in Alpha and Beta voted to adopt the comprehensive health education programs recommended by their respective community advisory councils.

NOTES

1. Schultz Interview, 8/29/94.
2. C. Sower, J. Holland, K. Tiedke, and W. Freeman, *Community Involvement* (New York: The Free Press, 1957), p. 96.

3. S. Patton, "Parents Wary of AIDS Education," *The Patriot Ledger*, 5/20/93, p. 10.

4. S. Patton, "Beta Proposes Early Start on AIDS Ed," *The Patriot Ledger*, 5/27/93, p. 1.

5. Editorial, "The AIDS Curriculum," *Beta Forum*, 6/9/93, p. 10.

6. Alexander Interview, 6/15/95.

7. At the AAC's April meeting, several requests were heard from Beta parents who were noncommittee members. The requests included: (1) a reasonable amount of time in which to review the curriculum (three weeks); (2) a reasonable amount of time for notice of the public hearing; (3) a sufficient quantity of available copies of the curriculum at each location; (4) and available copies of the AIDS curriculum at the public library. In *AIDS Advisory Committee Minutes*, 4/14/93.

8. After months of work, the AAC voted 15–3 on May 12, 1993 to submit the AIDS curriculum and a series of recommendations to the Beta School Committee. At this same meeting, Superintendent Kurtz explained the process of obtaining community input on the AIDS curriculum. These procedures were also made known to the general public in a letter Kurtz wrote to the *Beta Forum*. In Letter to the Editor, *Beta Forum*, 5/19/93, p. 10.

9. Kurtz letter, "15 Months Have Gone into AIDS Curriculum," *Beta Forum*, 5/19/93, p. 10.

10. Beta School Committee member Maureen Casey questioned this procedure:

How were people supposed to digest this material in the amount of time that they were allotted anyway? If they truly wanted to delve into it and invest the time, overnight was not enough. There's no way. So everybody was making copies. There were all kinds of copies floating around.

To limit the number of reproduced copies, Mary Custer added, "They made people start signing them out so you could only have it for so long and you were only supposed to have the grade that was applicable to your child." Both situations, however, presented potential problems. First, time constraints led people to create duplicate copies of the HIV/AIDS curriculum. These unofficial copies circulated throughout the community. As such, the opportunity to maintain a level of quality control of the curriculum was lost. Second, the time constraints did not allow community members enough time to review the scope and sequence of the *entire* curriculum. When misinformation about the AIDS curriculum began to circulate throughout the community, only those who read the curriculum in it's entirety could confirm/reject what they were hearing. Maureen Casey confirmed this in a presentation she made at the Harvard Graduate School of Education: "A lot of information being disseminated was second hand. It [the HIV/AIDS curriculum] became tarnished and exploited."

11. Murphy Interview, 10/27/95.

12. Bowman Interview, 10/6/95.

13. Nagel Interview, 10/27/95.

14. Kane Interview, 12/5/95.

15. Valley Interview, 1/15/96.

16. Bartow Interview, 10/27/95.

17. Kurtz Interview, 7/23/96.

18. Organizations that participated in this campaign included the PTA Council,

the League of Women Voters of Alpha, the Civil Liberties Union of Massachusetts (ACLU), Planned Parenthood, Fenway Community Health Center, Temple Israel, and the American Jewish Congress. Golden Interview, 8/17/94.

19. Golden Interview, 8/17/94.

20. On May 10, 1993, members of the Alpha Clergy Association unanimously adopted a statement to be read before the School Committee. Excerpts included,

The Alpha Clergy Association brings together clergy men and women from the diverse faiths found in Alpha to promote understanding, cooperation and mutual respect among Alpha's citizens, especially in relation to issues of faith. . . . The Health Education Task Force grew out of the concern on the part of students and parents for responsible and accurate information that will help them deal with the AIDS crisis. . . . We support the Health Education Task Force's open process which, on numerous occasions, has provided Alpha citizens with opportunities to express their views on the sex education curriculum.

We acknowledge that these discussions have the potential to polarize various constituencies within our city. . . . There are thoughtful people on every side of this issue from each of our faith perspectives. . . . We call upon the School Committee to continue its open process as it moves quickly to make and implement its decisions. (*Source*: Alpha Clergy Association, May 1993.)

21. Riley Interview, 9/7/94.

22. Andrews Interview, 9/16/94.

23. Golden Interview, 8/17/94.

24. Editorial, *The Patriot Ledger*, 6/23/93, p. 10.

25. K. Bartow (letter), "Put Away Phobias, Teach Our Children," *Beta Forum*, 7/14/93, p. 10.

26. Bowman Interview, 10/6/95.

27. CARE Critique of *Free Teens* Presentation (February 1994).

28. Devine Interview, 10/27/95.

29. Parker Interview, 8/12/94.

30. CARE Mission Statement Document (1994).

31. M. Goldberg, "Parents Take Sides on AIDS Education," *The Patriot Ledger*, 1/26/94, p. 14.

32. Bartow Interview, 10/27/95.

33. Alexander continued: "They [CPCB] used every sensitive issue that they could, that could confuse people. So we were getting to a point where we weren't using the word homosexual. We weren't using the word gay. . . . So we had this AIDS curriculum that had been so watered down, I would have been embarrassed to teach anyway, because kids are smarter than that." Alexander Interview, 6/15/95.

34. Nagel Interview, 10/27/95.

35. Dana Interview, 1/12/96.

36. Schultz Interview, 8/29/94.

37. Hale Interview, 8/24/94.

38. Sam Lyons, an *Alpha Graphic* reporter, explained why Carr received so much press coverage: "Bob would always talk to us and give us better quotes." Lyons Interview, 9/2/94.

39. Fenn Interview, 11/14/94.

40. N. Nadler (letter), "A Matter of Life and Death," *Tab*, 5/25/93, p. 29.

41. Editorial, "No Place for Hate," *Alpha Graphic*, 4/8/94, p. 18.

42. Riding Interview, 12/11/95. Other churches in Beta also had sexuality education programs. The *True Love Waits* curriculum developed by the Roman Catholic Archdiocese of Boston was in place at St. Timothy's Catholic Church in Beta.

43. Riding Interview, 12/11/95.

44. Alexander Interview, 6/15/95.

45. O'Neff Interview, 10/27/95.

46. C. Smith (letter), "Please Not in Beta," *Beta Forum*, 6/30/93, p. 14.

47. H. Moss (letter), "We Need AIDS, Sex, Drugs Education in Schools," *Beta Forum*, 7/7/93, p. 10.

48. J. W. Ferro, "Back to Square One on AIDS Course," *Beta Forum*, 2/23/94, p. 8.

49. Other supporters focused their comments specifically on the CPCB. Said one community resident: "I am tired of hearing about that Concerned Parent group. I feel that they do not represent every concerned parent in Beta, nor does every concerned parent share their views." In "Another View of Concerned Parents," *Beta Forum*, 2/2/94, p. 11. Another resident said, "We must be careful not to let a small vocal minority to dominate now that we have a broad-based poll of parental concerns." In "Time to Move Forward," *Beta Forum*, 3/15/95, p. 11.

50. Riley wrote, "Deliberately misleading statements made by extreme conservatives, seemingly to command media attention, have caused confusion in both the newspapers and on radio talk shows." S. Riley, Viewpoint: "Conservatives Mislead Public on Sex Education,"*Tab*, 5/4/93, p. 18.

51. Kanner Interview, 8/19/94.

52. In a letter to the editor of the *Alpha Graphic*, Tim Kane, a high school student member, wrote,

The travesty of justice I am referring to is the School Committee's and the local media's attempts to spread lies and misinform the general public on the beliefs and motives of the ACPE. They are not "Right-Wing Christian Fanatics" but concerned citizens of all faiths and political parties. Their main beliefs include the rights of parents to be involved in their child's education and they do not want the School Board to choose what their children will or will not value. (*Source*: T. Kane (letter), "ACPE Not Fanatics," *Alpha Graphic*, 10/14/93, p. 14.)

53. Kaplan Interview, 8/19/94.

54. Colin Interview, 1/23/95.

55. Ibid.

56. Devine Interview, 10/27/95.

57. Alexander Interview, 6/15/95.

58. Hampton Interview, 12/1/95.

59. B. O'Neff (letter), "Mailing Attacked Character of School Winners," *Beta Forum*, 5/10/95, p. 10.

60. "Spoke Loud and Clear," *Beta Forum*, 5/17/95, p. 11.

61. A. Hilton (letter), *Beta Forum*, 3/94.

62. M. Houston and R. Lear, "Officials Fear Religious Right Targeting Schools," *Tab*, 3/23/93, p. 1.

63. Caan presentation, *Alpha School Committee Minutes*, 5/10/93.

64. L. Pappano, "Alpha to Try Sex Education in 9th Grade," *The Boston Globe*, 5/11/93, p. 21.

65. L. Pappano, "A Fundamental Issue in Alpha? Sex Ed Supporters Say Religion Spurs Its Foes," *The Boston Globe*, 5/10/93, p. 17.

66. R. Aicardi, "Call for Calm About AIDS Education," *Beta Forum*, 6/30/93, p. 9.

67. This connection also surfaced in the School Committee elections. Candidate Dorothy Nedrick stated, "All over the country, there are people from the Christian Coalition getting school board seats and making decisions, and they've come to Beta. Their agenda is different from mine." In L. Pappano, "Little Sex-Ed Talk in Beta Race Some Voters Say Stance Unclear," *The Boston Globe*, 3/27/94, p. 4.

68. A. Reid, "Town Takes Breather in AIDS Tussle," *The Boston Globe*, 7/4/93, p. 1.

69. L. Kowalczyk, "Rev. Moon Linked to AIDS Course," *The Patriot Ledger*, 2/17/94, p. 1.

70. O'Neff Interview, 10/27/95.

71. O'Neff (letter), "The *Free Teens* Program Is Where It Belongs—in the Trash Heap," *Beta Forum*, 4/6/94, pp. 10, 11.

72. Kane Interview, 12/5/95.

73. Banner Interview, 12/5/95.

74. Whitmire Interview, 12/8/95.

75. Reid, "Town Takes Breather in AIDS Tussle," p. 1.

76. "AIDS Education a Good Idea," *Beta Forum*, 2/23/94, p. 11.

77. "More Kids Will Listen," *Beta Forum*, 3/30/94, p. 13.

78. *Alpha School Committee Minutes*, 4/26/94.

79. Bartow Interview, 10/27/95.

80. *Alpha School Committee Minutes*, 6/5/95.

81. D. Falbo, "Health Course Books Okayed," *Beta Forum*, 6/7/95, pp. 1, 9.

82. Sara Kanner, an Alpha parent and one of the group's founders, outlined why citizens of Alpha should support the effort. In summary, Kanner stated, (1) the Task Force is made up of a cross-section of professionals from the community who have long been involved in health and sexuality education, (2) children need to learn about sexuality in a healthy context, and (3) the statistics on adolescent sexual activity are alarming. In S. Kanner, Viewpoint: "Safe Crossing for Students," *Tab*, 5/4/93, p. 29.

83. Kanner Interview, 8/19/94.

84. Ibid.

85. Supporters of Student Health Education in Alpha, handout.

86. The ad read,

We support the efforts of the Alpha Health Education Task Force. We, members of the Alpha community, maintain that a sensitive and comprehensive health and sexuality curriculum will provide students with accurate and essential knowledge. This education will enable students to act responsibly and make healthier decisions, while respecting themselves and the worth of all individuals. (*Source: Tab*, 5/4/93, p. 25.)

87. Kanner Interview, 8/19/94.

88. Alexander Interview, 6/15/95.

89. Bowman Interview, 10/6/95.

90. Goldberg, "Parents Take Sides on AIDS Education," pp. 13, 14.

91. Nagel Interview, 10/27/95.

92. Alexander Interview, 6/15/95.

93. Ibid.

94. Bowman Interview, 10/6/95.

95. O'Neff Interview, 10/27/95.

96. Margola Interview, 10/27/95.

97. O'Neff Interview, 10/27/95.

98. Bowman Interview, 10/6/95.

99. See Part III: Findings and Analysis Introduction, note 10.

100. Stealth Candidates were identified as individuals who ran for public office under platforms that could not be readily identified nor recognized by the public.

101. Kanner Interview, 8/19/94.

102. Devine Interview, 10/27/95.

103. Bartow Interview, 10/27/95.

104. O'Neff Interview, 10/27/95.

105. Parker Interview, 8/12/94.

106. Margola Interview, 10/27/95.

107. Kanner Interview, 8/19/95.

108. Supporters of Student Health Education in Alpha document, 4/4/93.

109. Bowman Interview, 10/27/95.

110. Bartow Interview, 10/27/95.

111. *Alpha School Committee Minutes*, 1/21/94.

112. Other help came from a local political activist, Susan Shear. CARE member Valerie Devine shared, "She [Shear] also helped us organize. She does a lot of political stuff behind the scenes." In Devine Interview, 10/27/95. "She [Shear] suggested that we should get involved in the [school committee] elections," added CARE member Bill O'Neff. "She's very politically active in town. She gave us a lot of political advice. She was the one who suggested we put together a slate [card]. She helped us figure out how to go about backing a candidate." In O'Neff Interview, 10/27/95.

113. C. Brush and T. Coakley, "Alpha Approves Condom Distribution, Superintendent opposed but will implement," *The Boston Globe*, 1/28/92, p. 19.

114. Two days later an article titled "New York Catholics, Robertson in Alliance" appeared in *The Patriot Ledger*. The reporter wrote,

The Roman Catholic Archdiocese of New York, forging a tactical alliance with a group run by the Rev. Pat Robertson, will distribute to each of its 213 parishes a guide. . . . to help voters in school board elections pick candidates who are conservative on social issues. . . . The move shows the increasing involvement of the church in school politics [around] the recent controversies over the distribution of condoms and the teaching of tolerance for homosexuals. (4/16/93, p. 1)

CHAPTER 8

Implementing School-Based Health and Sexuality Education Programs

AVAILABLE RESOURCES

According to Sower et al.'s model, a plan is executed during the *implementation stage*. To be effective, it is necessary to have access to personnel, techniques, and other resources, usually from more than one organization.[1] Goodwill, knowledge, and skills may also be necessary resources in the implementation of community projects.[2] Now that the legitimizing bodies had given their approval, access to resources and public education were needed. Resources include: funding, review of existing curricula/materials, and personnel.

Funding

In Alpha and Beta, solicitation of funds occurred at many levels. In Alpha, school officials applied for federal, state, and local grants. In spring 1992, Task Force members worked with the Alpha School Department to submit grant applications for curriculum and staff development. In a report to the School Committee on May 26, 1992, Assistant Superintendent Redman reported,

Natalie Dixon and Miriam Ross have worked with me and John Feldman in submitting state and federal grant applications. We believe they are well developed and should be very competitive. Included in these applications are proposals for comprehensive health education programs and in-service training grants.[3]

In following discussions among Alpha School Committee members, Redman mentioned that "without additional assistance and staffing the program will not be implemented as envisioned." Superintendent Ivan Brown went on to add that he did not believe the short-term goals could be' met without funding summer workshops. He offered to identify areas where money could be transferred. He added, "The project could be done quicker and more comprehensively with additional staff and funding, but this is not a likely scenario. As with so many other areas in the system, this is operating a great deal on good will."[4] School Committee members voted to direct the Superintendent to allocate "a minimum of $5,000 out of surplus funds for summer workshops relating to health education issues."[5] Workshops included expanding the health education programs in Alpha's junior high schools, and revising the *Growing and Changing* curriculum in the upper elementary grades.[6, 7]

Task Force members worked collaboratively with school administrators to obtain possible federal funding. In one grant, "Education for Wellness," Alpha schools applied for $75,000 from the U.S. Department of Education. According to the proposal, funding would "coordinate existing and new curriculum innovations in the Alpha Schools into a single, comprehensive program serving 7,100 children in grades K–8."[8] This proposal, however, was not funded.

Members of this grant-writing team were successful in securing $45,000 in state funding from the Department of Education. In a memo to Superintendent Ivan Brown, Phil Redman announced that these funds would support the development of a comprehensive health education curriculum.[9,10]

In another attempt to locate funding, Jean Fisk, co-chair of the Task Force's curriculum subcommittee, informed the School Committee of funds available through the Massachusetts Department of Education's Health Protection Grant program. She stated, "There is possible funding from the tobacco tax that will provide money to municipal health departments and public school systems. Alpha is eligible for $300,000."[11] Eligibility required the Health Education Task Force be renamed and its composition slightly revised to represent a broader segment of the community.[12] The Health Education Task Force became the Health Advisory Council (HAC) and during the summer of 1993, three additional individuals—Bill Parker, Susan Simon, and Rob Pike—were asked to become members. Later that summer, the Alpha Public Schools received $310,000 from this grant program.

In Beta, the solicitation of funds occurred at the state and local levels. In spring 1993 and 1994, Beta school personnel worked with the Beta School Department to submit grant applications for curriculum and staff development to the state Department of Education. In the first year, Beta received $142,000 from the tobacco tax revenues. This enabled administrators to hire a school psychologist at the high school and a health teacher at one of the middle schools. In the second year, part of the $132,000 state grant was used to pay a health education coordinator, a school psychologist at Beta High School, and two health educators. One of the teachers would teach the ninth-grade course. The funding would also be used to purchase books and other teaching materials for students in grades 7 and 9.[13, 14] By the third year this funding had been reduced to $116,000.[15]

When I asked Jane Alexander about future funding for the comprehensive health education program, she commented, "Tobacco money. I haven't seen that money yet. I hope that's going to be level funded or we're going to be up another creek. It's my understanding that we are going to be level funded."[16] The uncertainty around funding, however, moved Alexander to reconsider developing the entire program. She stated, "The reason I didn't come up with a K–12 curriculum for the June 1995 School Committee meeting was because we didn't have the money or the time to do it properly. We could do a K–6 curriculum without any added personnel. So, that was feasible, doable, and affordable, grant-money wise."[17]

A few months after the School Committee adopted the second phase of a comprehensive health education program—a K–5 program—Beta school administrators learned that the Health Protection Grant money had been reduced to $116,000. Therefore, there wasn't enough funding to implement the curriculum in its entirety.[18] CARE member Linda Mazarella confirmed this with the statement, "[Jane] Alexander only got half of what she thought the grant was going to be. She could only institute [the curriculum] in two or three grades."[19] Kathy Bartow went on to add, "Yeah, but I heard Beta Medical Associates gave some money and somebody else was coming through with funds."[20] Additionally, Jane Alexander and Shirley Bowman are working with the Healthy People 2000 initiative to raise funds.[21, 22] According to Alexander,

The Great Body Shop—the K–5 curriculum—was approved unanimously by the School Committee. It hasn't been implemented in all the grades because of funding problems due to the $10,000 reduction in the Health Protection grant. We wrote letters to all medical people in Beta through Healthy People 2000. We got $1,800. In addition to money, physicians also came in and helped to teach the classes.[23]

Curricula and Materials

With regard to course content development, a variety of resources were utilized to develop Alpha's *Health and Sexuality* curriculum. In her master's thesis, which focused on implementing sexuality and HIV/AIDS education in Alpha's schools, Dixon wrote,

We examined many commercially developed curricula, reviewed programs from other school systems and searched through the professional literature to identify effective research-based programs. The most useful and most in harmony with Alpha's perspectives—were the National Guidelines for Comprehensive Sexuality Education published by SIECUS.[24, 25]

She concluded, "Our study led us to the decision to design our own curriculum and to integrate the commercially published skills-based curriculum, *Reducing the Risk*[26] into the ninth grade course."[27] The key concepts in this curriculum included: human development, relationships, personal skills, sexual behavior, health, and society and culture. Once the course content and outline had been designed, classroom materials needed to be selected. This was accomplished by establishing a set of criteria. Dixon wrote, "Early in the design of the 9th grade curriculum, Task Force members developed a set of criteria to help them evaluate and select materials for the course."[28, 29]

Caren Burke, the health education consultant and lead author of *Sexuality and Health* discussed the importance of resources in the form of both research materials and individuals. She stated,

I researched everything I could find. I read many articles. And then came up with a list of topics that I thought made sense. Given the guidelines and what was appropriate age-wise for ninth graders, I had this huge list. I organized it, and then Natalie and Cindy [Newman] and I sat together and culled from that.[30]

As Burke reflected on her experiences she said, "It was the longest process I've ever been involved in, in curriculum development or in Alpha." She went on to add, "The normal process is, they [teachers] spend a week together and they create this curriculum or you do it on your own at home. This [curriculum] is very thoughtful. . . . It involved so many people. We looked at every word."[31]

Although Beta School Committee members shunned the idea of developing a comprehensive program piecemeal, over a period of sixteen months committee members voted on implementing various components of the program. Initially, on February 28, 1994, the Beta School Committee adopted a series of lesson plans on AIDS education for seventh graders. This instructional program was implemented in the fall of 1994. Teaching materials came from a publication by the Weekly Reader Instructional Materials entitled *AIDS, What Teens Need To Know*. The material includes information on: the medical information about the AIDS virus, how AIDS affects the body's immune system, and how AIDS is and is not transmitted from one person to another.[32]

Four months later, the Beta School Committee approved a 60-session, ninth-grade health education curriculum with three sessions focusing on AIDS education. This curriculum was in place by the spring of 1995. Educators would use the textbooks *Health Promotion Wave* and *Discover: Decisions for Health* to help them talk about alcohol and drug abuse, nutrition, and personal hygiene. Before the vote, School Committee chairman Joseph Ponds made an impassioned plea to other members of the committee:

We agree there needs to be AIDS instruction and we agree that no curriculum is going to satisfy everybody. This may not be the best there is out there, but, damn it, let's put our foot down once and for all. For the sake of the community, the school, and the students, we need to begin with something, we need to start somewhere and now is the time to do it.[33]

One year later, on June 5, 1995, the Beta School Committee would vote to consider two textbooks for grades K–6. On the morning of the vote, I interviewed Jane Alexander, who provided a brief overview of the curriculum development process:

They voted 6–1 that I was to come up with a K–12 health education plan by June 5th. So I put together another committee, the curriculum committee. We met, and there were principals and teachers and a couple of parents. Only people that wanted to help. We just wanted people who knew about teaching. So they looked it all over and we made the proposal that's on the table. Anyway it'll get voted in. There'll be a lot of talk and it will get voted in 6–1.[34]

That evening, Alexander presented plans for the curriculum which was developed by a twelve-member panel and approved by the HAC. The Beta School Committee voted to implement the curriculum by a 6–1 vote. By September 1996, second through fifth graders would have a new curriculum from *The Great Body Shop*. Topics covered in the elementary curriculum included: bodily functions, nutrition, fitness, safety, illness prevention, substance abuse, emotional health, growth, consumer and community health. Sixth graders would have a course taught by a health education specialist using the *Health Promotion Wave* curriculum. The proposed 30-session sixth-grade course covered: personal hygiene, mental health, family life, first aid, HIV/AIDS, stress management, drug and disease prevention, human development, and sexuality.[35]

While School Committee members voted to implement programs at the elementary and middle school levels, some members expressed concern that the proposal did not begin to address health education for grades 10, 11, and 12 until the 1996–1997 school year. "Instead of beginning in the elementary school," said School Committee member Al Bari, "I think you should begin in the higher grades and then work down. We should focus on HIV/AIDS so more kids don't graduate without having this instruction."[36] School Committee member Karen White expressed concern that: "We will have another senior class going out ignorant, without having learned this [AIDS education]."[37] Alexander replied that there was no money in the budget to hire the health educator needed to teach the high school level courses.

In spring 1996, the Beta School Committee approved two 45-session courses for grades 11 and 12. These courses, which will address contemporary health and sexuality issues, will be offered as electives in fall 1996. In an interview with Alexander, she commented, "This year my job will be to try to get these courses required."[38]

Shirley Bowman, a Beta parent who has seen the state's initial recommendation evolve from the development of an HIV/AIDS program into a comprehensive K–12 health education curriculum, commented on the community decision-making process. She said, "We do have a K–6 curriculum. We also have School Committee approval to put in AIDS education for [grades] 9–12. It's been a lot of work, four years worth of work and an epidemic that's been here for twenty years."[39]

Personnel

With regard to personnel, two issues emerged in Alpha: the criteria for teacher selection and staff development. As curriculum development progressed, the Health Education Task Force looked ahead to the selection of teachers for the course. Dixon writes, "Realizing we needed a set of guidelines to help us in selecting the best teachers for the course, we combined and adapted recommendations from SIECUS and the American School Health Association."[40]

A series of teacher qualifications were developed.[41] Regarding staff development, faculty interested in teaching this curriculum were drawn from various disciplines. In the first year, two teachers from each high school pilot-tested the program. The following spring, three teachers from the guidance, home economics, and physical education departments taught the pilot program. During the 1994–1995 academic year, a total of thirteen teachers from both high schools taught sections of the curriculum. Faculty were drawn from a variety of disciplines, including administration, guidance, history/social studies, home economics, physical and special education.[42] Approximately 800 ninth-grade students at Alpha North and Alpha South were enrolled in the program. One hundred sixty-two (17%) ninth-grade students opted out of the program, many due to scheduling conflicts. In anticipation of full implementation in fall 1994, the thirteen faculty members and other interested colleagues participated in a five-day summer training.

In Beta, there are currently three certified health education instructors. Two additional Beta public school educators, who are currently home economic instructors, will be certified to teach in fall 1996 to accommodate the expanding health education program. Alexander was plain and simple about teacher qualifications: "They [teachers] can't teach health education unless they are qualified and certified." She continued, "If the high school course electives become mandatory we would require additional staff. Possibly, two more teachers. I can't see us expanding without at least one and a half more certified teachers."[43] During the 1995–1996 academic year, 6 (2%) out of 356 students opted out of the seventh-grade program and 3 (1%) out of 350 students opted out of the ninth-grade program.[44]

With regard to staff development, Beta school administrators have applied for funding of teacher development workshops for grades K–2. Additionally, Alexander will train and support elementary school staff as the health curriculum is implemented. Certified health educators will teach the upper grade courses.[45, 46] Alexander commented,

We're now in fine shape. We've had a hard time with training and development although grant money was not the issue. I couldn't get the money [from the school administration] to pay for substitutes for staff release time. We need *more* of a commitment for staff development.[47]

Alexander also mentioned that as Beta looks to implement the comprehensive health curriculum framework[48] developed by the Massachusetts Department of Education: "There will be a multidisciplinary approach. Through a series of workshops teachers will be taught to integrate health across subject areas."[49]

Public Information Campaigns

Another important component of the implementation stage was public education. Both Health Advisory Councils have educated and continue to educate the larger community about their respective work. In Alpha, HAC member Rob Pike recalled, "I had always pushed the [curriculum sub] committee to be more public with its findings and to communicate more openly to the parents."[50] Burke concurred, stating, "The curriculum subcommittee needed to be more public. There needed to be correspondence with community members. Parents and other community members needed to be prepared for the curriculum and its contents."[51] To rectify this problem, one of the first steps carried out by the HAC was to develop an informational packet to provide background and factual information on the program. Materials in this packet included the scope and sequence and core values of the program, criteria for selecting teachers, questions and answers regarding sexuality education, and the Task Force report of parent perspectives.[52] The community was also kept informed through public meetings. From January through September 1994, the HAC held meetings for eighth- and ninth-grade parents to discuss the curriculum. Dixon commented, "These meetings were well received and were helpful in providing parent education in the area of sexuality and health."[53] In addition, the Teacher's

Guide and student activity sheets were available to the public in high school and town libraries.[54]

In December 1993, the School Committee approved the new curriculum. In a memo to the School Committee, Superintendent Brown wrote, "I am extremely pleased and proud of the work that these people have done . . . in developing this pilot program. It is a program that will meet the needs of Alpha students and represents efforts that we should all be proud to support."[55] This sentiment was echoed in an editorial in the *Tab* entitled "Sex ed long overdue." The author wrote, "This is a thorough pilot program dealing with a complex, controversial subject. It is a subject that can no longer be ignored by schools or taught as a small section of health class. It is well thought out and represents careful, methodical work by the Task Force."[56]

In Beta, Alexander discussed future opportunities to develop greater community awareness of the HAC's work. The first was related to a formalized assessment of the health education curriculum at the elementary level. According to Alexander, "None of these courses [K–6] are graded. I would like to see them graded for assessment purposes. We need to grade them [the students]. It would be a good PR thing because parents could see the grades on report cards."[57] She discussed the importance of this tactic as a public relations strategy that might increase the credibility of elementary health education.

Additionally, the HAC membership is interested in conducting an in-depth, community-wide assessment on school-based health education. This strategy would "keep a pulse on community views towards health education and could also shed some light on an earlier community-wide assessment." Alexander continued, "We'd like to ask more in-depth questions to understand why parents of elementary school children were not interested in having HIV/AIDS taught in the lower grades. We also want to know why there wasn't an interest in consumer health."[58]

Additionally, the HAC membership will work with the school administration and the Beta PTO to continue to host public health forums on HIV/AIDS for Beta residents. Superintendent Kurtz commented on the health education program that is currently being implemented:

The program now reflects what the community wants. It's a program that will provide our students with the tools to make healthy decisions and choices through their years. We've made a tremendous amount of progress with the help of our staff and parents in the community.[59]

The effectiveness of the HAC's and school administration's efforts in the implementation of the respective health education curricula in both Alpha and Beta was due to their ability to access resources and to develop public information campaigns. The goodwill displayed by HAC members and school administrators in both communities was illustrated in their willingness and ability to work together. Through this collaborative effort, individuals were able to exchange knowledge and skills to obtain sources of funding and materials for the development and implementation of both comprehensive health education curricula.

NOTES

1. C. Sower, J. Holland, K. Tiedke, and W. Freeman, *Community Involvement* (New York: The Free Press, 1957), p. 126.

2. C. V. Willie, *Theories of Human Social Action* (Dix Hills, NY: General Hall, Inc., 1994), p. 59.

3. *Alpha School Committee Minutes*, 5/26/92, p. 11.

4. Ibid.

5. Ibid., p. 16.

6. Redman Memo, 9/8/92.

7. R. Lear, "AIDS/HIV Curriculum Slated for '93," *Tab*, 6/2/92, p. 3.

8. Education for Wellness Grant, 2/10/92.

9. Redman Memo, 9/12/92.

10. A press release from the Office of Grants Management/Alpha Public Schools, read,

The grant will support the first year of a three year project to plan and implement a course on human sexuality for 650 ninth graders in Alpha's two high schools. Central to this project is the development of an effective curriculum, staff development and in-service trainings for teachers who will teach the curriculum. . . . A part-time health education consultant [Caren Burke] will assist teachers and coordinators in conducting this project. (*Source*: Alpha School Department Press Release, 9/14/92.)

11. *Alpha School Committee Minutes*, 5/10/93, p. 15.

12. Ibid.

13. "Tobacco Tax to Bolster Health Education," *The Patriot Ledger*, 5/25/94, p. 11.

14. D. Falbo, "Still Working on AIDS Course," *Beta Forum*, 5/25/94, p. 23.

15. Alexander Interview, 6/15/95.

16. Ibid.

17. Ibid.

18. However, under the direction of Superintendent Kurtz, materials for the program had been approved under the school budget and were not dependent on the funds form the Health Protection Grant. In Alexander Interview, 6/15/95.

19. Mazarella Interview, 10/27/95.

20. Bartow Interview, 10/27/95.

21. Devine Interview, 10/27/95.

22. Beta Healthy People 2000 is a coalition of health professionals, businessmen, educators, clergy, students, and parents who have come together to "take the pulse of the health needs of the town and prescribe some remedies." In C. Conley, "Beta Healthy People 2000—Its Goal Is in Its Name," *Beta Forum*, 2/2/94, p. 3.

23. Alexander Interview, 6/15/95.

24. Dixon, *Educating for Life: Implementing Sexuality and HIV/AIDS Education in the Alpha Schools* (Master's Thesis, Cambridge, MA: Cambridge College, 1993), p. 59.

25. These guidelines were based on four goals:

• to provide accurate information about human sexuality;

• to provide an opportunity for young people to develop their values, attitudes, and beliefs about sexuality;

• to help young people develop relationships and interpersonal skills;

• to help young people exercise responsibility regarding sexual relationships, including addressing abstinence and encouraging the use of contraception and other sexual health measures. (*Source*: National Guidelines Task Force, SIECUS, 1991.)

26. *Reducing the Risk* curriculum is based on active learning and skill-building. This curriculum uses fifteen structured lessons to help teenagers gain skills and confidence to either abstain from sex or if sexually active to use birth control.

27. Dixon, *Educating for Life: Implementing Sexuality and HIV/AIDS Education in the Alpha Schools*, p. 55.

28. Ibid., p. 66.

29. The curriculum/materials must: (1) Support the core values and specific goals of the ninth-grade Human Sexuality curriculum, (2) Be accurate and reflect the most current knowledge in the field, (3) Promote abstinence as a positive, healthy choice, (4) Help students to think critically about decisions and to consider a range of alternatives and possible consequences, (5) Recognize and respect the diversity and differences in our society (race, religion, income, ethnicity, family structure, and sexual orientation), (6) Present various points of view on issues related to the curriculum, (7) Provide specific ways to promote/facilitate parent-student communication, (8) Be developmentally appropriate for the intended group, (9) Not rely on scare tactics, (10) Be free from bias and gender stereotypes, 11) Support the development of positive, nonexploitive relationships, (12) Enjoy a variety of effective teaching strategies to help students acquire knowledge and develop the skills, attitudes, and behaviors that promote healthy living. In *Health Education Task Force Report*, 1993.

30. Burke Interview, 11/21/94.

31. Ibid.

32. M. Goldberg, "Former Foes Accept Class Program," *The Patriot Ledger*, 2/1/94, p. 1.

33. J. C. Perez, "Beta School Committee Adopts AIDS Class," *The Patriot Ledger*, 12/6/94, p. 8C.

34. Alexander Interview, 6/15/95.

35. In Spring 1996, the Beta School Committee approved a 45-session eighth-grade program using the *Into Adolescence* curriculum. This course addresses health education and sexuality. With regard to the tenth-grade curriculum, Alexander is currently working with the director of the Life Science program to incorporate additional health material into the syllabus.

36. D. Falbo, "Health Course Books Okayed," *Beta Forum*, 6/7/95, p. 9.

37. Ibid.

38. Alexander Interview, 6/15/95.

39. Bowman Interview, 10/27/95.

40. Dixon *Educating for Life: Implementing Sexuality and HIV/AIDS Education in the Alpha Schools*, pp. 69–70.

41. A series of teacher qualifications were developed. These included:

- a commitment to and support of the rights of parents as the primary sexuality educators of their children;

- a belief that sexuality education is important in helping young people develop healthy attitudes and responsible behavior;

- a motivation to teach human sexuality;

- an understanding and acceptance of one's own sexuality and a comfort with topics to be covered;

- a personal code of ethics/values;

- knowledge about anatomy, physiology, developmental sexuality, and marital and family dynamics;

- an awareness of community standards and sensitivity to parental and administrative concerns;

- a respect for different cultural and religious values and beliefs;

- open-minded and nonjudgmental; and

- a willingness to learn, develop new teaching strategies. (*Source*: Dixon, *Educating for Life: Implementing Sexuality and HIV/AIDS Education in the Alpha Schools*, pp. 69–70.)

42. The American School Health Association (ASHA) cited a 1989 Alan Guttmacher Institute study that reports 31% of teachers of sexuality education are physical educators, 26% are health educators, 23% home economics teachers, 17% biology teachers, and 3% school nurses (Kent, Ohio: ASHA, 1991), p. 8. In Dixon, *Educating for Life: Implementing Sexuality and HIV/AIDS Education in the Alpha Schools*, p. 68.

43. Alexander Interview, 6/15/95.

44. Ibid., 6/15/95.

45. Beta Public Schools, *Health Protection Grant*, 1995–1996, p. 2.

46. Falbo, "Still Working on AIDS Course," p. 23.

47. Alexander Interview, 6/15/95.

48. The comprehensive health curriculum framework is one of seven curriculum frameworks that, together with the Common Core of Learning, lay the foundation for Massachusetts Education Reform in learning, teaching, and assessment. The comprehensive health curriculum framework was developed by educators, parents, and students working with staff from the Massachusetts Department of Education. In *Massachusetts Comprehensive Health Curriculum Framework*, November 1995, Draft, Preface.

49. Alexander Interview, 6/15/95.

50. Pike Interview, 11/9/94.

51. Burke Interview, 11/21/94.

52. Dixon Interview, 6/30/94.

53. Health Education Update, 1/23/95.

54. Simon Interview, 8/24/94.

55. Brown Memo to the Alpha School Committee, 12/93.

56. Editorial, "Sex Ed Long Overdue," *Tab*, 12/28/93, p. 30.
57. Alexander Interview, 6/15/95.
58. Ibid.
59. Kurtz Interview, 7/23/96.

PART IV

Conclusion and Implications

CHAPTER 9

Conclusion and Implications

Sower et al.'s Community Action model has provided a framework to understand the process by which community members in Alpha and Beta decided to implement respective school-based comprehensive health education curricula. Through the use of this model and insights from community organizing practice I will present additional learnings on creating social change at the community level. Additionally, I would like to discuss some learning opportunities for those who are interested in building local support for school-based health education programs.

With regard to the Community Action model, Sower et al. present community organization as a process consisting of three stages: *initiation*, *legitimation*, and *implementation*. In the *initiation stage*, they present a framework for the effective operation of the initiating set. This includes specific internal and external characteristics and the ability of the group to initiate action.

In Alpha, the initiating set was the Student Committee on Sexual Awareness and in Beta the initiating set was the AIDS Advisory Committee (AAC). Even though the student group was a grassroots movement and the AAC was driven by state policy, both groups possessed the necessary internal characteristics to operate effectively. Both groups had a level of internal organization (the AAC's internal organization was more formalized), clear goals and objectives, and had identified proposed action.

With regard to internal organization, it was interesting to note how both groups operated. The members of the Student Committee on Sexual Awareness made decisions based on a consensus model of leadership. This was evident in how the students, as a collective, arrived at their goal. As time went on the students' goal *evolved* into a broader vision based upon the relationships they developed with members of the larger Alpha community. In Beta, the AAC operated under a bureaucratic style of leadership. This model was illustrated by the school administration's motivation in forming the AAC, how this group's goal was determined, and how objectives were identified and operationalized. In their Community Action model, Sower et al. discuss the importance in the distinction between individual goal(s) and group goal(s) in effective groups. The goal of the Beta school administration was *not* distinct from the goal of the AAC. In fact, unlike the student group, as the AAC grew to include student voices and dealt with community members opposed to its work, the AAC's goal did not evolve over time. Additionally, this bureaucratic leadership style determined the proposed action of the AAC. This was illustrated when the AAC did not assess community views on a school-based health education curriculum because of the belief by the AAC leadership that Beta community members already supported such a program.

With regard to the development of external relationships, it became evident that members of the Student Committee on Sexual Awareness forged alliances with adults and other students within and outside the community to accomplish their goal. These alliances provided guidance, direction, and understanding of a political system that was unfamiliar to the students. Through their common goal and collaboration with adults, the students developed a level of prestige and credibility that enabled them to bring their public health message to the larger community. Their collaboration with other students provided the group with the critical mass as seen in the student petition, to demonstrate to the School Committee and the larger adult community in Alpha their commitment to their cause. Their efforts initiated a community-wide discussion. In Beta, however, the school administration and the AAC did not take advantage of the resources within their community. While they provided *updates* on their work to community members, they did not actively solicit community input or support from individuals and community groups that could have legitimized their work.

Interestingly, while the AAC held prestige within the Beta community and had access to resources to accomplish its goal, it was unsuccessful in carrying out its goals and objectives and dealing with opposition. Part of this was attributed to the internal organization of the AAC and its bureaucratic leadership style. Part of this can also be explained by the group's inability to actively forge alliances with members of the Beta community. Both of these circumstances influenced the lack of community debate about the issue of a school-based HIV/AIDS education program and the formation and initial effectiveness of the chief opposition group—the Concerned Parents and Citizens of Beta (CPCB).

In the *legitimation stage* the sponsoring set has three tasks to move a proposal toward implementation. These include: justifying the proposed action as "good" for the welfare of the community, gaining support from appropriate legitmizers, and being able to counteract any possible opposition. In Alpha, students worked effectively with adults to demonstrate to the larger community the need for a condom availability and expanded sexuality education program. Both students and parents, and the Alpha School Committee members had attempted similar initiatives in the past but each of these efforts was unsuccessful. In Beta, the AAC leadership and the school administration did not communicate the need for a school-based HIV/AIDS education program to the larger community. This lack of action is partly explained by the school administration's belief that such a program would ultimately be a "done deal" based on the perception of forthcoming state legislation and the belief that the Beta community supported such an initiative. To the surprise and dismay of school officials, community residents in Beta turned down *two* proposed HIV/AIDS education programs.

Over time in both communities, proponents of school-based health and sexuality education programs conducted community outreach to solicit community support. In Alpha, the school administration and the Task Force leadership decided to solicit community input from youth and adults early on. This was done through a series of surveys and parent Information Nights. After two failed attempts to implement a school-based HIV/AIDS education program, the Beta school administration and the HAC decided to solicit community input before developing a comprehensive health education program. In both communities, this activity provided important information in the development of the respective curricula and also served as a mechanism to create community awareness and discussion about the need for school-based health and sexuality education programs.

In both communities individuals and organized community groups opposed their proposed plans. This was seen in the emergence of Alpha Citizens for Public Education (ACPE) and Concerned Parents and Citizens of Beta (CPCB). In Alpha and Beta, these groups demonstrated their opposition by providing school administrators with alternative abstinence-based curricula, namely, the *Free Teens* program, questioning the selection and legitimacy of the Task Force/HAC, taking on the school administration's "opt in/opt out" policies, conducting community forums, and ultimately running a slate of candidates in their respective School Committee elections.

Initially, in Beta, school officials were not able to counteract opposition voices as effectively as in Alpha. As such, the AAC's proposed HIV/AIDS curriculum and the *Free Teens* program were scrapped. In contrast, Alpha officials successfully counteracted the activities of the opposition within their community. During the months after the *Free Teens* debacle, Beta officials were finally able to accomplish this same task. Their success was related to the lessons they learned from past experiences, the influence of outside experts from across the Commonwealth of Massachusetts including Alpha residents, and the emergence of adult and student voices who decided to publicly speak out for the need of a school-based comprehensive health education program.

With regard to *implementation*, both communities were able to obtain funding from resources within and outside their communities, including state and local dollars. Funding, however, became an issue in Beta after the school administration learned that funds under the Health Protection Grant Program had been reduced by almost one-quarter. While proponents were initially disillusioned, they did not give up. In fact, some HAC members worked with Beta school administrators to actively solicit funds from community resources, such as the Beta's Healthy People 2000 initiative.

Presently, both Alpha and Beta are implementing the next phases of their respective comprehensive health education programs. In Alpha, school administrators are working with the HAC and Health Education Office to implement the next phase of the program. In Beta, school administrators are working with the HAC and the Health and Human Development Office to implement the eleventh- and twelfth-grade high school electives and the grades 2–5 elementary program.

Sower and associates discuss the importance of initiation, legitimation, and implementation. The findings in these case studies confirm that these components of the model are important. However, when we look at community action as a process, we may need to add a fourth stage for analysis—evaluation, through which individuals and community groups can assess the impact of their actions. Such information has been invaluable to school administrators and HAC members in Alpha and Beta as they develop a plan to implement their respective health education curricula in other grade levels.

Along with understanding the community decision-making process within Alpha and Beta, the success of these initiatives was also based upon the initiating/sponsoring sets' ability to frame the issue, assess current curricula materials and resources, and create alliances with key community leaders. One reason for the success of these initiatives was related to how the curricula components were presented to the community. While the state guidelines recommended the expansion of HIV/AIDS instruction in all grades in Massachusetts Public Schools, Alpha school administrators, Task Force members, students, and parents discussed the need for a *comprehensive* health and sexuality education program from the outset. It was almost two years into the debate in Beta before school administrators, the HAC, School Committee members, and parents from Community Advocates for Responsible Education successfully refocused their discussion from the creation of an HIV/AIDS education program to the discussion of HIV/AIDS within the framework of a school-based *comprehensive* health education program. This strategy circumvented some of the virulent debate that is associated with the stigma and discrimination faced by people with HIV/AIDS.

In both communities, a significant amount of time was devoted to the assessment of current programs, curriculum development, and the solicitation of community members' views on health education and school-based comprehensive health education programs. As HAC members in both communities were collecting and analyzing this data, other advisory council members were involved in the assessment of health and sexuality curricula in place in other communities across Massachusetts and the nation. Additionally, advisory councils were created in both communities to build alliances between school administrators and community members. These councils were responsible for building community support and securing funding for their respective programs.

As I have used Sower et al.'s Community Action model to analyze the process of social change in Alpha and Beta around the issue of the development of comprehensive health education curricula, I learned that the early stages of the community decision-making process were different in each community. This difference may have been impacted by factors such as: individual/cultural differences in Alpha and Beta, the religious diversity in Alpha compared to Beta, differences in socioeconomic status and levels of educational achievement among individuals across communities, differences in leadership style among the Task Force and the AAC, involvement of students, the emergence and organization of groups opposed to the respective initiatives in each community, and/or how the issue was framed in Alpha and Beta. While there are a variety of factors that may have influenced this initial difference in the community decision-making process in Alpha and Beta, over time the process was similar in both communities.

Based upon my findings from this research study and my own experiences as a community organizer, I would like to discuss some lessons for school administrators and community members who are interested in building local support for school-based health education. According to Sower et al. (1957) and Hawkins, Catalano, and associates (1992), these points can be subdivided into six areas: internal organization and development, community mobilization, assessment, implementation, evaluation, and sustainability (see Figure 9.1).[1, 2] With regard to internal organization and development, it is important to provide opportunities for community involvement. This idea of inclusion can be accomplished by encouraging and fostering a broad representation of people that reflects the diversity of the community (race/ethnicity, religion, economic class, age, ability, sexual orientation) that can participate in the planning, development, and implementation of local efforts. As increasing numbers of community members become part of a decision-making structure, the initiating/sponsoring set may need to adopt a consensus style of decision-making to operate effectively. This can be done through training participants in the use of a consensus decision-making model as they develop group goals, objectives, and proposed action. Additionally, it is important for the group to maintain a

Figure 9.1
Community Organization Principles

- *Inclusion.* Encourage and foster, through coalition building, a broad representation of people that reflects the diversity of the community (race/ethnicity, religion, economic class, age, ability, sexual orientation) who can participate in the planning, development, and implementation of local efforts.
- *Adopt a consensus style of decisionmaking.* Train participants in the use of a consensus decision-making model as they develop group goals, objectives, and proposed action.
- *Flexibility.* Maintain a level of flexibility and fluidity as new individuals, events, and ideas may influence the community decision-making process.
- *Conduct community outreach.* Build relationships with community members and groups.
- *Increase public awareness.* Conduct public forums and information campaigns to present new information, solicit community input, and address people's questions and concerns.
- *Data collection.* Identify community risks and resources and gaps in services in the community. Prioritize risks to be addressed.
- *Selection and implementation of programs.*
- *Evaluation.* Evaluate efforts.
- *Sustainability.* Identify funds at the national, state, and local levels. Solicit in-kind contributions through private individuals, businesses and community support. Identify future leadership and funding sources to sustain project efforts.

level of flexibility and fluidity as new individuals, events, and ideas may influence the group decision-making process.

It is important for the initiating/sponsoring set to mobilize community members and groups. This can be accomplished by building alliances with community members and groups and increasing public awareness through the dissemination of information to the community at large. This practice will educate the larger community about local initiatives, dispel misinformation and provide an opportunity to solicit community input.

With regard to assessment, it is important to conduct a community-wide risk and resource assessment. This activity will enable planners and community members to identify gaps in services within the community and prioritize risks to be addressed. With this information community members can select and implement programs. It is also important to evaluate the effectiveness of local efforts. This can be done through the use of process and outcome evaluation measures.

To ensure implementation and sustainability of local efforts it is important for the sponsoring group to identify future leadership potential and funding sources. Funding is often available at the national, state, and local levels. Additionally, community groups can solicit in-kind contributions through private individuals and businesses at the local level.

As local officials seek to create and implement social policy, it is important for them to understand the process of social change. This process typically involves "a social system of different individuals, groups, and institutions." As a result, it is important for policy makers to use a collaborative model. This model, which includes a diversity of community voices, also fosters a sense of ownership and empowerment among those involved. Embedded in most definitions of community empowerment is a philosophy that members of a community are their own best resources for effecting change in the community. In both Alpha and Beta, community advisory councils comprised of school personnel, parents, youth, and other community members continue to work together to evaluate their respective comprehensive health education curricula. These data will be invaluable in assessing each program's impact and guiding its implementation.

NOTES

1. C. Sower, J. Holland, K. Tiedke, and W. Freeman, *Community Involvement* (New York: The Free Press, 1957), p. 126.

2. J. D. Hawkins, R. F. Catalano, Jr., and associates, *Communities That Care: Action for Drug Abuse Prevention* (Seattle, WA: Developmental Research and Programs, Inc., 1992).

Appendices

APPENDIX A

Methodology

Through my work and research in community organization, I found little information relating to the *process* by which individuals and community-based groups create change through social action. As such, this research study has enabled me to analyze this process. Over the past few years, while many Massachusetts communities have debated the adoption of comprehensive health education programs within their respective schools, Alpha has begun to implement one. The Beta School Committee just recently voted to adopt a similar program. Through comparative case study analysis using a revised version of Sower et al.'s Community Action model, I have explored how individuals, institutions, and groups have influenced or hindered the development of comprehensive health education programs in these two respective communities.

Merriam defines a case study as, "a detailed examination of one setting, or a single subject."[1] And as Robert Yin discussed in *Case Study Research*, "the essence of a case study, the central tendency among all types of case study, is that it tries to illuminate a decision [process] or set of decisions: why they were taken, how they were implemented, and with what result." Yin goes on to define a case study as "an empirical inquiry that investigates a contemporary phenomenon within a real-life context; when the boundaries between phenomenon and context are not clearly evident; and in which multiple sources of evidence are used."[2] Specifically, through the use of comparative case study, I have been able to consider the appropriateness of using a revised Community Action model in understanding the process of social change in two Massachusetts communities.[3]

SITE SELECTION

In this study, I focused on the Massachusetts communities of Alpha and Beta, both of which have been dealing with the issue of comprehensive health education. In the past three years, debate has captured much attention at public meetings and in the media. And although debate is occurring in many communities in the Commonwealth of Massachusetts, Alpha has begun to implement a comprehensive health and sexuality education program in its schools. Recently, the Beta School Committee voted to adopt the first phase of a comprehensive K–12 health education program for its schools. In studying these two sites, I have compared and contrasted how and why community support and opposition developed in response to these two proposed comprehensive health education programs.

Alpha and Beta are comparable because they are two inner-ring suburbs of Boston with populations under 100,000. In addition, both communities, which are under the same state jurisdiction, had local school committees that served as the chief policy makers in carrying out the Massachusetts State Board of Education's recommendations. These communities are different demographically. For example, the religious diversity in Alpha is reflected in the demographics of its School Committee membership. In 1993, four committee members were Jewish, three Catholic, and one Protestant. In contrast, all seven members on the Beta School Committee in 1993 were Catholic. With regard to socioeconomics, Alpha's per capita income is $28,840 and nearly 70% of Alpha adults are college educated, whereas, in Beta, the per capita income is $18,624 and approximately 25% of Beta adults are college educated.

DATA COLLECTION AND ANALYSIS

Over three years, I analyzed documents, observed videotapes of public meetings, and conducted interviews with over 60 community members.[4]

Document Analysis

Documents were used to recreate a historical account of events that occurred in Alpha and Beta around the development and eventual implementation of each community's respective comprehensive health education program.[5] Additionally, documents were used to help frame questions in my interviews and to corroborate or raise questions about evidence collected from other sources."[6] (A copy of the Interview Guide is in Appendix E.) The information from documents was analyzed in relationship to information provided in interviews and videotaped sessions of School Committee meetings and Community Forums to minimize potentially conflicting evidence.

Initially, I created a document data base to provide an account of events in Alpha and Beta. The information for this database was collected from newspaper articles, editorials, and letters to the editor from *The Boston Globe*, *Alpha Graphic*, *Beta Forum*, *The Patriot Ledger*, and *Tab*. I collected additional information from other primary documents, including: minutes of Alpha and Beta School Committee, Task Force, AIDS Advisory Committee and Health Advisory Council meetings; internal memoranda from both School Departments and community-based groups; copies of grant proposals and curricula; letters from community members, and selected videotaped School Committee and Community Forum meetings. I also collected demographic data on the communities, surveys conducted by the Massachusetts Departments of Public Health and Education, and recreated membership lists of community-based groups including Alpha Citizens for Public Education (ACPE), Committee '93, Concerned Parents and Citizens of Beta (CPCB) and Community Advocates for Responsible Education (CARE), Restore American Values in Education (RAVE), and Supporters of Student Health Education in Alpha (SSHEA).[7]

Documents were coded as data using Sower et al.'s three-stage model (*initiation*, *legitimation*, and *implementation*) to determine whether or not these were useful stages in explaining how the comprehensive health education programs were developed.[8–10] As a guide for coding, I generated categories from my literature review.[11–13] This listing is in Appendix B.

Data as coded and analyzed revealed two distinct but interrelated sets of issues in Alpha. The first set concerned a proposal to make condoms available in the high schools. The second set concerned the development of a comprehensive health education curriculum. For example, in November 1991, students initiated action by petitioning the Alpha School Committee to make condoms available at the city's two high schools.[14] After soliciting community input, the School Committee approved the students' requests in January 1992. Throughout the coming months, school administrators and city Health Department officials developed and implemented a condom availability program. The Alpha School Committee also charged school administrators with forming a Task Force to explore the components of a comprehensive health and sexuality curriculum. In May 1993, the School Committee legitimized the work of the Health Education Task Force by adopting its final recommendations concerning the proposed ninth grade pilot program. The *Health and Sexuality* curriculum was implemented in September 1994.

In contrast, my findings in Beta revealed that community members did not support a school-based condom availability program. This was exemplified in the comments made by a Beta School Committee member at a candidates' rally in March 1992. "I would never entertain the thought," said Joseph Ponds. "The idea of condom distribution is absolutely ludicrous."[15] Beta school administrators did initiate action around the development of an AIDS curriculum by creating an AIDS Advisory Committee (AAC). However, there were few opportunities for students or parents to publicly support the AAC's recommendations. These recommendations were not endorsed by the whole community as seen in the emergence of the opposition group Concerned Parents and Citizens of Beta (CPCB). The CPCB's efforts were realized when the School Committee voted to reject the proposed HIV/AIDS curriculum. However, at the School Committee's request, a newly formed Health Advisory Council (HAC) worked over the next two years to create community support for a comprehensive health education curriculum. In June 1995, the School Committee legitimized the work of the HAC by adopting its recommendations for a comprehensive K–12 health education program.

Interviews

To understand the community decision-making process from a variety of individual perspectives, I interviewed 35 community leaders in Alpha. The interviewees were identified from a list of groups I created to ensure that respondents represented a broad segment of Alpha (Appendix C). Through both document analysis and the assistance of initial interviewees, I identified over 60 Beta community members to be interviewed (Appendix D). I interviewed 28 Beta community members. Sampling was purposeful[16, 17] and the interviewees included students, parents, School Committee members, educators, school administrators, clergy, media, and other community members/groups. In some instances, I returned to respondents in both communities to ask additional questions. In the early stages of interviewing in both communities, individuals emerged as key "informants."[18, 19] These individuals provided me with personal documents and, in some instances, strategies to obtain further documents.

Due to the sensitive nature of the subject, and in order to gain access to certain individuals, I changed the names of both the community and individuals involved in these debates. As a result, individuals seemed to more freely share their thoughts, views, and feelings (and in some cases information from their own files) about teaching health education in a public school setting.

Interviews were in-depth, lasting from one to three hours[20] (an Interview Guide is in Appendix E). From these interviews, I collected a tremendous amount of information which was provided neither by the media nor in other reports available to the public. The interviews provided data to confirm, disconfirm, or elaborate information collected in earlier interviews/documents and helped me to determine where gaps in information existed.[21] With respondents' approval, interviews were recorded on audiotape and transcribed. I maintained two folders of interview transcripts, one in the original interview format and another based on the coding procedures generated for document analysis. Within each community grouping, such as educators, parents, and students, I interviewed at least one person who supported and one person who opposed the health education plan in each community.[22] Only two individuals were unavailable for interview. However, their views have been obtained from comments recorded at School Committee meetings.

Interview Analysis

I analyzed and coded interview data in the same manner as document data.[23, 24] In an effort to make sense of these data and identify their relevance to the revised Community Action model, I wrote memos to myself recording my thoughts and ideas.[25] This "thinking on paper" enabled me to reveal associations and distinctions in the data collected.[26] In one instance, this process helped me to distinguish between the issues/arguments concerning condom availability and comprehensive health education. I then applied the tenets of inductive analysis. Patton writes, "An evaluation approach is inductive to the extent the researcher attempts to make sense of the situation without imposing preexisting expectations on the phenomenon or setting under study. Inductive analysis begins with specific observations and builds toward general patterns. The strategy of inductive design is to allow the important analytic dimensions to emerge from patterns found in the cases under study without presupposing in advance what the important dimensions will be. The qualitative methodologist attempts to understand the multiple interrelationships among dimensions that emerge from the data without making prior assumptions."[27]

Using this method, I analyzed data, using Sower et al.'s framework as a guide to examine how individuals and community groups in Alpha interacted to support or oppose the development and adoption of a school-based health and sexuality education program. For example, in Alpha I concluded that *initiation* began when students became leaders, alerting the School Committee and larger community to the need for a school-based condom availability program and an expanded sexuality education program. Analysis of the data helped me to further explain how and why both the School Committee and other Alpha community individuals and groups supported the student's requests. In one instance, members of Supporters of Student Health Education in Alpha (SSHEA) placed a full-page ad in the *Alpha Graphic* to show community support. The ad included over 800 signatures.[28]

I also used inductive analysis and Sower et al.'s framework as a guide to analyze the community decision-making process around the development of a health education curriculum in Beta. My initial findings in Beta revealed that initiation occurred when school administrators responded to the State Board of Education's policy that urged school systems to develop

HIV/AIDS educational programs. Within four months, school administrators created a nineteen-member AIDS Advisory Committee (AAC) to develop recommendations for an AIDS curriculum in Beta's schools. Interestingly, in Alpha the request to create a school-based health and sexuality education program came from both state-level administrators and community members, namely, Alpha High School students and their adult supporters. In Beta, local school administrators responded solely to the state initiative since community members did not initially mobilize around this issue.

With regard to the *legitimation* stage, I discussed with interviewees how community groups established credibility to execute their proposals. For example, it was during this stage that both support for and opposition to Alpha's condom availability and comprehensive health education program emerged. Various community groups established credibility to execute their proposals including the students who obtained over 1,500 signatures to petition the School Committee.[29] This credibility was reinforced when the School Committee approved their request for a condom availability program and then charged the school administration to create a Task Force to explore the development of an expanded educational program. Over the next year, various individuals and community groups publicly supported the work and recommendations of the Task Force. Individuals and groups opposed to the curriculum also had the opportunity to demonstrate their opposition. However, the main opposition group, ACPE, lost credibility in response to its March forum. This was evident in the *Alpha Graphic*'s editorial entitled "No Place for Hate."[30]

My findings in Beta revealed that CPCB was formed in opposition to the AAC's recommendations. In a short period of time, through petitions and community-wide information forums, CPCB gathered enough community support against the proposed HIV/AIDS curriculum.[31] In June 1993, the Beta School Committee voted against the adoption of the proposed curriculum. However, over the next two years, the Health Advisory Council (HAC) and the community-based group, Community Advocates for Responsible Education (CARE) mobilized community support for a comprehensive health education curriculum. In June 1995, the School Committee legitimized the work of the HAC by adopting its recommendations for a comprehensive K–12 health education program.

In Alpha, school administrators worked closely with the School Committee and later the Health Education Task Force in hosting a series of open meetings to solicit community input before developing a health education curriculum. In Beta, however, the AAC worked for more than twelve months developing an HIV/AIDS education curriculum before soliciting community input. In contrast, the HAC conducted a community-wide needs assessment before developing recommendations for a comprehensive health education program.

Finally, I investigated the strategies that both supporting and opposing sides employed for *implementation* of their respective proposals for community action. In Alpha, the effectiveness of the Task Force's and school administration's efforts in the implementation of the ninth-grade *Health and Sexuality* curriculum was due to their ability to access resources and to develop a public information campaign. Through this collaborative effort, individuals were able to exchange knowledge and skills to obtain sources of funding and materials for the development and implementation of the *Health and Sexuality* curriculum. With regard to the opposition, I learned that ACPE's lack of internal organization was part of the reason why this group was not successful. This was confirmed in interviews with Mary Citron, ACPE spokeswoman and Bob Carr, ACPE co-founder.[32, 33]

My findings in Beta revealed that the School Committee initially voted against the adoption of an AIDS education curriculum. However, in June 1995 they voted to adopt the first phase of a comprehensive health education program. Presently, Alpha school administrators have begun to implement the next stage of a comprehensive K–12 curriculum, a ninth-grade program, while Beta school administrators work with the HAC to implement elementary and middle school programs.

BIASES/THREATS TO VALIDITY

As I conducted my research, I was mindful of my own views on health and sexuality education. These views are shaped by my personal and professional experiences as a gay male and an educator. For the past ten years I have worked in educational and community settings, discussing health promotion through prevention education. In my position at the Massachusetts Prevention Center, I assisted individuals and community groups in building their capacity to improve the health and well-being of their respective communities.

Before beginning my study, I considered my biases as they related to the need for school-based comprehensive health education programs.[34] And as I continued my research, I tried to remain cognizant of these biases. I have not been interested in determining who is right or wrong in this debate. Rather, I have been interested in analyzing the process of community decision-making that has supported or opposed the development and adoption of comprehensive health education programs in Alpha and Beta. I knew that during my analysis biases could potentially impact my research methods and/or analysis of the data. To minimize this, I employed a series of strategies. First, I created and followed a consistent set of research procedures. These procedures related to both data collection and analysis. For example, I reviewed and then sorted documents both chronologically and by subject area. I then compiled this information into a database that chronicled events as they occurred in the community. Second, throughout this study I maintained a healthy sense of benign skepticism, listening and looking at each piece of data carefully. I looked to individuals and/or additional documentation to assist me in clarifying unclear information. Third, I continuously checked and cross-checked my findings using data collected from document review, interviews, observations of videotaped meetings, and my field notes. Fourth, I consistently shared drafts of my written work with the four members of my dissertation group. Finally, as another means of fact-checking, I shared drafts of my case study report with key informants and other community members.

NOTES

1. S. B. Merriam, *Case Study Research in Education: A Qualitative Approach* (San Francisco: Jossey-Bass, 1988), p. 62.

2. R. K. Yin, *Case Study Research Design and Methods* (Newbury Park, CA: Sage Publications, Inc., 1989), p. 23.

3. Ibid., pp. 80–83.

4. C. Marshall and G. B. Rossman, *Designing Qualitative Research* (Newbury Park, CA: Sage Publications, Inc., 1989), p. 58.

5. Ibid., p. 95.

6. Yin, *Case Study Research Design and Methods*, p. 86.

7. Ibid., p. 87.

8. R. C. Bogdan and S. K. Biklen, *Qualitative Research for Education* (Boston: Allyn and Bacon, 1992), pp. 164–172.

9. A. Strauss and J. Corbin, *Basics of Qualitative Research* (Newbury Park, CA: Sage Publications, Inc., 1990), pp. 61–143.

10. M. Q. Patton, *Qualitative Evaluation and Research Methods* (Newbury Park, CA: Sage Publications, Inc., 1990), p. 381.

11. Bogdan and Biklen, *Qualitative Research for Education*, pp. 176.

12. Patton, *Qualitative Evaluation and Research Methods*, pp. 381–382.

13. Marshall and Rossman, *Designing Qualitative Research*, p. 113.

14. In a petition presented to the Alpha School Committee the students requested: (1) the expansion of sex education addressing students in small groups; (2) the availability of pamphlets discussing the correct usage of condoms; and (3) the installation of condom vending machines. Student Petition, 1991.

15. J. Reardon, "School Board Hopefuls Focus on Realignment," *Beta Forum*, 3/11/92, p. 18.

16. Bogdan and Biklen, *Qualitative Research for Education*, p. 71.

17. Patton, *Qualitative Evaluation and Research Methods*, pp. 169–198.

18. Yin, *Case Study Research Design and Methods*, p. 89.

19. Bogdan and Biklen, *Qualitative Research for Education*, p. 67.

20. Marshall and Rossman, *Designing Qualitative Research*, p. 82.

21. Yin, *Case Study Research Design and Methods*, p. 89.

22. Bogdan and Biklen, *Qualitative Research for Education*, pp. 96–104.

23. Marshall and Rossman, *Designing Qualitative Research*, pp. 114–118.

24. Patton, *Qualitative Evaluation and Research Methods*, pp. 169–198.

25. J. T. Murphy, *Getting the Facts* (Glenview, IL: Scott, Foresman and Company, 1979), p. 145.

26. Marshall and Rossman, *Designing Qualitative Research*, pp. 112–120.

27. Patton, *Qualitative Evaluation and Research Methods*, p. 44.

28. The text of the ad read,

We support the efforts of the Alpha Health Education Task Force. We, members of the Alpha community, maintain that a sensitive and comprehensive health and sexuality curriculum will provide students with accurate information and essential knowledge. This education will enable students to act responsibly and make healthy decisions, while respecting themselves and the worth of all individuals. (*Source*: *Alpha Graphic*, 5/4/93.)

29. C. Brush and T. Coakley, "Alpha Approves Condom Distribution, Superintendent Opposed But Will Implement," *The Boston Globe*, 1/28/92, p. 19.

30. Editorial, "No Place for Hate," *Alpha Graphic*, 4/8/93, p. 18.

31. A. Reid, "Foes of Teaching on AIDS Test Clout," *The Boston Globe*, 6/27/93, p. 1.

32. Citron Interview, 9/16/94.

33. Carr Interview, 1/13/94.

34. Strauss and Corbin, *Basics of Qualitative Research*, p. 43.

APPENDIX B

Coding Categories

BACKGROUND HISTORY
  Demographic Profile
INITIATION STAGE
  Internal Characteristics
    Internal Organization
    Development of Common Goals/Objectives
    Identification of Proposed Action
  External Relationships
  Initiation of Action
    Prestige
    Gaining Access
    Community Welfare
LEGITIMATION STAGE
  Tasks of the Sponsoring Set
    Benefits to the Community
    Obtaining Approval
    Opposition
    Neutralizing Opposition
    Mediation
IMPLEMENTATION STAGE
  Resources
    Funding
    Curricula/Materials
    Personnel
  Public Information Campaigns
SEXUALITY EDUCATION
  Analysis of

National, State, Local Initiatives
in Alpha/Beta Public Schools
Gaps in Services
OTHER
Influence of Outside Events/Individuals

List of Primary Interviewees in Alpha

Students
- Mark Fleming, former Alpha South High School student;
- Tim Kane, former Alpha North High School student, opposed sex. ed.;
- Regina Sidell, former Alpha South High School student;
- Miriam Stall, Alpha North High School student;

Educators
- Caren Burke, Health Education consultant;
- Bill Parker, Alpha South High School History and Sexuality Education teacher;
- John Simon, Alpha North High School teacher;

Parents
- Martha Kaplan, past co-president, City-wide PTA Council;
- Sylvia Healey, president, Alpha South PTA;
- Ron Kiley, member of Alpha Citizens for Public Education;
- Cindy Newman, co-chairwoman, Health Education Task Force;
- Rob Pike, member of Health Education Task Force;

School Committee/School Committee Candidates
- Diane Eisen, Alpha School Committee member;
- Allison Levy, Alpha School Committee member;
- Howard Rosen, Alpha School Committee member;
- Sandra Riley, Alpha School Committee member;

- Sonya Schultz, chairwoman, Alpha School Committee;
- Anthony Valle, Alpha School Committee candidate, Ward 1;

School Administration

- Ivan Brown, superintendent, Alpha Public Schools;
- Paul Redman, assistant superintendent, Alpha Public Schools;

Alpha Citizens for Public Education

- Bob Carr, co-director, Alpha Citizens for Public Education;
- Mary Citron, spokeswoman, Alpha Citizens for Public Education;
- Linda Hale, co-director, Alpha Citizens for Public Education;

Health Education Task Force

- Natalie Dixon, Health Education specialist and member of the Task Force;
- Susan Simon, Alpha parent and member of Task Force;

Religious Institutions

- Reverend Jack Andrews, president, Alpha Clergy Association;
- Reverend Harold Hart, pastor, Myrtle Baptist Church, Alpha;
- Reverend James Manning, pastor, Corpus Christi Parish;
- Reverend Matthew Barker, pastor, Second United Church of Christ;

Media

- Sheila Fenn, producer, "Response to The Gay Agenda";
- Rhonda Lear, reporter, *Tab*;
- Sam Lyons, reporter, *Alpha Graphic*;

Other Community Members

- Daniel Colin, Massachusetts State Representative;
- Hanah Golden, local activist and Alpha resident;
- Sarah Kanner, chairwoman, Supporters of Student Health Education in Alpha.

List of Primary Interviewees in Beta

Students

- Brendon Borman, former Beta High School student;
- Ann Murphy, former Beta High School student;

Educators

- Jane Alexander, health educator, Beta schools, chairwoman, AIDS Ad. Council;
- Joe Gray, headmaster, Beta High School;
- Chris Valley, Home Economics educator, Beta High School;

Parents

- Mary McPherson;
- Michael Murphy;

Beta School Committee

- Jean Anderson, member for 16 years;
- Maureen Casey, member;
- Joseph Ponds, chairman;

AIDS Advisory Committee

- Jane Alexander, chairwoman and health educator, Beta Public Schools;
- Shirley Bowman Books, parent;
- Alice Dowling Elstermeyer, parent;
- Elaine Kane, CPCB director and former Special Needs teacher;
- Mary McPherson, R.N., CPCB member;

- Ellen Nagel, parent, CARE spokeswoman;
- Kate Pagano, parent, CARE member;

School Administration
- Superintendent Peter Kurtz;

Concerned Parents and Citizens of Beta
- Carolyn Banner, R.N., co-founder and member;
- Mary Custer, co-founder and member;
- Thomas Hampton, founding member and founder, Restore American Values in Education (RAVE);
- Elaine Kane, leader of CPCB;
- Linda Whitmire, spokeswoman;

Community Advocates for Responsible Education (CARE)
- Kathy Bartow, member;
- Shirley Bowman, founding member;
- Valerie Devine, founder;
- Ellen Nagel, member, spokeswoman;

Religious Institutions
- Bill O'Neff, Unitarian Universalist Church, Social Action Committee;
- Reverend Richard Riding, pastor, Second Church of Christ;
- James Russo, pastor, St. Timothy's Roman Catholic Church;

Media
- Cathy Collins, *Beta Forum*;
- Alice Dana, resident; local host, cable television program;

Others/Community Members
- Thomas Hampton, founding member and founder, Restore American Values in Education (RAVE);
- Beverly Wiggins, Center for Prevention.

APPENDIX E

Interview Guide

Research Question: What was the decision-making process by which individuals, community-based groups, and institutions influenced the development of comprehensive health education programs in two Massachusetts communities?

1. How did you become involved in this issue?

2. Would you say that you were a member of any particular group? If so, which one?

3. How did your particular group come into existence?

4. What was the internal organization of this group? How did you/your group function?

5. The goals/objectives of Concerned Parents and Citizens of Beta (CPCB)/Community Advocates for Responsible Education (CARE) were reported in an article in *The Patriot Ledger*. Did you/the group of which you were a member have specific goals/objectives? What were they? Were your goals similar to or different from the group's goals? If they were different was this reconciled? How?

6. Did you/your group propose action? If so, what type?

7. Did conflict emerge within the group? If so, please explain.

8. Did you/your group develop relationships within the community? How? With whom?

9. Did you/your group conduct any type of needs assessment to support your goals/objectives? Who was involved? Was this data presented/discussed within the community? How?

10. Did you/your group obtain approval for your goals/objectives? From whom? How was this accomplished?

11. How did you/members of your group support/or oppose the HIV/AIDS education curriculum?

12. What strategies did you/your group employ?

13. Did you/your group have to deal with individuals/community groups opposed to your efforts? If so, how was this handled?

14. What other individuals/groups and/or factors supported/hindered the development of the HIV/AIDS education curriculum? How? Why?

15. Did conflict emerge in the community? At what point? Between which individuals/groups? Were you/ was your group involved? How?

16. What strategies/techniques, if any, were used to reduce/resolve conflict? By whom? What other strategies could have been used?

17. Could the conflict have been avoided? How?

18. What types of resources were available to implement your/your group's goals/objectives? How/where were these resources obtained?

19. Was the community at large aware of your/your group's efforts? How? What was the community response? Please elaborate.

20. As you/your group implemented your proposed action, did conflict arise? If so, how was conflict mediated? Please explain.

21. Based on your experience from this situation, what would you do differently today if your community was faced with this same issue? What did you learn from this experience?

22. What recommendations would you make to other individuals/community groups dealing with the same situation in their community?

23. Who/what other groups should I speak with concerning this issue?

Selected Bibliography

Alinsky, S. D. *Rules for Radicals*. New York: Random House, 1972.

Biddle, W. W., and L. J. Biddle. *The Community Development Process: The Rediscovery of Local Initiative*. New York: Holt, Rinehart & Winston, 1965.

Bogdan, R. C., and S. K. Biklen. *Qualitative Research for Education*. Boston: Allyn and Bacon, 1992.

Centers for Disease Control and Prevention. Division of STD/HIV Prevention, Annual Report.

Citizen Action Seminar Manual. Chesapeake, VA: Christian Coalition, 1992.

Clinard, M. B. *Slums and Community Development: Experiments in Self-Help*. New York: Free Press, 1970.

Cox, F. M., J. R. Erlich, J. Rothman, and J. E. Tropman, eds. *Strategies of Community Organization: Macro Practice*, 4th ed. Itasca, IL: F. E. Peacock Publishers, 1987.

Dixon, N. *Educating for Life: Implementing Sexuality and HIV/AIDS Education in the Alpha Schools*. Master's Thesis, Cambridge College, 1993.

Governor's Commission on Gay and Lesbian Youth. *Making Schools Safe for Gay and Lesbian Youth, Breaking the Silence in Schools and in Families*, February 1993.

Green, L. W. *Toward A Healthy Community: Organizing Events for Community Health Promotion*. Washington, DC: U.S. Department of Health and Human Service, U.S. Public Health Service, 1985.

Harper, E. B., and A. Dunham. *Community Organization in Action: Basic Literature and Critical Comments*. New York: Associated Press, 1959.

Hawkins, J. D., R. F. Catalano, Jr., and associates. *Communities That Care: Action for Drug Abuse Prevention*. Seattle, WA: Developmental Research and Programs, Inc., 1995.

Heller, K., R. Price, S. Reinharz, S. Riger, and A. Wandersman. *Psychology and Community Change*. Homewood, IL: Pursey, 1984.

Henderson, P., and D. N. Thomas. *Skills in Neighborhood Work*. Winchester, MA: Allen & Unwin, 1980.

Hirschmann, A. O. *Exit, Voice and Loyalty, Responses to Decline in Firms, Organizations and States*. Cambridge, MA: Harvard University Press, 1970.

Kirby, D. *Sexuality Education: An Evaluation of Programs and Their Effects*. Santa Cruz, CA: Network Publications, 1984.

Kirby, D., J. Alter, and P. Scales. Analysis of U.S. Sex Education and Evaluation Methods. Washington, DC: U.S. Department of Health, Education and Welfare, 1979.

Koop, C. E. *Surgeon General's Report on Acquired Immune Deficiency Syndrome*. Washington, DC: Office of the Surgeon General, 1986.

Marshall, C., and G. B. Rossman. *Designing Qualitative Research*. Newbury Park, CA: Sage Publications, Inc., 1989.

Massachusetts Department of Education. *Policy on AIDS/HIV Prevention Education*, April 24, 1990.

Massachusetts Department of Education, Bureau of Student Development and Health. *Massachusetts 1993 Youth Risk Behavior Survey*, June 1994.

Massachusetts Department of Public Health. *Comprehensive Curriculum Guidelines on HIV/AIDS: Grades K–12*, September 1991.

Merenda, D. W. *A Practical Guide to Creating and Managing Community Coalitions for Drug Abuse Prevention*. Alexandria, VA: ACTION: The Federal Domestic Volunteer Agency.

Merriam, S. B. *Case Study Research in Education: A Qualitative Approach*. San Francisco: Jossey-Bass, 1988.

Morris, R., and R. H. Binstock. *Feasible Planning for Social Change*. New York: Columbia University Press, 1966.

Murphy, J. T. *Getting the Facts*. Glenview, IL: Scott, Foresman and Company, 1979.

National Research Council. *Risking the Future: Adolescent Sexuality, Pregnancy and Childbearing* (vol. 1). Washington, DC: National Academy Press, 1987.

Parents United for Responsible Policies on Sexuality Education. *Massachusetts Advocacy Kit*. Planned Parenthood League of Massachusetts, 1994.

Patton, M. Q. *Qualitative Evaluation and Research Methods*. Newbury Park, CA: Sage Publications, Inc., 1980.

Perloff, H. S. *Planning and the Urban Community*. Pittsburgh: Carnegie Institute of Technology, 1961.

Sower, C., J. Holland, K. Tiedke, and W. Freeman. *Community Involvement*. New York: The Free Press, 1957.

Strauss, A., and J. Corbin. *Basics of Qualitative Research*. Newbury Park, CA: Sage Publications, Inc., 1990.

Sullivan, T. J., and K. S. Thompson. *Social Problems: Divergent Perspectives*. New York: John Wiley and Sons, 1984.

Warren, R. *The Community in America*. Chicago: Rand McNally and Company, 1963.

Watzlawick, F., J. H. Weakland, and R. Fisch. *Change Principles of Problem Formation and Problem Resolution*. New York: W. W. Norton, 1974.

Weed, S. E., J. A. Olsen, and J. Hooper. *Sex Respect First Year Evaluation Report.* Salt Lake City: Institute for Research and Evaluation, 1987.

Willie, C. V. *Theories of Human Social Action.* Dix Hills, NY: General Hall, Inc., 1994.

———. *Effective Education.* Dix Hills, NY: General Hall, Inc., 1987.

Yin, R. K. *Case Study Research Design and Methods.* Newbury Park, CA: Sage Publications, Inc., 1989.

Index

Adolescent sexual activity and practices, 9, 11 n.3, 14 n.47, 22–24, 32 n.14, 56 n.7, 83 n.8

AIDS Advisory Committee, 40–42, 65–68, 78–81; conflict on, 41–42, 64, 67–72, 82; curriculum development and recommendations of, 66, 85–86 n.57, 130–131 n.34, 153 n.10; external relationships of, 43, 75–77, 93–96, 137, 174, 175; formation of, 40–41, 103; goals of, 41, 64, 65; internal organization of, 61–63, 174; opposition to, 96, 103, 106 nn.34, 35; support for, 105. *See also* Initiation stage

AIDS education: in Alpha, 55; in Beta, 38–40, 44–45

AIDS statistics, 4, 9, 11 n.3, 53, 56 nn.3, 7

Alexander, Jane, 40–43, 45, 46, 60–68, 70, 76, 93–94, 97, 101, 102, 115, 120, 124, 128, 137–38, 141, 144, 148, 149, 161–66

Alinsky, Saul, 6

Alpha, 21–35; community leaders and organizations in, 23; demographics of, 21, 22; school committee membership, 22

Alpha Citizens for Public Education, 27–29, 111, 116–28, 142–44; external relations of, 127; formation of, 115–19; goal of, 125–26; internal organization of, 125–26; link between organized regional and statewide opposition groups and, 30, 145, 155

Alpha Clergy Association, 95, 154

American Family Foundation, 54

American Freedom Coalition, 54

Anderson, Jean, 44, 47, 94, 101, 117, 149

Anderson, Patricia, 6

Andrews, Jack, 140

Andros, Paul, 44

Banner, Carolyn, 116, 117, 119, 120, 126, 146

Bari, Al, 49, 163

Barker, Matthew, 119

Bartow, Kathy, 49, 140, 141, 147, 149, 150, 151, 161

Beta, 37–57; community leaders and organizations in, 39; demographics of, 37, 38; school committee membership, 38

Binstock, Robert, 5

Bowman, Shirley, 41, 44, 62, 66, 68, 72, 75, 94, 99, 137, 140, 141, 146, 148, 150, 151, 164
Bradbury, Lisa, 22
Brown, Ivan, 26, 31, 121, 160, 166
Burke, Caren, 162, 165

Caan, Melvin, 29, 145
Carlson, John, 120, 132
Carr, Brian, 28, 113, 116, 120–23, 125, 127, 142, 150
Casey, Maureen, 38, 41–44, 47, 61, 67, 83, 97, 113, 118
Catalano, Richard, 177
Catholic Alliance. See Christian Coalition
Christian Coalition, 54
Citron, Mary, 30, 114, 125, 145
Clinard, Marshall, 5
Colin, Daniel, 29, 144
Committee '93, 29, 144
Committee on the Prevention of AIDS, 25, 26, 74
Community, definition of, 4, 5
Community action model, 4, 7
Community Advocates for Responsible Education, 7, 8, 45–46, 140–41, 147–52; conflict, 150; external relationships of, 149, 151, 157; formation of, 45; goals of, 92, 141, 144; internal organization of, 148–52; opposition to Free Teens program by, 99, 140
Community organization models, 5–8
Community organizing, principles of, 177–79
Community support, 3, 10, 11, 27, 47–48, 60–61; obtaining approval and, 94–109. See also Legitimation stage, neutralizing opposition and
Comprehensive curriculum guidelines on HIV/AIDS for grades K–12, 40, 53, 62, 66, 70
Concerned Parents and Citizens of Beta, 7, 42–43, 111–13, 116–28; external relations of, 126–28, 133 n.94, 134 n.103; formation of, 42, 77, 116–19; goal of, 42, 125–26; internal organization of, 124, 125, 128; link between organized regional and statewide opposition groups and, 48, 145–46, 156 n.67
Concerned Women for America, 54
Condom availability, 75; community input on, 25, 26, 32–33 nn.28, 29, 40, 57, 79–80, 150
Condom distribution, 74–75
Custer, John, 47
Custer, Mary, 42, 76, 115, 117, 126

Dana, Alice, 141–142
Devine, Valerie, 44, 46, 48, 77, 83, 100, 120, 144–47, 150
Dixon, Natalie, 28, 31, 74, 75, 92, 93, 116, 117, 161, 165
Dominants, 71, 81, 87 n.92
Donovan, Lorraine, 10, 47, 55
Dorman, Patricia, 40, 44, 55, 97, 98
Dowling, Alice, 37, 43, 62, 64, 68, 69, 71, 112
Dunham, Arthur, 5

Earl, Sarah, 146
Eisen, Diane, 114

Fenn, Sheila, 29, 142
Ferguson, Pam, 29, 142
Fisch, Richard, 5
Fisk, Jean, 30, 130, 160
Fleming, Mark, 22, 24, 60, 63, 65, 72–75, 80, 82
Focus on the Family, 54
Forbing, Shirley, 6
Fox, C. Lynn, 6
Free Teens program, 45, 46, 48, 116, 128, 175; association with Unification Church, 99, 100, 141; community input, 95; community opposition to, 99–100, 140–41; community support for, 98–99; description of, 107 n.54

Golden, Hannah, 139–140, 150
Governor's Commission on Gay and Lesbian Youth, 53–54, 56 n.8

The Grassroots Forum, 47, 123; opposition to, 144–145. *See also* Concerned Parents and Citizens of Beta

Gray, Jim, 38, 77, 94

Green, L. W., 5

Hale, Leslie, 28, 113, 115, 117, 120, 125, 127, 142

Hampton, Thomas, 42, 100, 123–24, 126–27, 145

Harper, Ernest, 5

Hawkins, J. David, 177

Healey, Sylvia, 24, 65, 79, 115

Health Advisory Council, 46–47; community assessment conducted by, 92, 94, 95, 100–103; external relations of, 94; formation of, 46, 55, 92, 94, 104 n.14, 118–20, 160; goal of, 94; internal organization of, 102; opposition to, 132, n.70; public awareness conducted by, 165–66; recommendations of, 102. *See also* Legitimation stage

Health Education Task Force, 26–27; community assessment conducted by, 33–34 n.43, 38, 92–94, 102–3, 104 n.9, 131 n.55; community support for, 34 n.47, 95, 96, 105 n.33, 156 n.82; formation of, 33 n.41, 91, 103 n.5; goal of, 27; recommendations of, 30, 95, 104. *See also* Legitimation stage

Healthy People 2000: National Health Promotion and Disease Prevention Objectives, 9, 53

Implementation stage, 4, 7, 159–70; curricula and materials, 161–64, 168 nn.25, 29; definition of, 159; funding, 159–61; personnel, 164–65, 169 n.41; public awareness, 165–67

Initiation stage, 4, 7, 59–89; conflict, 67–72, 82; definition of, 59; development of goals, 63–65; external relationships, 65, 72–78; initiating action, 78–83; initiating set, 59, 81–83 n.6, 173; internal organization,

60–63, 84 n.13; proposed action, 65–68

Interfaith Coalition, 127. *See also* Opposition voices, organized regional and statewide

Kane, Elaine, 41, 42, 45, 62, 66–72, 77, 97, 114–16, 118, 122, 124–26, 139, 146

Kanner, Sarah, 29, 143, 144, 147–51

Kaplan, Martha, 144

Kiley, Rob, 112

Kurtis, John, 25, 74, 80

Kurtz, Peter, 40, 43–47, 55, 61, 97–98, 100, 101, 117, 118, 120, 138, 139, 151, 166

Lawson, Patrick, 25, 74, 75

Lear, Rhonda, 119

Legitimation stage, 4, 7, 91–157; benefits to the community, 92–94; definition of, 91; mediation, 128–29; neutralizing opposition, 29, 30, 137–47, 153–54 nn.18, 20; obtaining approval, 94–109; opposition, 101, 111–24; sponsoring set, 91, 92

Levitt, Peggy, 5

Libow, Alex, 123

The Lighthouse Institute for Public Policy, 57

Margola, Linda, 149, 150

Massachusetts Department of Education, recommendations of, 9, 62

Massachusetts Department of Public Health, recommendations of, 9, 53

Massachusetts Family Institute, 57, 127

Massachusetts State Board of Education, recommendations of, 1, 40, 53

Massachusetts Youth Risk Behavior Survey, 14 n.47, 94

Mazarella, Linda, 49, 161

McPherson, Mary, 41, 62, 66–71, 114, 115, 122

Miller, Mike, 5

Moore, C. M., 4, 5

Moore, Michael, 38, 41, 44, 61, 64, 66, 70, 75, 80, 115
Morris, Robert, 5
Murphy, Ann, 44, 138, 146
Murphy, Michael, 146

Nagel, Ellen, 7–8, 42, 62, 63, 69, 71, 99, 138, 141, 149
National Research Council of the National Academy of Sciences, 8, 13 n.40
Nedrick, Dorothy, 41, 66, 100
Neutralizing opposition, 137–47. *See also* Community Advocates for Responsible Education; Supporters of Student Health Education in Alpha
Newman, Cindy, 73, 75

O'Neff, Bill, 45, 48, 143, 144, 146, 149, 150
Opposition voices, 4, 10, 11, 47–48, 111–24, 137–39, 175; on the AIDS Advisory Committee, 114–18; on the Health Education Task Force, 114–17; organized regional and statewide, 54, 57 n.11, 127. *See also* Alpha Citizens for Public Education; Concerned Parents and Citizens of Beta

Pagano, Kate, 62, 63
Parker, Bill, 24, 30, 72–74, 79
Parker, Nan, 81, 98, 141, 150
Pell, Lisa, 30, 96
Pentz, Maryann, 5
Peters, Richard, 127
Pike, Rob, 30, 114, 117, 165
Pilgrim Family Institute. *See* Massachusetts Family Institute
Planned Parenthood League of Massachusetts, PURPOSE campaign of, 10, 54–55, 56–57 n.10
Political Action Committee. *See* Alpha Citizens for Public Education; Community Advocates for Responsible Education; Restore American Values in Education; Supporters of Student Health Education in Alpha

Political Research Associates, 57
Ponds, Joseph, 44, 55, 61, 62, 97, 100, 118, 161
Porter, Nan, 63, 99

Redman, Paul, 26, 30, 116, 119, 120, 159, 160
Rein, Martin, 5
Restore American Values in Education, 123–25, 145
Riding, Richard, 142
Riley, Sandra, 22, 60, 119, 140, 143
Report of the Health Needs of the Beta Public Schools, 46, 101, 108–9 n.79
Rosen, Howard, 26
Rothman, Jack, 5
Russo, James, 120–21

Sanders, Mary, 41, 66, 75
Sawyer, Mark, 125
Schock, Verna, 22
Schultz, Sonya, 6, 26, 80, 91, 114–15, 119, 137, 142
Sex Information and Education Council of the U.S., 54, 56 n.9, 162. *See also* Implementation, curricula and materials
Sexuality education, 8–11; definition of, 13 n.37; definition of comprehensive health and, 13 n.37; research on, 10, 16 n.87; strategies of, 15 n.59; types of instruction and programs, 8–10
Sidell, Regina, 22, 24–26, 60, 63–65, 73–75, 78, 79, 81
Simon, Susan, 30, 114, 120
Sinclair, Jamie, 25, 26, 74
Social change, definition of, 4, 11 n.4
Student Committee on Sexual Awareness, 22–25, 60–65, 72–75, 78–82; activities of, 24–26, 65, 74, 78–80; external relationships, 24, 25, 32 n.19, 65, 72–75, 81, 87 n.101, 174, 175; goals of, 24, 63–64, 74; internal organization, 60–61, 173. *See also* Initiation stage
Student voices, 48, 60, 79–80, 98, 146–47, 152. *See also* Committee on the

Prevention of AIDS; Student Committee on Sexual Awareness
Subdominants, 71, 72, 78, 81
Supporters of Student Health Education in Alpha, 29, 34 nn.54, 57, 95; activities of, 142–44; conflict, 149, 150; external relations, 150–52; internal organization, 147–52

Tropman, John, 5

Valley, Chris, 42, 61, 62, 66, 67, 71, 75–76, 139
Vanderbilt, Edward, 24, 60, 73

Watzlawick, Paul, 5
Weakland, John, 5
White, Karen, 44, 49, 163
Whitmire, Linda, 42, 43, 45, 48, 75, 80, 113, 117, 121, 123, 124, 127, 146
Whitmire, Sharon, 43, 146
Wiggins, Beverly, 32, 73, 75, 149
Williams, Kathy, 48, 147
Wiseman, Jason, 26
Willie, Charles, 87 n.92

Zabin, Laurie, 10

About the Author

STEVEN P. RIDINI, a graduate of the Harvard School of Public Health and Harvard Graduate School of Education's Administration, Planning, and Social Policy program, is vice-president of programs at The Medical Foundation in Boston, Massachusetts.

ISBN 0-89789-570-3

90000>

EAN

9 780897 895705

HARDCOVER BAR CODE